D0912885

Modern Heroism

MODERN HEROISM

Essays on D. H. Lawrence,
William Empson, & J. R. R. Tolkien

Roger Sale

UNIVERSITY OF CALIFORNIA PRESS
BERKELEY, LOS ANGELES, LONDON
1973

University of California Press
Berkeley and Los Angeles
University of California Press, Ltd.
London, England
ISBN: 0-520-02208-4
Library of Congress Catalog Card Number: 73-186106

1736010

for Dorothy

Contents

Civilization has absolutely no need of nobility or heroism. These things are symptoms of political inefficiency. In a properly organized society like ours, nobody has any opportunities for being noble or heroic.

—Aldous Huxley, *Brave New World*

Preface

This book was begun in the spring of 1965 when Catharine Carver, then of the Viking Press, wanted to know if I was working on a book. I was not, so far as I knew, but I was plagued by the idea that various authors on whom I had been working—Lawrence, Empson, Tolkien, Henry Adams—were similar in a way I had not yet realized. After a number of false tries I came up with the "idea" of modern heroism, which increasingly seemed to me interesting and important yet also not so much an idea as a sort of magnetic field in which I might locate these apparently very different authors. The more I worked at creating this magnetic field, the more Henry Adams did not seem to belong, and the more the others did. In the introduction I try to describe in more detail what this idea or magnetic field looks like to me, in the conclusion I return briefly to Adams, in between are the essays on Lawrence, Empson, and Tolkien.

But 1965 was some years ago, and as the book has taken on various shapes I have become greatly indebted to a number of people who have given help, advice, insight, and support. First, parts or versions of the three main chapters have appeared in different journals and books, and I am grateful to the editors of *The Massachusetts Review*, *The Hudson Review*, and the University of Notre Dame Press for help given me in the past and for permission to reprint versions of those parts and versions here. Second, Catharine Carver and Hugh Kenner, both acting in quasi-official capacities, read different versions with great kindness and insight, helped to identify snags and helped clear them away; acting less officially William E. Coles, Jr., Anne Howells, and Marvin Mudrick read parts or wholes and made differences to the final version in ways that they, at least, can see. Third, Elaine McKay Smith showed me at a crucial point how to create and trust my reading of Empson so that Empson himself became richer for me and the whole idea of modern heroism seemed more attractive and possible. Fourth, the Dean of the Graduate School of the University of Washington gave me a grant which helped me take the summer of 1968 to work and complete the essential sentences and form of the book.

Two debts remain, neither easy to explain, of different and greater magnitude. The first is to Empson, who is not only one of the heroes of this book but who seemed to me the architect of my mind during the years of its becoming written. The second is to Dorothy Sale, who at many times seemed to be everything else essential: goad, critic, champion, guide. I only hope that my pages on the one and my dedication of the book to the other begin to express the depth of my sense that this is really their book.

For permission to use copyrighted material, I wish to express my thanks to the following:

The Massachusetts Review, Inc. for "D. H. Lawrence, 1912–1916," by Roger Sale.

Harcourt Brace Jovanovich, Inc. for quotations from "To An Old Lady" and "Aubade" in *Collected Poems,* by William Empson, and for a quotation from "Gerontion" in *Collected Poems 1909–1962,* by T. S. Eliot.

The Viking Press for quotations from "Ah oh—That The

Man I Am Might Cease To Be" and "Both Sides of the Medal," from *The Complete Poems of D. H. Lawrence,* edited by Vivian de Sola Pinto and F. Warren Roberts.

Random House, Inc. for the quotation from "In Memory of W. B. Yeats," from *Collected Shorter Poems, 1927–1957,* by W. H. Auden.

Faber and Faber Ltd. for quotations from "Gerontion" from *Collected Poems 1909–1962* by T. S. Eliot, and from "To the Memory of W. B. Yeats" from *Collected Shorter Poems 1927–1957* by W. H. Auden.

Chatto & Windus Ltd. for quotations from *To An Old Lady* by William Empson.

Hudson Review, Inc. for the essay "The Achievement of William Empson" by Roger Sale.

Houghton Mifflin Company for quotations from *The Fellowship of the Ring* by J. R. R. Tolkien.

George Allen & Unwin Ltd. for quotations "Three for the Elven Kings under the Sky" and "Seek for the Sword that was Broken" from *The Fellowship of the Ring* by J. R. R. Tolkien.

University of Notre Dame Press for the chapter "Tolkien and Frodo Baggins" by Roger Sale from the book *Tolkien and the Critics.*

R. S.

I. *Introduction*

To find a hero one tells a story: there has never been any
other way. Most of this book, thus, is made up of stories about
the heroism of D. H. Lawrence, William Empson, and J. R. R.
Tolkien. Any attempt to bring together under a single rubric
three writers so obviously different from one another is bound
to seem a little willful; a number of people to whom I have
described my notion of modern heroism have said, in effect,
"Well, yes, but why those three? And if them why not others?"
Though I have no quick or easy answer to those perfectly legiti-
mate questions, it does seem arrogant just to reply: "Read the
book." Heroes may demand stories, and if my sense of modern
heroism has any validity, it may well have to lie in the three
essays that follow, but these stories are literary criticism, and a
critic has no business being coy when asked to explain what he
thinks he is doing. What I can offer by way of introduction and
explanation is not a convincing answer to the questions asked
above, or a strict definition of modern heroism, but rather a
statement of the ground rules I have used. Anyone for whom
such preliminary statements are a waste of time is urged to start
reading elsewhere, choosing whatever subject he likes. I have
not designed this book so as to impede or discourage anyone
who simply wants to treat it as three unrelated essays on three
major writers.

Introduction

Let me begin by rehearsing certain well-known facts about "modern," especially "modern literature." The great burst of the years 1910–1940 still seems to dominate the way we think about the literature of the whole century, and writers who have been dead as many as forty years are easily called "modern." Yeats, Eliot, Lawrence, Joyce, Pound, Forster, Ford, Lewis, Frost, Hemingway, Stevens, Faulkner—give or take a name or two, the roll call is always about the same. These writers are so obviously different one from another in subject, temperament, and range that we seldom try to find a single common denominator to call "modern"; it is one of those terms we all know the meaning of until we are asked to define it. There are, though, one or two strains of the "modern" that can help create a context for the essays that follow; they are familiar enough that they can be evoked without needing a lengthy description or explanation.

The first strain or theme in at least some important modern writers is that in this century heroism as it has been known in the Western world is dead. I offer Leslie Fiedler's summary here, but many others are easy enough to come by:

> . . . the Christian heroic tradition proved viable for ten centuries, as viable in the high verse of Dante and Shakespeare and Chaucer as in folk ballads and the sermons of country priests. Yet all the while it lived, of course, it was dying, too, dying with the civilization that had nurtured it, already mourned for by the time of Sir Walter Scott. So slowly did it die, however, that only under the impact of total war were those who fought shocked into admitting that perhaps they no longer believed in what they fought for. (*Collected Essays* [New York, 1971], II, 226)

Epic and tragedy are the traditional literary forms for heroes, and we do not write epics and our good writers, at least, do not not write tragedies. Our major forms are the novel and the extended lyric, and the best known "heroes" of these forms—Prufrock, Leopold Bloom, Jake Barnes, Flem Snopes, the Catcher in the Rye, Lucky Jim—are decidedly not heroic. They live in worlds much more restricted than those of earlier heroes, and they hold modest views of themselves; Bloom is no Ulysses, Prufrock is not Prince Hamlet nor was meant to be. Perhaps the classic statement of this theme is made in the voice that seemed for a long time to speak for all of us:

> After such knowledge, what forgiveness? Think now
> History has many cunning passages, contrived corridors
> And issues, deceives with whispering ambitions,
> Guides us by vanities. Think now
> She gives when our attention is distracted
> And what she gives, gives with such supple confusions
> That the giving famishes the craving. Gives too late
> What's not believed in, or if still believed,
> In memory only, reconsidered passion. Gives too soon
> Into weak hands, what's thought can be dispensed with
> Till the refusal propagates a fear. Think
> Neither fear nor courage saves us. Unnatural vices
> Are fathered by our heroism. Virtues
> Are forced upon us by our impudent crimes.
> These tears are shaken from the wrath-bearing tree.

Belief, passion, courage, heroism, and virtue are for Eliot the old terms, the ancient guides to life that now produce deceit, unnatural vices, and impudent crimes. He who seeks to mold a heroic destiny is deceived, and dangerous.

"Gerontion" comes in 1920 and immediately follows the war that, as Fiedler indicates above, was the single event most responsible for shaping the modern idea that heroism is dead. It began as the last of the old wars and ended as the first of the new, the most cunning passage of history in our century. Ever since, the spring of 1914 has been idealized as our last moment of innocence, and if the civilization that ended then was "an old bitch gone in the teeth," it was nonetheless the civilization one had known and assumed. French and German soldiers celebrated Christmas together in 1914, and lances were used in some early battles, but by 1916 the baffled generals were reduced to barbed wire, machine guns, and poison gas, while the politicians could only offer propaganda, the awful remedy of democratic tyrannies. In *No More Parades* Ford's Christopher Tietjens makes the classic statement about what had happened:

"At the beginning of the war," Tietjens said, "I had to look in on the War Office, and in a room I found a fellow . . . What do you think he was doing. . . . what the hell do you think he was doing? He was devising the ceremonial for the disbanding of a Kitchener battalion. You can't say we were not prepared in one matter at least. . . . Well, the end of the show was to be: the adjutant would stand the battalion at ease: the band would play *Land of Hope and Glory*, and then the adjutant would say: *There will be no more parades*. . . . Don't you see how symbolical it was: the band playing *Land of Hope and Glory*, and then the adjutant saying *There will be no more parades*? . . . For there won't. There won't, there damn well won't. . . . No more Hope, no more Glory, no more parades for you and me any more. Nor for the country . . . Nor for the world, I dare say . . . None . . . Gone . . . Na poo, finny! No . . . more . . . parades!"

Those who knew "Land of Hope and Glory" or Elgar's equally famous piece whose title derives from Othello's exultation in the pride, pomp, and circumstance of glorious war were beached, confused, resentful. No wonder that shortly after "Gerontion" Eliot wrote his famous sentences about the way Othello uses his language to cheer himself up. The big wars that had made ambition virtue now could only be arenas for self-delusion.

This strain or theme of modern literature is accompanied by one even more central to our present concern: a version or idea of history that explains how all this had come about, and why regret, confusion, and resentment are the best honest tones left available to us. It is "History" that is the overpowering "She" in "Gerontion," history that happens so decisively that its victims are left with the sense that all real and good human possibilities lie in the past. In many respects the versions of history created in these years are only variations on the ancient myth of a Golden Age. There was a time when the world made sense and men knew how to live in it, and that time was followed by a long period of disintegration into the muddle, chaos, and catastrophe of the modern world; such is the argument of all such myths. But those made in the twentieth century differ from earlier myths of the Golden Age by trying to place the Golden Age in an actual and relatively recent historical time rather than in a more simply mythic Eden or Camelot. I call this the Myth of Lost Unity, a cumbersome term, but it does identify its central qualities. Its earliest full version is created by Henry Adams at the turn of the century: unity lies in the cult of the Virgin in the twelfth century; chaos and multiplicity are symbolized by the Dynamo in the twentieth. Eliot's best known statement of his version is in "The Metaphysical Poets": the unified sensibility of the dramatists of the sixteenth and the poets of the early seventeeth becoming gradually dissociated later, especially under the decisive influence of Milton and Dryden. Yeats's *Trembling of the Veil* imagines the period of "unity of Being" falling "somewhere about 1450." Pound's search for alternatives to the iambic pentameter line that had dominated English verse during its decline led him to medieval Provence, Anglo-Saxon England, ancient Rome, Confucian China. Bernard Berenson outlined the "decline of art" in Italy after the precious "tactile values" of the quattrocento painters were lost during the brilliant generation of Leonardo, Michelangelo, Raphael, and Corregio. In all these versions of the Myth of Lost Unity the motion of history is linear, not cyclical, so that something lost cannot be regained, and the present time is the latest or last step in a process of disintegration that has gone unchecked since it began a number of centuries ago. The Myth of Lost Unity invites nostalgia and despair and the sense that large and heroic actions are possible now only as the schemes of fools and lunatics.

Given the emphasis that the Myth places on the great difference between "Then" and "Now," it is easy to see that if heroism was appropriate "Then," it could not be so "Now." Unfortunately, what this way of thinking ignores or overlooks is the fact that heroism is not and never has been a constant set of values or actions; what has proven to be heroic in one age is always different from the heroic actions or values of the previous age. The heroism of any period dies when the period itself dies, and the heroism that replaces it implicitly finds the old heroism inadequate. Epic is not romance, romance is not tragedy: Beowulf, Gawain, and Antony all are heroes, but all are very different one from another. Fiedler says in the passage I quoted earlier that the Christian heroic tradition was dying for many centuries. That is one way of saying it, and perhaps a better way is to say that it was constantly undergoing change and redefinition. This point does not demand elaborate demonstration, but I would like here to take two major moments in the history of our literature and indicate how at these moments new tasks were being forged for new heroes.

First, Hamlet. Immediately after Hamlet viciously shouts at Ophelia to get herself to a nunnery, she describes him as he had once been, and, at the same time, gives us a description of heroes in the age before her own:

> O, what a noble mind is here o'erthrown!
> The courtier's, soldier's, scholar's, eye, tongue, sword!
> The expectancy and rose of the fair state,
> The glass of fashion and the mold of form,
> The observed of all observers, quite, quite down!
> [III, 1, 153–157]

Ophelia's Hamlet is a focus for the values of the entire society because he has the courage, nobility, and sense of honor demanded of its leaders and heroes by the state. The virtues are public, a model to inform and educate others. So too Troilus wants to make of the stolen Helen a "theme of honor and renown," so too Hotspur wants to make the easy leap that would pluck bright honor from the pale-faced moon, so too Octavius Caesar praises the fortitude and courage of the soldier Antony was but is no longer.

But Ophelia, Troilus, Hotspur, and Octavius Caesar, we know, do not tell Shakespeare's story. Ophelia sees a madman where she once saw a hero, but Shakespeare's Hamlet is heroic precisely because he is willing to insist upon and explore that madness. Hamlet grows up as the rose and expectancy of the fair state, when the earth was a goodly frame, the sky a majestical roof, and man the paragon of animals. But he is thrust from that world, the garden is suddenly unweeded, the earth is a sterile promontory, and man is errant knave crawling between earth and heaven. Everyone else in the play, like Ophelia, lives in a world defined by clear boundaries and codes. Horatio knows the rules for talking to ghosts, the Ghost himself knows the code and ethics of revenge, Claudius knows just how to deal with balky foreign powers and bereaved children, Polonius is an entire jam pot of proverbial and traditional wisdom. But Hamlet is different, and as he explores that differentness, he alters the world's sense of what it is to be a hero. He is historically decisive because after him heroes will resemble him much more closely than they will Beowulf or Gawain or the Red Crosse Knight. Hamlet does display all the virtues for which Ophelia praises him, but his heroism lies elsewhere. Instead of simply revenging his father's foul and unnatural murder, he must try to set right the time gone out of joint; he must explore his private awareness that no clock can ever be turned back. His heroism lies, in effect, in repudiating an understood public code in the name of making one's murky way through the twilight. After him heroic action will be much more inward and personal than it ever was before.

If there is a second moment in the history of heroism in English literature as important as Hamlet's it is Wordsworth's. Beowulf can save his world and Macbeth can destroy his because in earlier times it was possible for one man to shape the destiny of a whole country. But by the beginning of the nineteenth century that was no longer possible, and most earlier ideas and ideals of heroism had thereby become obsolete. At the opening of *The Prelude,* Wordsworth is filled with a sense of great and unused powers and he is searching for a subject for a major poem. He has assumed it would be like other major poems, an epic or a tragedy, and so he looks into history and the Bible for "some old Romantic tale by Milton left unsung." He discovers that none of these tales holds any magic for him, that the past is indeed past. He then lapses into reminiscence, only to discover within his memory the autobiography that is the poem, "philosophic song Of Truth that cherishes our daily life." At that moment two important things happen to alter our sense of what heroism is and can be. First, the arena for heroic action is not courts and battlefields, but the woods and lakes surrounding a small boy; second, the boy shares the heroic burden and achievement with his maker, the poet, so that Wordsworth himself becomes heroic as he writes:

> O Heavens! how awful is the might of souls,
> And what they do within themselves while yet
> The yoke of earth is new to them, the world
> Nothing but a wild field where they were sown.
> This is, in truth, heroic argument,
> This genuine prowess, which I wished to touch
> With hand however weak, but in the main
> It lies far hidden from the reach of words.   [III, 180–187]

The duality of the heroism is explicitly stated here, implicitly present throughout the poem. The boy is heroic in the might of his soul when the earth is new to it, the poet is heroic as he makes a heroic argument out of the power of the young soul, as he touches, with hand however weak, what had hitherto lain hidden from the reach of words. The boy skates, or steals a boat, or poaches a trap; these are prosaic events only in the sense that Hamlet is an adolescent mooning after a dead father and a remarried mother. Such statements render prosaic what the poet makes heroic, and in Wordsworth's case the making itself becomes heroic action:

Points have we all of us within our souls
Where all stand single; this I feel, and make
Breathings for incommunicable powers;
But is not each a memory to himself,
And, therefore, now that we must quit this theme,
I am not heartless, for there's not a man
That lives who hath not known his god-like hours,
And feels not what an empire we inherit
As natural beings in the strength of Nature.   [III, 188–196]

The key point is that Wordsworth's assertions here are not true. Many of us have not known godlike hours as inheritors of an empire in the strength of nature, and were it not for Wordsworh, many more would not ever have seen the possibility. That we all stand single is something many others were coming to learn at the turn of the nineteenth century, but that there were moments when that singleness could become the experience of a god, that the poet in remembering and creating those spots of time convinces us the possibility is there—the mightiness and awfulness of the soul within nature's grasp—this is Wordsworth's heroic activity. If it is the boy who is godlike, it is the man whose imagination can create the heroic argument and make the individual mind not only the haunt and main region of his song but also space large enough for that heroism. *Caverns* there were, he says, within my mind which sun could never penetrate. To make one's poem imitate the sun, to make it illuminate at least as much as the sun could, is to be a romantic poet and a romantic hero. Just as he gives us a new definition for "romantic," Wordsworth gives us a new definition for "hero."

To some this way of speaking of Wordsworth as a hero is only another sign that the real heroism, the old heroism, is dead. If someone wants to say it will not do to call Wordsworth a hero, and that the word should be used only to refer to the central figures of epic, romance, and tragedy, so be. There is no need to quarrel about a particular word as long as we are clear about the way it is being used, and why. The nature of heroism changes, and I think it is also true that the possibilities for heroism do diminish, that it is less important in the nineteenth century that there be any heroes at all than it was, perhaps, in the twelfth. Wordsworth's heroic argument is different from Shakespeare's, just as Shakespeare's is different from Virgil's, and inevitably as the sphere or the arena of the heroic action diminishes, it will be less crucial that we identify heroic action at all. Still, we must remember that at every key moment in the history of heroism in the last five centuries sane and important people have said heroism was dead, and they were wrong. The Ophelia who mourns the madness of Hamlet, the Wordsworth who feels there are no more heroic songs to be sung, the Eliot of "Gerontion" are completely right on their own terms: the heroism they are thinking of is dead. But they are wrong, too.

In our century those who believe in the Myth of Lost Unity assume that if one knows that mere anarchy is loosed upon the world, that it is going to end not with a bang but a whimper, then the proper response is a range of tone that runs from cynicism and despair through bitterness and resentment to resignation and nostalgia. If the examples of Hamlet and Wordsworth show us anything, it is that heroes are bred in the same milieu as others of their time, which will lead us to believe that our modern heroes too will learn the modern world's sense of history and know what are considered to be the appropriate tones and responses. Also, they will differ from others around them in ways that are personal and mysterious: Hamlet has bad dreams; Wordsworth is haunted by the fears that haunted his childhood. What later in each becomes heroic action has origins as apparently insignificant as these, though the difference, that which sets them apart, will turn out to be crucial, and will lead them down paths others would not take. So too the modern hero is not a different breed of man; he will live in the world lived in by the makers of the Myth of Lost Unity, of which many despaired and from which they sought retreat. If the despair is created by the sense that History has overwhelmed the world, then the heroism will be created in defiance of that same History. This means the modern heroes must be themselves historians, else they might qualify as saints or fools but never as heroes; their defiance of history will seem the more heroic, the more we sense what they had to overcome to do as they did. Jay Gatsby may seem to some great or gorgeous, but he cannot be in this sense a modern hero because he is innocent of what history has created. To know what the creators of the Myth know, to feel that history may indeed have led us to a dead end, to be tempted to weep and despair, but then to defy, to weave active and new human possibilities out of all the unraveled threads of the cloth that was once whole, to insist that the human spirit need not be overcome despite all that is eager to annihilate it—that, it seems to me, is heroic activity for a modern man.

It is not their ability to fit a definition that makes Lawrence, Empson, and Tolkien heroic, which is why it is always in the storytelling that heroism is known and felt to be heroic. The fact that others have written about my three heroes, often very well, and that they have seen no need to make them into heroes is not, so far as I can see, any deterrent at all. Hamlet when seen through the eyes of any character in his play, Wordsworth as seen in the very good criticism of Peacock or the very good parodies of Lewis Carroll, are not the least heroic. In the Old Testament Adam's fall is barely noticeable, while in *Paradise Lost* it is grand and heroic indeed. Which is only to say that it must be in the stories themselves that Lawrence, Empson, and Tolkien will seem heroic, if they do.

Nonetheless there are similarities in the careers of Lawrence, Empson, and Tolkien which might begin to suggest why they, though apparently and really very different one from another, seem subjects for heroic stories. All three are historians of the Myth of Lost Unity, though each became such a historian in a different way. Lawrence seems to have been driven to discover the history for himself as he was struggling over the book that was to become *Women in Love,* when he understood that before he could write that book as it should be written he had first to write a historical novel, *The Rainbow.* In his case World War I was an integral event both in his struggle and in his understanding. Tolkien too was ravaged by the war, but in his case there was no immediate and direct response. He withdrew more completely from the modern world than almost any other maker of the Myth of Lost Unity, and in his more dogmatic pronouncements Tolkien has always spoken as though the Myth were not a myth at all but the literal truth, and as though only madmen or fools would contemplate the twentieth century without horror. Yet during the long years of his withdrawal, his imagination was coming to terms with the inescapable fact that he is a modern man and not an elf or an ent. At his best he is a writer about modern rather than ancient things, and his work reveals the differences between the two as well as any more conscious historian. For Empson the question of being a historian was never really a decision, it would seem. He was born some years later than either Lawrence or Tolkien, which means he was coming to his maturity when the Myth of Lost Unity was gaining widespread popular acceptance, which in turn means that he seems to have felt its truths in his bones from the very beginning.

We can note also that the struggle against the implications of the Myth that each waged in his own way took place in a relatively short period of time, and the price each paid for even that much struggle is very great. About the struggles it is harder to be clear in a summary way than it is about the prices. But, if the central fact about modern experience is that its voice is individual, wry, lonely, lyrical, and lost, speaking of its powerlessness as if from a void, then one sign of heroic achievement will be the creation of a space for more than one, a sense of human possibility that creates a community even as it acknowledges the atomized or alienated lot of the individual. The heroic voice insists that such communities are possible, that their achievement is a struggle and a noble act, that we can do more than wait silently for the end. Nothing like the unity of a whole society can be imagined—except for satires and utopias, that unity has not been imaginable for more than two centuries —but any community created from a genuine sense of possibility and not from a huddled sense of loss is too rare and too precious not to be valued very highly.

As for the prices each paid for his struggle to achieve such a community, it is easier to be clear about Lawrence and Empson than about Tolkien. Lawrence and Empson both, having come to their climactic moment and heroic achievement relatively early in life, are left to reveal the cost. Each simplifies the truths he has gained, each becomes more dogmatic and therefore more liable to outbursts of terror or hysteria. For all three, including Tolkien, the period following the heroic achievement seems a reversion as well as a simplification. The later work shows old individual fears returning, fears that earlier helped give courage to defy that now come back as if from childhood. When the self can no longer sustain the great imaginative energy, then the fears can dictate and dominate. But if we remember the fate of some earlier heroes this need not surprise us much. Hamlet in Act V is a much simplified figure from the hero he had been, and he speaks to Laertes as though none of what has happened had happened and they were still lads together, sharing a code of honor. Wordsworth has not finished the first version of *The Prelude* before he begins to turn his back on his fears and the caverns of his mind and starts speaking about an imperial palace whence he came. In our later centuries, when heroism has almost always been unsought and when it has not been achieved by fitting oneself into some prescribed role, the hero has had to face as his risk and his danger not so much death as the diminution or the extinction of his imagination. Though the self may remain alive, the qualities that created the heroism often do not.

We have, then, a rough outline: a writer driven to become a historian of the Myth of Lost Unity who, at that moment or later, then refuses to accept the generally held attitudes toward the Myth, and whose refusal or defiance is achieved in the creation of a small community that shows us that the isolated or alienated voice is not the only one in which we can speak. This period of defiance and creation is then followed by another, of retreat, not into modernism but into some more personally needed code or dogma. Put that crudely, this outine does justice to none of the three writers in question, and, of course, some of its terms fit one author better than the others. In the essays that follow I will not be trying to make sure that Lawrence, Empson, and Tolkien each fit every item in the outline, and I offer it here more as an indication of the general boundary lines of my territory than as specific signposts down the three roads I will be taking. Finally, I want to add that two of my heroes, Empson and Tolkien, are very much alive as I write, which means that the time to conceive their biographies is far from having arrived. Concerning both I make some assertions about their lives that may be questionable, at least by them. I hope there are not very many. In any event, the absence of biographical material anything like as rich as we have for Lawrence is not much of a deterrent, as it is the published record that counts, that creates the heroism, that is the basis for those speculations I do offer.

The important thing, of course, is not to make patterns out of the private lives of Lawrence, Empson, and Tolkien, any more than it is to offer a rigid definition of modern heroism into which they fit neatly and from which everyone else is excluded. It is, simply, to say the right things about each writer in turn, to find the appropriate terms for each particular case. It would not be interesting to try to make Lawrence, Empson, and Tolkien into heroes were one not also trying to say what is best or most important about them, were one not convinced that there is no better way to approach their individual greatness. There are a number of things I hope to have achieved by enclosing my subjects in a magnetic field called modern heroism. I would like to convince admirers of one of these writers that there are qualities shared by all three that contribute to the individual greatness of each one. I would like to demonstrate how the heroism of one age has to be different from the heroism of earlier or later ages. But these are relatively minor goals. Most of all I am trying to find a way to talk about the best each writer wrote, and though I agree with almost everyone as to which are each writer's major works, I do not think any of them has been adequately described. Probably no one who is not himself interested in heroism would undertake such a task, but many who are not should understand that the point of the undertaking is not to create partisans of heroism but to find a different way to expand our sense of the possibilities of greatness.

II. *D. H. Lawrence, 1910–1916*

Chronology

	1910
October	—begins third novel, *Paul Morel*.
December	—Lawrence's mother dies.
	—first novel, *The White Peacock*, published (written 1905–1910).

	1911
	—"A Modern Lover," "The Old Adam," "Daughters of the Vicar" written while Lawrence is teaching at Davidson School, Croydon.
October	—Lawrence shows first draft of his novel *(Paul Morel A)* to Jessie Chambers. Work on it has come to a standstill.

	1912
January–February	—Lawrence on leave from teaching while recovering from pneumonia. Jessie Chambers sees new version of the novel *(Paul Morel B)* and is delighted with the much different early chapters.

March	—Lawrence resigns teaching position to write full time.
March–April	—Lawrence shows Jessie Chambers middle chapters (about Miriam) of *Paul Morel B*. She protests bitterly and their relationship collapses.
Early April	—Lawrence meets Frieda von Richthofen Weekley, wife of a former teacher of his at Nottingham.
May 3	—Lawrence and Frieda elope: London, then Germany.
May	—Lawrence's second novel, *The Trespasser,* published (written early 1910).
Summer	—first poems written for *Look! We Have Come Through!*
	—first sketches written for *Twilight in Italy*.
Sept. 12	—Lawrence and Frieda settle in Gargnano, Lago di Garda, Italy.
Fall	—Lawrence revises his novel, now called *Sons and Lovers*. Finished November 14.
December	—begins "Burns novel"; this is abandoned quickly.

1913

January–February	—begins "The Insurrection of Miss Houghton." Works on and off on this, then lays it aside. Later revised and published as *The Lost Girl*.
	—begins "The Sisters."
February	—*Love Poems and Others* published (written 1903–1910).
Spring	—"The Prussian Officer" and "Thorn in the Flesh" written.
	—*Sons and Lovers* published.

17

June– September	—Lawrence and Freda return to visit Frieda's children. They meet John Middleton Murry and Katherine Mansfield.
September	—return to Italy, settle in Lerici. "I am working away at *The Sisters*."

1914

February 9	—"I have begun my novel *(The Sisters)* again —for about the seventh time."
May 9	—"I have about three thousand more words to write"; "Frieda wants the novel to be called *The Rainbow*."
June	—return to England.
July 13	—Lawrence and Frieda married.
September– October	—working on "Study of Thomas Hardy" (never finished, published posthumously in *Phoenix*).
December	—*The Prussian Officer and Other Stories* published.
December 4	—"I am writing over my novel."

1915

January 7	—"I am going to split the book into two volumes."
March	—*The Rainbow* finished. —meets Bertrand Russell, Keynes, G. E. Moore in Cambridge; "one of the crises of my life."
September	—*The Rainbow* published.
November	—*The Rainbow* prosecuted as an obscene book. The pubisher Methuen offers no defense and book is withdrawn.
Fall	—"The Crown" published in Murry's magazine, *The Signature*.

1916

January	—"I'm doing my philosophy" (presumably

	Psychoanalysis and the Unconscious, published in 1921).
May 1	—"I have begun the second half of *The Rainbow*" (*Women in Love*).
24	—"I have got a long way with my novel."
June	—*Twilight in Italy* published.
June 19	—"I have nearly done my new novel."
July	—a book of poems, *Amores,* published.
	—*Women in Love* finished.

(This chronology makes no effort to be complete. It is designed as an outline to the story that follows.)

– 1 –

In the autumn of 1910, Lawrence began his third novel, which he called *Paul Morel*. In strange places and barely explicable ways, modern literature was beginning to happen. If literary England had a center or a dictator at the time, it was the *English Review* and its editor, Ford Madox Hueffer. It was to him that Jessie Chambers, the girl of Lawrence's youth, had sent some of his early poems and stories, and it was in the *English Review* that Lawrence was first published and achieved mild fame. Hueffer had published the work of Conrad, Wells, Galsworthy, and some of the first work of Wyndham Lewis and a young American, Ezra Pound. But equally important events were happening elsewhere, in obscurity, and without apparent connection one to another. Yeats, though a poet for many years, was just beginning to discover the fascination for what's difficult. Joyce had recently finished *Dubliners* and *Stephen Hero*. Eliot had written "Portrait of a Lady" and had begun work on "Prufrock." Thus most of the first work of the major architects of the modern consciousness was written between

1905 and 1910, the year, Virginia Woolf later claimed, human nature changed. But if any of this was apparent to anyone at the time, it was only as part of the rhetoric of Ezra Pound's or Hueffer's restless, decent egotism. There was no dawn in which it was bliss to be alive, no sense that modern literature was not Conrad, Bennett, Hardy, and Shaw.

Of all the group, Lawrence was certainly the most English, the most obviously traditional, the one most likely to achieve popular success and least likely to achieve greatness. His first two novels, *The White Peacock* and *The Trespasser,* show "genius" only if one makes many allowances for youth, inexperience, clumsiness, and aimlessness. The stories of the period, "The Shades of Spring," "Goose Fair," "Odour of Chrysanthemums," are much better. In a way the most promising sign of what is to come is Lawrence's awareness of what is wrong with the novels. He says in a letter of October 18, 1910, *"Paul Morel* will be a novel—not a florid prose poem, or a decorated idyll running to seed in realism: but a restrained, somewhat impersonal novel." (*The Collected Letters of D. H. Lawrence,* ed. Harry T. Moore, 2 vols. [New York, 1962.] All quotations from the letters will be from this edition and will be cited hereafter by date of letter.) He adds, with pretentious youthful precision, that he is about one-eighth done.

At the time Lawrence was teaching unhappily at the Davidson School in Croydon, and he was going home as often as possible to be with his mother, who died in December of 1910 after a long, painful, battle with cancer. Writing was his way of holding on to himself, and he saw that it could not do this for him if he relaxed and tried to escape into decorated idylls or florid prose poems. If only his own life mattered, then the writing had to be autobiographical, but restrained, impersonal. The novel he wrote, or tried to write, in the months just before and just after his mother's death, I will call *Paul Morel A,* following Harry T. Moore who first described it, in *The Life and Works of D. H. Lawrence.* From what we can gather it only partly resembles the *Sons and Lovers* it became two versions and two years later. The longest description of *Paul Morel A* is Jessie Chambers's; she first saw it late in 1911, the year that Lawrence later called the worst of his life, and she makes clear that the effort to be restrained and impersonal had been defeated under the pressure of Lawrence's sense of pain and loss. If *Paul Morel A* is not a decorated idyll or a florid prose poem, it is clearly an escape into daydream:

He had written about two-thirds of the story, and seemed to have come to a standstill. The whole thing was somehow tied up. The characters were locked together in a frustrating bondage, and there seemed no way out. The writing oppressed me with a sense of strain. It was extremely tired writing. I was sure that Lawrence had had to force himself to do it. The spontaneity that I had come to regard as the distinguishing feature of his writing was quite lacking. He was telling the story of his mother's married life, but the telling seemed to be at second hand, and lacked the living touch. I could not help feeling that his treatment of the theme was far behind the reality in vividness and dramatic strength. Now and again he seemed to strike a curious, half-apologetic note, bordering on the sentimental. . . . A nonconformist minister whose sermons the mother helped to compose was the foil to the brutal husband. He gave the boy Paul a box of paints, and the mother's heart glowed with pride as she saw her son's budding power. . . . It was story-bookish. The elder brother Ernest, whose short career had always seemed to me most moving and dramatic, was not there at all. I was amazed to find there was no mention of him. The character Lawrence called Miriam was in the story, but placed in a bourgeois setting, in the same family from which he later took the Alvina of *The Lost Girl.* He had placed Miriam in this household as a sort of foundling, and it was there that Paul Morel made her acquaintance. [E. T. (Jessie Chambers), *D. H. Lawrence* [London, 1965), pp. 190–191.)

Jessie Chambers is not a great writer, but she was a very intelligent person and the passage above makes very clear how Lawrence had gone wrong and finally had come to a standstill. He is working off his animus against his father, glorifying his mother, and seeking the major virtues for himself. Including the nonconformist minister makes it easy to simplify his father into a lower-class brute; Lawrence Clark Powell, discussing a manuscript of what is probably *Paul Morel A*, adds that Morel is jailed for accidentally killing one of his sons. Leaving out his older brother makes it easy for Lawrence to give himself the center of the stage. Making Jessie Chambers a foundling who must be grateful to the lad who rescues her allows Lawrence to turn Paul Morel into Galahad. Because it is all daydreaming, it is bound to lead to a point where "the whole thing was somehow tied up." Lawrence's world had collapsed and the only writing he could force himself to do led to this glorification of himself at the expense of his father and his girl.

Jessie Chambers told Lawrence as she returned his novel to him that he should stick to what had happened, and he implicitly agreed by asking her to write down what she remembered of their early years together. Her sketches became the basis for a number of scenes in later versions. He began rewriting the book in January of 1912 while he was at home recovering from pneumonia, determined to pull himself out of his lethargy, and sent it, *Paul Morel B* as Moore calls it, to Jessie Chambers as it was being written. She was very enthusiastic:

The early pages delighted me. Here was all that spontaneous flow, the seemingly effortless translation of life that filled me with admiration. His descriptions of family life were so vivid, so exact, and so concerned with everyday things we had never even noticed before. There was Mrs. Morel ready for ironing, lightly spitting on the iron to test its heat, invested with a reality and significance hitherto unsuspected. . . . He did not distinguish between small and great happenings; the common round was full of mystery, awaiting interpretation. [E. T., pp. 197–198]

Here almost certainly the first six chapters of *Sons and Lovers* are being described, in something like the form in which they were published. In the early months of 1912 Lawrence achieved his first great triumph, one hardly worth calling heroic, but worth attention for its own sake and for the way it seems like a small wave heralding the much bigger one to come later. Lawrence had momentarily escaped from the bondage of his love for his mother. Perhaps living once again near his father, perhaps the relief of not having to teach, perhaps the decision to devote all his time to writing, helped give him the freedom so obviously felt by the writer of this first third of *Sons and Lovers,* the chapters Frank O'Connor once called "the finest thing in English fiction."

What Lawrence had achieved here is a plateau, reached not by climbing unknown paths but by seeking his own way up the familiar slopes of nineteenth-century fiction. Here the tradition of provincial culture in which he had been raised—the culture of which he and Jessie Chambers were so shyly proud—is expressed in the tradition of the novels of Jane Austen, George Eliot, and Hardy which had been created out of that culture. The impersonality he had known he must seek had been found; during the writing of *Paul Morel B* Lawrence repeatedly refers to the book simply as "my colliery novel," as though it had no closer connection with his family than that implies. Its strength derives from Lawrence's profound respect for his family, a respect he achieved rather than simply felt all along.

The most marked change between the fantasy of *Paul Morel A* and the early chapters of *Paul Morel B* is in the treatment of the father, Mr. Morel, which is why it is tempting to say that living in Eastwood again after Mrs. Lawrence died may have made a crucial difference. He had tried in the first version to make his father into a monster, but he could not bring it off, and in the implicit realization of his failure shown by his revision, Lawrence expresses the depth of his respect and love for the man he fully hated as well. We will see Mr. Morel transformed over and over in the next few years—into Baxter Dawes late in *Sons and Lovers,* into the orderly in "The Prussian Officer," into Tom and Will Brangwen in *The Rainbow,* into

Gerald Crich in *Women in Love*. We can see, looking back, that versions of the figure had already appeared, in Annable in *The White Peacock* and as the suitor of a figure modeled on Jessie Chambers in "A Modern Lover," "The Old Adam," "The Shades of Spring," stories of the Croydon years. But in some ways the change from *Paul Morel A* to *Paul Morel B* was the crucial one; having transformed the monster into a man Lawrence was then able to have a base from which the later mutants came. The description of Morel eating his breakfast, letting the bacon drippings fall on his bread; the alterations in the whole household that come when Morel is home, and cheerful; the fights in each of the first two chapters when the Morels discover their passion has locked them into antagonism—this is what Jessie Chambers calls Lawrence's refusal to "distinguish between small and great happenings" because "the common round was full of mystery, awaiting interpretation." No need here for the nonconformist minister, or for the deletion of Ernest who, as William Morel, becomes as moving in the book as Jessie Chambers says he was in life.

As the scenes are thrust before us, so plain and strong they seem to exist only for their own sake, we slowly begin to see the outlines of a larger action and become aware for the first time of Lawrence's magnificent way of making events seem causally connected even though they are not. This is Lawrence's intuition of literary form, his equivalent of plot, and he never needed another. Here, for instance, is part of the account of the Morels after Mr. Morel has been hurt in the mine, a passage that tempts one to say novels should always be like this:

> During his recuperation, when it was really over between them, both made an effort to come back somewhat to the old relationship of the first months of their marriage. He sat at home and, when the children were in bed, and she was sewing—she did all her sewing by hand, made all shirts and children's clothing—he would read to her from the newspaper, slowly pronouncing and delivering the words like a man pitching quoits. Often she hurried him on, giving him a phrase in

anticipation. And then he took her words humbly.

The silences between them were peculiar. There would be the swift, slight "cluck" of her needle, the sharp "pop" of his lips as he let out the smoke, the warmth, the sizzle on the bars as he spat in the fire. Then her thoughts turned to William. Already he was getting a big boy. Already he was top of the class, and the master said he was the smartest lad in the school. She saw him a man, young, full of vigour, making the world glow again for her.

And Morel sitting there, quite alone, and having nothing to think about, would be feeling vaguely uncomfortable. His soul would reach out in its blind way to her and find her gone. He felt a sort of emptiness, almost like a vacuum in his soul. He was unsettled and restless. Soon he could not live in that atmosphere, and he affected his wife. Both felt an oppression on their breathing when they were left together for some time. Then he went to bed and she settled down to enjoy herself alone, working, thinking, living. [Compass ed., pp. 46–47]

Sons and Lovers, we know, is "not like" the later Lawrence, but the method of this passage is Lawrence's from here on. It is an account of an evening, but also an account of many evenings, and no word in it makes it exclusively one or the other. The shift in tense in the second sentence, from the simple past of "He sat at home" to the imperfect of "he would read to her," is one of Lawrence's most powerful weapons for simultaneously giving his scene the particularity of a specific event, as though it happened only once, and the generality of a pattern in the relationship, as though it happened in effect many times over. Mr. and Mrs. Morel try to come together but fail, so she turns in her thoughts to William. Morel, thus, without a word said between them to indicate her thoughts, feels shut out. As a result they both feel constrained, Morel can only go to bed, and Mrs. Morel is left free and powerful and alone. No causal connections are stated, but many are made. The web of impulse and action spun in every sentence is woven tightly enough so after a while we are witnessing that rarest of literary creations, domestic family relations working out a logic of their own.

To achieve this Lawrence did not simply substitute "real

life" for fantasy and thereby achieve greatness. The events described above had their counterpart in life when Lawrence was far too young to remember them even if he had seen them. Rather, he seems to have seen what his father must have been in order for his mother to be as she was, and to have recognized he could not suit his wishes about one without affecting the way he wrote about the other. In other words, he comes to see people in relationship rather than separately. Compared to Lawrence's later characters, Walter and Gertrude Morel are full and vivid personalities, but this vividness is achieved by seeing men and women locked together in a relationship. Morel is sometimes brutal, he whines, he whistles as he makes household things, he is genial and blustering in his efforts to be a father; his wife is fierce, tired and tiring, tough and humorless. But the book does not treat them this way, as sketched-in creatures with decisively individual traits. It sees Morel's whining as both a cause and a result of her fierceness, his brutality as a cause and a result of her toughness. It is Emma and Mr. Knightley, Lydgate and Rosy, Heathcliff and Catherine, but compressed so that plot is unimportant and individual events are free of the taint of seeming set pieces or melodramatic.

But this achievement, better known and honored as it is by those who shy away from Lawrence's later work, is only a plateau. Lawrence could not settle himself once and for all, as later parts of *Paul Morel B* and *Sons and Lovers* make clear. The impersonal passion in Part I of *Sons and Lovers* is only temporarily sustained. Even as he was writing it in the early months of 1912, strain was showing, and Jessie Chambers reports that "we were back in the old dilemma" because "I began to realize that whatever approach Lawrence made to me inevitably involved him in a sense of disloyalty to his mother" (E. T., pp. 200–201). None of this mattered greatly as long as the focus remained on the elder Morels, but trouble began the moment Lawrence came to Miriam. Only fragments of *Paul Morel B* still exist, but by looking at them, at Jessie Chambers's account of the book as it came to her, and at Lawrence's comments on it as he revised the book into *Sons and Lovers* that fall, we can see what *Paul Morel B* is like in the crucial middle third, the part dominated by the lad-and-girl love of Paul and Miriam. I will assume that the really significant alterations made in *Paul Morel B* to make it into *Sons and Lovers* come in the last third, the part dominated by Clara and Baxter Dawes, and that the middle chapters in the published novel are substantially those Jessie Chambers saw and resented in *Paul Morel B*.

The parts of *Paul Morel B* described by Harry T. Moore all show Lawrence working with accounts of the lad-and-girl relationship written, as he had asked her to do, by Jessie Chambers. In most cases Lawrence is much the better writer and he clarifies and heightens what she has written. Lawrence tends to idealize Paul Morel in most of these, and at Miriam's expense, but it is different from the fantasizing that had brought *Paul Morel A* to a standstill. Others as well as Jessie Chambers have testified to "what really happened" so as to make clear that Lawrence often altered his experience to cover up some unpleasantness or to heighten Paul's brilliance, but Paul in *Sons and Lovers* is not the simple dream figure the outline of the first version suggests he was. What Jessie Chambers disliked so about *Paul Morel B* was not this sort of thing at all, but what she took to be a more fundamental betrayal of her that resulted when Lawrence fit their relationship into a mold that would give, in her words, "his mother the laurels of victory."

Lawrence and Jessie Chambers had known each other for fifteen years when Lawrence was working on his novel, and had been very close and important to each other, but never in decisive ways. In the years after Lawrence began teaching in Croydon, they saw each other less often and, to judge from stories like "A Modern Lover" and "The Shades of Spring," with a false intensity and an aimlessness that was perhaps inevitable

in a relationship that never developed sexually, that had little
internal coherence of impulse, habit, and action. The more
Lawrence simply wrote down what happened, the more ram-
bling he would eventually become, and he felt compelled to
try to give the relationship a shape in his book that it had never
had in life. To do this he set Miriam off against Mrs. Morel;
Jessie Chambers says in her memoir that "whatever approach
Lawrence made to me inevitably involved him in a sense of
disloyalty to his mother," and by making the relation between
mother and girl a fighting one, Lawrence thought he could
resolve his dilemma. But in the doing he got into terrible difficulties.

In the early scenes of lad-and-girl love between Paul and
Miriam there are no signs that anything is amiss, and some
moments in the middle chapters are as good as the best in the
first six. Here, for instance, is part of the lovely swinging scene
of Paul and Miriam's early adolescence:

> "It's so ripping!" he said, setting her in motion. "Keep your heels
> up, or they'll bang the manger wall."
> She felt the accuracy with which he caught her, exactly at the right
> moment, and the exactly proportionate strength of his thrust, and she
> was afraid. Down to her bowels went the hot wave of fear. She was in
> his hands. Again, firm and inevitable came the thrust at the right
> moment. She gripped the rope, almost swooning. [P. 151]

Jessie Chambers could not have written that, and she may not
even have liked it when she read it, but it is intrinsic to Lawrence's conception of Miriam in all three versions, and it is very
good. The simple sexuality of the swinging is created by Miriam's innocence about what is happening to her. A little later
Paul asks her why she is always sad, and she denies that she is
until he says "even your joy is like a flame coming off sadness,"
and she admits he is right. This is all very typical of her. She is
innocent, intent, humorless, shocked at discovering herself,
reverent, clumsy, an easy target because she tries to do algebra,

and everything else, with her soul. Miriam is not a very attractive person, but she makes sense, both as someone to whom Paul can turn and for whom Mrs. Morel can feel an instinctive dislike. Jessie Chambers herself seems less self-conscious and more self-aware than Miriam, more able to share Lawrence's joys in reading and in the natural world, but nonetheless, in his early handling of Miriam, Lawrence has shaped a recognizable character and has left Jessie Chambers with no justifiable complaint.

As long as Miriam is innocent and passive, however, she gives Lawrence no way to direct his story. She can arouse dislike in Mrs. Morel and a sense of disloyalty to his mother in Paul, but she is not responsible for either feeling. Had he been completely honest, Lawrence would have had to make it clear that Mrs. Morel's dislike and Paul's sense of disloyalty are strictly the result of who they are, not of who Miriam is. But he was not honest, or not honest enough. In the closing episodes of "Strife in Love" Lawrence begins to manipulate his characters so he can resolve his feelings and his story. The scene begins as the last in the novel in which the Morel family has the vitality of the opening chapters, and it ends as melodrama. One Friday night Morel returns from the mines to enact his weekly ritual of dividing his earnings with some other miners and leaving his wife her weekly allowance. When he is through he goes out to a pub, and Mrs. Morel leaves shortly after to go to the market, asking Paul to mind the bread in the oven. Miriam comes, and for a few minutes they discuss some designs Paul is making and "all his passion, all his wild blood, went into this intercourse with her, when he talked and conceived his work." But then another girl, Beatrice Wyld, comes, and the whole atmosphere changes. Out of spite or embarrassment Beatrice taunts Miriam, who is humble and silent in response, and she flirts with Paul, who responds playfully, leaving Miriam in the lurch. It is wonderfully done: the simple and mindless rudeness of

Beatrice, the hurt recoil of Miriam, the siding of Paul against Miriam, himself in recoil against her helplessness. During all this, Paul has let the bread burn in the oven:

> "My word, Miriam! you're in for it this time," said Beatrice.
> "I!" exclaimed Miriam in amazement.
> "You'd better be gone when his mother comes in. *I* know why King Alfred burned the cakes. Now I see it!" [P. 205]

Unjust though she is, Beatrice is perfectly right about Mrs. Morel. Beatrice leaves, Paul walks Miriam home, and when he returns his mother and sister are sitting in accusing silence. Paul confesses his negligence about the bread, and then the three argue, mostly about Paul's neglect of his mother for the sake of Miriam.

Up to this point Lawrence is at his *Sons and Lovers* best; forlorn Miriam, wretched and passionate Paul, beleaguered and therefore aggressive Mrs. Morel, all rendered neatly in the domestic details of a Friday night. But then, after Annie retires, we have this:

> He had taken off his collar and tie, and rose, bare-throated, to go to bed. As he stooped to kiss his mother, she threw her arms round his neck, hid her face on his shoulder, and cried, in a whimpering voice, so unlike her own that he writhed in agony:
> "I can't bear it. I could let another woman—but not her. She'd leave me no room, not a bit of room—"
> And immediately he hated Miriam bitterly.
> "And I've never—you know, Paul—I've never had a husband—not really—"
> He stroked his mother's hair, and his mouth was on her throat.
> "And she exults so in taking you from me—she's not like ordinary girls."
> "Well, I don't love her, mother," he murmured, bowing his head and hiding his eyes on her shoulder in misery. His mother kissed him a long, fervent kiss. [P. 213]

In a flash Mrs. Morel has become mother-lover, Paul has become son-lover, and we are back in effect to the fantasy figures of *Paul Morel A*. In order to be Paul's lover Mrs. Morel must insist she has had no husband and condemn Miriam as a conscious rival who "exults so" in taking Paul away. But one mark of the great success of the novel to this point is the way it shows that Mrs. Morel is not telling the truth here: she has indeed had a husband, though not the one she thought she was getting when she married, and Miriam is innocent, solemn, forlorn, no conscious or exulting rival.

That Mrs. Morel might be driven to such a version of the facts is possible, if not entirely in keeping with her usual effort to be honest with herself. But for Lawrence to accept her version is disastrous, and we can see from the rendering of the scene and the rest of the book that he does so accept and alters his characters to fit it. Paul and Mrs. Morel change right here; Mr. Morel changes a moment later when he returns in the middle of the lovemaking and fills his newly created role as Laius by saying: "At your mischief again." That mischief, at any rate, had never happened before. The change in Miriam comes more slowly, and is not really clear until after Paul insists they become lovers. Though Lawrence is inventing here, what happens has its own kind of sense. The trouble is that Lawrence asks us to make of it something different from the conclusion to which we are naturally drawn. Paul, having in effect become his mother's lover, being unable to admit this to Miriam, is driven to destroy Miriam in a sequence of rape and desertion. That is what happens, but it is not what Paul or Lawrence would have us believe. The Miriam we have known could accept the insistence of Paul's passion, and even the brutality of his subsequent rejection of her, but no Miriam could be like the Miriam of the scene of their parting:

> "Why, I want us to separate. We have lived on each other all these years; now let us stop. I will go my own way without you, and you will go your way without me. You will have an independent life of your own then."

There was in it some truth that, in spite of her bitterness, she could not help registering. She knew she felt in a sort of bondage to him, which she hated because she could not control it. She hated her love for him from the moment it grew too strong for her. And, deep down, she had hated him because she loved him and he dominated her. She had resisted his domination. She had fought to keep herself free of him in the last issue. And she *was* free of him, even more than he of her. [P. 296]

There is no way except by authorial fiat for the intense, innocent, passive Miriam to become this girl who hates her bondage to Paul, hates the strength of her love for him, resists his domination, and wants to be free. Then, when Miriam says "It has always been you fighting me off," Paul twists her words to mean she had never loved him, and Lawrence lets Paul get away with it:

And she—she whose love he had believed in when he had despised himself—denied that their love had ever been love. . . . Then it had been monstrous. There had never been anything really between them; all the time he had been imagining something where there was nothing. [P. 297]

Lawrence even has Miriam feel what Paul has accused her of feeling:

She sat full of bitterness. She had known—oh, well she had known! All the time he was away from her she had summed him up, seen his littleness, his meanness, and his folly. [P. 298]

This is what Jessie Chambers hated, this conversion of herself into a conscious and cunning rival of Mrs. Morel. All Lawrence had to do to make the conversion was to invent a layer of consciousness in Miriam at this point and then insist it had been there all along. It was clearly a desperate move. His novel and his sense of life demanded some kind of form, and the most he could offer is the display of self-pity and self-justification we see here. In point of fact Lawrence had told Jessie his feelings for his mother:

Lawrence looked at me with intensity. "You know—I've always loved mother," he said in a strangled voice.

"I know you have," I replied.

"I don't mean that," he returned quickly. "I've *loved* her, like a lover. That's why I could never love you." [E. T., p. 184]

But Lawrence could not have Paul say this to Miriam without releasing Miriam from any complicity in their failure, and doing that would make it Mrs. Morel, not Miriam, who "exults so" as she steals Paul from her rival. This Lawrence could not do, and so he lets Mrs. Morel become the book's spokesman; he lets Paul pity himself as the victim of the battle between mother and girl; he lets the melodramatic pattern of his fantasies distort a great deal that was most interesting in his life and that was finest in the early parts of his novel.

But at the very time that *Sons and Lovers* was being cruelly fit into a mold and Lawrence's relationship with Jessie Chambers was collapsing, Lawrence met and fell in love with Frieda von Richthofen Weekley. He had planned a trip to Germany on his own, and by mid-April of 1912 that trip had become an elopement for them and a return to her parents for her. They left England in early May and lived nomadically for the next few months. It was a terrifying experience for both of them, as their letters and the early poems in the sequence that later became *Look! We Have Come Through* make clear. Lawrence had just finished making a ramshackle truce with his feelings for his mother and suddenly he was embarked on what he knew to be the great adventure of his life. Lawrence did not know how he was to live and he was resentful of all he often felt Frieda had heaped upon him—her estrangement from her children, her confusion at shuttling from aristocratic parents to working-class lover, her love for him. He was alone, in a country whose language he did not really know and whose people he generally did not like. He was committed to someone he barely knew, and he could see her only when she could free herself from her family.

But because of or in spite of this, Lawrence worked away at his novel. He wrote Edward Garnett, who for some time had been serving as his literary mentor and unpaid agent, that he was revising it. He finished *Paul Morel B* in early June and sent it off to Garnett for advice, knowing it was not yet right. But he did not really get at this revision until he and Frieda completed their walk through the Alps and settled in the first of their many permanent homes at the Villa Igéa, Lago di Garda, Gargnano, on September 12. Two weeks later he wrote Garnett: "I do my novel well, I'm sure. It's half done," and a month after that the title is changed to *Sons and Lovers* and is finished except for the last hundred pages. Finally, on November 14 he is done, "I tell you I have written a great book."

The differences between *Sons and Lovers* and *Paul Morel B*, to repeat, are uncertain, but it is clear that the last hundred pages were much revised or begun from scratch at the very end, in November. So the first six chapters, which Jessie Chambers saw and loved, were done in something close to published form at the end of the winter, as were the middle five, which Jessie Chambers saw and disliked intensely. The last four were probably written in the fall. What they show is that Lawrence, having cruelly and precariously shifted the book's bearings to accommodate his feelings for his mother, set off into new territory and explored his commitment to those feelings and to his parents who generated them. Lawrence insisted often that his book "had form," and he was obviously very excited at having fought through to what he believed was an artistic whole. The curious account he sent to Garnett shows us the novel he thought he had written:

a woman of character and refinement goes into the lower class, and has no satisfaction in her own life. She has had a passion for her husband, so the children are born of passion, and have heaps of vitality. But as her sons grow up she selects them as lovers—first the eldest, then the second. These sons are *urged* into life by their reciprocal love of their mother—urged on and on. But when they come to manhood, they can't love, because their mother is the strongest power in their lives, and holds them. . . . As soon as the young men come into contact with women, there's a split. William gives his sex to a fribble, and his mother holds his soul. But the split kills him, because he doesn't know where he is. The next son gets a woman who fights for his soul—fights his mother. The son loves the mother—all the sons hate and are jealous of the father. The battle goes on between the mother and the girl, with the son as object. The mother gradually proves stronger, because of the tie of blood. The son decides to leave his soul in his mother's hands, and, like his elder brother go for passion. He gets passion. Then the split begins to tell again. But, almost unconsciously, the mother realizes what is the matter, and begins to die. The son casts off his mistress, attends to his mother dying. He is left in the end naked of everything, with the drift towards death. [November 14, 1912]

1736010

This is indeed repellent, pathetic because Lawrence really believed it, the most misleading statement of an author about his work since Spenser's letter to Raleigh at the beginning of *The Faerie Queene*. I have said enough about the early and middle sections of the novel to indicate the ways I think this statement makes of them a distorted and simple pattern. Perhaps the most interesting question one can ask of this account, however, concerns the later chapters, the ones on which Lawrence had just been working: Where is Baxter Dawes?

In the last four chapters of *Sons and Lovers* Lawrence gropes toward a solution of his feelings for his parents, and the fact that the description above says so little about this means the solution the book arrives at was probably not achieved consciously. In transforming the elder Morels and Miriam to fit his desire for his mother, Lawrence had to face in some way the implications of that desire. What is crucial for our purposes about the solution he made is that it gave him a way to render all his characters from then on. The key figures are Clara and Baxter Dawes, the only major figures in the book not taken over directly from Lawrence's experience. Clara "is" Alice Dax and "is" Louise Burrows and "is" the woman who told Mrs. William Hopkin she "gave Bert sex" when he was having trouble finishing a poem. So too Baxter "is" Alan Chambers and "is" Ernest Weekley. But from their entrance in the novel they are characters with assigned roles, unlike the elder Morels and Miriam who are wrenched into their roles later on in their careers. So far as I know, Frank O'Connor was the first to identify these roles:

Dawes is really Paul's father, and Paul, through his relationship with Clara, which gives him the opportunity of probing Dawes's relations with his wife, is not only able to repeat the offense against his father by robbing him of his wife, but is also, in the manner of a fairy tale, able to undo the wrong by reconciling them. [*The Mirror in the Roadway* (New York, 1956), p. 278]

Of the thousands of sentences I have read on Lawrence, this is the one that has made the most difference to me. It not only clarified what had seemed puzzling about *Sons and Lovers,* and showed me the form the novel had and which excited Lawrence for reasons he could not quite grasp, but it also pointed the way to the kind of writing Lawrence was to do for the rest of his life. O'Connor himself is unsympathetic to the later Lawrence, and he insists that his parents were the only people who were ever real for Lawrence, but his insight does show how Lawrence could move from the bright realism of the novel's opening toward the modes he was to explore in the next two novels. It has always seemed to me that this sentence, which has gone virtually unnoticed in later commentary on Lawrence, is the best possible introduction to Lawrence as hero. His handling of the Daweses shows us both his dilemma and the ways in which he could confront it. His marriage and the war subsequently gave him and forced upon him a sense of history and urgency not felt here, at the end of *Sons and Lovers,* but his need and his ability not to rest defeated are first apparent here.

The one critic who also has seen what Frank O'Connor sees is Daniel Weiss, whose careful and scrupulous *Oedipus in Nottingham* is the one indispensable book, after Jessie Chambers's, for those reading early Lawrence. Weiss stresses the way the Daweses are used to reconcile to himself Lawrence's desires for his parents. Clara, of course, is mostly just there, an object for Paul's passion; she bears only slim resemblance to Mrs. Morel when they are compared as characters. But, as Frank O'Connor says, Clara allows Paul to seek out Baxter, the shadowy "other man" who is so central in Lawrence and for whose sake, after a while, the relationship with Clara seems to exist. Quotation cannot indicate the spooky quality of Paul here, because what is striking about his questioning of Clara about Baxter is its suddenness, its coming on the scene without preparation or explanation. He begins his exploration shortly after he meets Clara:

> "How old were you when you married?" he asked quietly.
> "Twenty-two."
> Her voice was subdued, almost submissive. She would tell him now. [P. 274]

She answers him by giving a version of her marriage similar to the one Mrs. Morel has given him about hers:

> "He—he sort of degraded me. He wanted to bully me because he hadn't got me. And then I felt as if I wanted to run, as if I was fastened and bound up. And he seemed dirty." [P. 275]

Soon Paul is back, again raising the issue without explanation:

> Mrs. Dawes and he had many periods of coolness, when they saw little of each other; but they always came together again.
> "Were you horrid with Baxter Dawes?" he asked her. It was a thing that seemed to trouble him. [P. 276]

Later he asks, "Why did you hate Baxter Dawes?" and this third time the line is simply there, without antecedent or succeeding conversation, and can be explained only by saying Lawrence had to keep having Paul ask the questions without either of them knowing why.

The "form" of the early chapters has by now completely disappeared. There the logic of the family builds into unstated causalities that link sentence to sentence and paragraph to paragraph. Here the writing is by one who seems drugged, in a trance. Almost certainly Lawrence was unaware that he calls Paul "Morel," the name otherwise reserved for Paul's father, about twenty times late in the book, and each time Paul is with Baxter Dawes. Their affection and hatred is enacted without semblance of explanation, but the result, Baxter's reconciliation with Clara, is unmistakable. It is not at all in the manner of the early or the middle chapters, but in an obscure pattern of repetition of the marriage of the elder Morels done in a dream landscape, rather like the second half of *Wuthering Heights*. Out of the implacable antagonism of Paul and Baxter emerges whatever of true intent Paul has in these later chapters: Baxter must not be fought, and he must be returned to his wife. Because, we can add, it is Paul's only way of completing his passion for his mother and of releasing himself from its bondage.

Baxter Dawes does not appear as a distinct character in *Sons and Lovers*; no one knows much about him and Paul does not care about him as a separate being but only as Clara's husband, as a shadow father figure. Such a figure, as I have indicated, has appeared before in Lawrence's work. In "A Modern Lover" and "The Shades of Spring," both written at Croydon as efforts to work out the failed relationship with Jessie Chambers, the Lawrence figure returns home to the midlands to find the heroine being courted by a silent young man who lives close to the soil and who has none of the intellect or talent of the Lawrence hero. Such a man did not in fact exist in Jessie Chambers's life. He appears again as a young miner in "Daughters of the Vicar" and more indistinctly as a former lover in "The Shadow in the Rose Garden." In "The Old Adam" he is the husband of the older woman the Lawrence figure is courting, just as he is in

Sons and Lovers. In all cases where the two men meet there is a sudden and unexplained bond between them: "The two men grasped hands," "The two men walked almost like friends," " 'After all,' said Mersham, 'he's very beautiful; she is a fool to give him up.' " The relationship seems to demand but never receives explanation. In the stories perhaps no such explanation is really needed, but in *Sons and Lovers*, rich as it is earlier in all sorts of explanation, the relationship of Paul and Baxter, by its very unannounced and eerie quality, shows that Lawrence is moving out into new territory, experimenting with what might be called symbolical characters and relationships, but still, here, in a book where they do not quite belong but where nothing else would have served to release Lawrence and Paul from the brutal impasse reached by the transformation of the elder Morels and Miriam. It was the most and best Lawrence could do in the fall of 1912 to square himself with his family now that he had left them to go off with Frieda.

That Lawrence did not know what was happening or what he had done can be seen, first, in the absence of any mention of Baxter Dawes in his account of the novel to Garnett. It is also apparent in the first of the new projects he undertook on finishing *Sons and Lovers.* The Burns novel has a short career:

> I am thinking so hard of my new novel, and since I am feeling hard pushed again, am in the right tune for it. It is to be a life of Robert Burns—but I shall make him live near home, as a Derbyshire man and shall fictionise the circumstances. I think I can do him almost like an autobiography. [December 17, 1912]

But exactly a month later, the project is abandoned: "As for the book, my novel on the subject [Burns], I wonder if I shall ever get it done" (January 17, 1913). The book could have been only *Sons and Lovers* warmed over, and the fragment that remains begins resolutely in the old manner: "There was the clear sound of a man whistling, but no one was to be seen on the common. The afternoon of the beautiful November day was drawing to a close"—and continues in the vein of the early stories. Even as he was working on the Burns novel, he was indicating in his letters that he was beginning to see much newer and more important things to do:

> I shall do a novel about Love Triumphant one day. I shall do my work for women, better than the Suffrage. [December 23, 1912]

> I'll do my life work, sticking up for the love between man and woman. [December 25, 1912]

But after dropping the Burns novel, Lawrence did not immediately turn to his "life work," his "work for women," his "novel about Love Triumphant." Instead he starts on *The Insurrection of Miss Houghton,* which, he says in a letter of February 1, "might find a good public amongst the Meredithy public." He is excited about it all winter, saying it is very different "from my other stuff—far less visualised." Judging from the early chapters of *The Lost Girl,* the novel it eventually became, it is not in the early manner but not in any manner Lawrence worked in later, either. It is, as he says, outspoken, but more in the sense that he is working off animus against some people he knew in Nottingham than in the sense that he is saying what is most urgent in him. It is remarkably impersonal, detached, strong in feeling, very good but curiously hard to read. It is easy to see why Lawrence liked its manner, yet understandable why, after working on it for two months, he did not go on. His life work, Love Triumphant, demanded something different.

That he should want to do his "work for women" by writing a novel about Love Triumphant is of course testimonial to Frieda and to the relationship they were creating. But it should be remembered that he had never before been able to write about such a love—women had been for him objects or else creatures to be fought off. The end of *Sons and Lovers* suggests Lawrence had achieved at least partial release from the mother love that had so restricted him, but the means of that release,

Clara and Baxter Dawes, seems to create almost as many problems as it solves; to do one's work for women in *Sons and Lovers* is to seek out the woman's husband. It should not be surprising, therefore, that when Lawrence set out later to do this work, he did so both excitedly and fumblingly:

> I am a damned curse unto myself. I've written rather more than half of a most fascinating (to me) novel. But nobody will ever dare to publish it. I feel I could knock my head against the wall. Yet I love and adore this new book. It's all crude as yet, like one of Tony's clumsy prehistorical beasts—most cumbersome and floundering—but I think it's great—so new, so really a stratum deeper than I think anybody has ever gone, in a novel. [March 11, 1913]

> I have written 180 pages of my newest novel *The Sisters*. It is a queer novel, which seems to have come by itself. I will send it you. You may dislike it—it hasn't got hard outlines—and of course it's only first draft—but it is pretty neat, for me, in composition. Then I've got 200 pages of a novel which I'm saving—which is very lumbering—which I'll call, provisionally, *The Insurrection of Miss Houghton*. That I shan't send you yet, but it is, to me, fearfully exciting. It lies next my heart, for the present. But I am finishing *The Sisters*. It will only have 300 pages. It was meant to be for the *"jeune filles,"* but already it has fallen from grace. I can only write what I feel pretty strongly about: and that, at present, is the relation between men and women. After all, it is *the* problem of today, the establishment of a new relation, or the readjustment of the old one, between men and women.—In a month *The Sisters* will be finished. [April 18 (?) , 1913]

Nothing we know of either *Miss Houghton* or early versions of *The Sisters* makes them candidates for a book that is "so new, so really a stratum deeper than I think anyone has ever gone, in a novel," but *The Sisters* certainly comes closer. In any event, by April it has taken over as the main object of his attention; the first revealing description of it comes in a letter written six weeks later:

> I was glad of your letter about *The Sisters*. Don't *schimpf*, I shall make it all right when I rewrite it. I shall put it in the third person. All along I knew what ailed the book. But it did me good to theorise

myself out, and to depict Frieda's God Almightiness in all its glory. That was the first crude fermenting of the book. I'll make it into art now. I've done 256 pages, but still can't see the end very clear. But it's coming. Frieda is so cross, since your letter came, with the book. Before that she was rather fond of her portrait in straight pleats and Athena sort of pose. [Late May or early June, 1913]

The Sisters at this point is a first person narrative, presumably told by the sister who represents Frieda. She seems to be named "Ella," as Frieda speaks of herself as "Ella-ing" earlier in the same letter. Lawrence's work for women has turned into a rendering of Frieda's "God Almightiness," giving voice to Lawrence's theorizing about women. The result is not right and Lawrence knows it, but he seems convinced he is on the right track and will finish soon. Back in April he had written to A. W. McLeod:

I am doing a novel which I have never grasped. Damn its eyes, there I am at page 145, and I've no notion what it's about. I hate it. F. says it is good. But it's like a novel in a foreign language I don't know very well—I can only just make out what it is about. [April 26, 1913]

So after 145 pages Lawrence could not grasp what he was doing, and after 256 he knew what he had done, knew it was not yet "art," yet still could not see the end clearly. Though no manuscript of this version exists, it is clear from the hints given here, and especially from remarks made a little later, that the two sisters at the opening of the novel resemble those at the beginning of *Women in Love* and their situation is like Paul Morel's at the end of *Sons and Lovers*. Of *The Rainbow* to be we have no hint, and no sense that any of Lawrence's thinking is as yet historical.

At this point Lawrence and Frieda returned to England for the summer and we learn nothing more of *The Sisters* until they returned to Italy in the fall. What Lawrence does mention are the stories he had been writing and the best of these, "The Prussian Officer," plus the poems of 1913 which belong to

Look! We Have Come Through!, show us the problems with which he was wrestling about the time he finished *The Sisters* for the first time.

The sequence of poems opens with bitter ones from the early days of the elopement, followed by some spiteful ones about Frieda's "God Almightiness." Then come the first group that asserts triumph—"New Year's Night," "Birth Night," "Paradise Re-Entered"—but in such an insistent way—we will come through, we have come through, now you are mine—as to indicate more doubt than assurance. Along with these is the very curious "Both Sides of the Medal," written late in 1912:

> And because you love me,
> think you you do not hate me?
> Ha, since you love me
> to ecstacy
> it follows you hate me to ecstacy.

This curious and shaky logic, with its theorizing based on intuition, is probably what fills the early versions of *The Sisters*. As the poem proceeds it becomes clear that what she hates is not him but confinement with and to him:

> Since you are confined in the orbit of me
> do you not loathe the confinement?
> Is not even the beauty and peace of an orbit
> an intolerable prison to you,
> as it is to everybody?

> But we will learn to submit
> each of us to the balanced, eternal orbit
> wherein we circle on our fate
> in strange conjunction.
> What is chaos, my love?
> It is not freedom.
> A disarray of falling stars coming to nought.
> [*The Complete Poems of D. H. Lawrence*, ed. V. de Sola
> Pinto (New York, 1964), I, 235]

This is an early version of what was to become standard Lawrentian doctrine, stated flatly enough here to make a meager
poem but well enough to show us that he saw this early that the
positive alternative to God Almightiness is "the beauty and
peace of an orbit" where the man and woman "circle on our
fate in strange conjunction."

The poem makes clear that one source of strain in the relationship between Lawrence and Frieda is her urge to be somehow free, independent, and his insistence that such freedom is
chaos. All this is central to the relationship between Rupert
Birkin and Ursula Brangwen in the novel that grows directly
from *The Sisters* begun shortly after the poem was written. The
novel gives us the doctrine but drama too, because it provides
the answering voice of the "you" that hates to ecstasy. Yet the
novel, at least in the early versions, could not avoid Lawrence's
theorizing about the need for a new relationship between men
and women. That is, both the poem and *The Sisters* seem to
have had the doctrine more than the reality. There had been,
we all know, a breakdown in the old relationship between men
and women in which the men had been dominant. The best
known and most obvious alternative was independent women,
the ideal of the suffragettes. But Lawrence had said he would
do more for women than that. Still, in Lawrence's deciding on
his own what was really good for Frieda and for women, one
detects, and one knows Frieda detected, a note of the old Adam
of masculine domination. Behind the poem's assertion about
submitting "to the balanced, eternal orbit" one can hear the
arguments between Lawrence and Frieda in their first year together.

But if one source of strain was what Lawrence wanted to call
Frieda's "God Almightiness," then another source was the
"other man" or, more strictly speaking, whatever it was in Lawrence that was drawn to such a man. In "The Prussian Officer,"

written in the spring of 1913, we can see what has happened to this figure since his creation as Baxter Dawes. It is not, given his entire work, a typical Lawrence story, but it is very suggestive about its author nonetheless. The Prussian officer is haughty, handsome, tight-lipped, educated, cruel, and attracted to his orderly, who is silent, lithe, uneducated, and baffled by the officer's attention. The officer is more open in his pursuit than Paul Morel is with Baxter, and the absence of an intervening woman makes the word "homosexual" appropriate here in a way it is not in any earlier treatment of the two figures:

[The officer has just brutally interrogated the orderly and discovered the boy has been writing poetry to his girl.] The officer, left alone, held himself rigid, to prevent himself from thinking. His instinct warned him that he must not think. Deep inside him was the intense gratification of his passion, still working powerfully. Then there was a counter-action, a horrible breaking down of something inside him, a whole agony of reaction. He stood there for an hour motionless, a chaos of sensations, but rigid with a will to keep blank his consciousness, to prevent his mind grasping. And he held himself so until the worst of the stress had passed, when he began to drink, drank himself to an intoxication, till he slept obliterated. [*The Complete Short Stories* (London, 1955), I, 103]

The discovery of his passion engages the officer in a way he cannot face or fathom. Because it can be expressed only by cruel and repressive gestures that seek to keep it from becoming fully expressed, the orderly is only hounded and whipped and so he soon seeks his revenge. The story insists that this revenge, which comes when the orderly strangles the officer on a march, kills both of them because it brings them consummately together in an act of mutual self-destruction. Frieda Lawrence said of the two men that they "seemed to represent the split in [Lawrence's] soul, the split between the conscious and the unconscious man." Such an assignment of roles is too simple, but accurate as far as it goes. The power of the captain, the "conscious man," can express itself only in acts of cruelty and domination, and these really are also acts of self-destruction. The homosexual passion of the conscious Lawrence is too much for him, and the only way he can handle it in the story is to seek means for its ultimate obliteration, in sleep, in drink, and ultimately in death.

Lawrence's homosexuality and the various sexual "perversions" that accompany it, have come in for much tongue-clucking, especially after F. R. Leavis tried to insist that Lawrence was a figure of health and normality. Coming to it as we have, via "The Prussian Officer" and the other early stories that involve the "other man," we can perhaps begin to see it for what it is and for what it implies about his relationship with Frieda and his struggle for the sexual relations between men and women. Throughout his life Lawrence sought to dominate other men—that is the explanation for his predilection for second-rate men—and to idealize the man he was not and his father almost was, a physically and emotionally strong man, calm, knowing, unintellectual—the gamekeeper of his first and last novels is the "ideal" solution. But the more these feelings became conscious, the more they became subject to the will of the volatile, intelligent, self-conscious Lawrence, the more they became destructive and therefore suicidal. The will to dominate in Lawrence is not so much homosexuality as it is an evasion of the ideal heterosexuality. The ideal, the Love Triumphant, the eternal orbit wherein the man and woman circle in strange conjunction, is threatened, then, by both the hensure man and the cocksure woman, as Lawrence later called them, by the impulses toward independence and domination which are the same or similar.

But in 1913 Lawrence "knew" all this at best fleetingly, and the impulse that could make the doctrine vital and not jargon was beset by Frieda and even more by passions inside himself. Perhaps the greatest temptation and danger for him lay in his sense that on the other side of the passion to dominate and hurt lay consummation and death:

I wish that whatever props up the wall of light
would fall, and darkness come hurling heavily down,
and it would be thick black dark forever.
Not sleep, which is grey with dreams,
nor death, which quivers with birth
but heavy, sealing darkness, silence, all immovable.

[*Poems*, I, 205]

Here there is no mention of the passions that in "The Prussian Officer" lead to the desire for obliteration; the desire is simply felt, rather the way Paul Morel feels it after his mother dies. It seems the obverse of some other poems in *Look! We Have Come Through!* For just as the idea of "coming through" implies struggle and new birth, so the desire for obliterating darkness implies a desire to end the struggle, a doubt that "coming through" is possible, a frustration at its difficulty. What made the difficulty may have been Frieda's "God Almightiness," but probably much more contributory was Lawrence's own "God Almightiness," his similarity to the Prussian officer, his passion to dominate, to destroy himself by such dominating, and to be sealed in darkness as an end or as punishment for the passion to dominate. The closer Lawrence came to seeing his life work made real, to coming through, to realizing the implications of Love Triumphant, the closer he also came to its opposite and its enemy: the passion to control, to dominate other men. The heroism of Lawrence lies in his moving closer to the light even as he moves and knows himself to be moving closer to the darkness at the same time.

I have said all this while using "The Prussian Officer" and some poems as evidence, and to do so implies that the case is incontrovertible and not in need of further support. Further support, however, is amply available in *The Rainbow* and *Women in Love,* and I have tried to extract a Lawrence of 1913 from the lesser works to provide a context for the details of his struggle to write those novels.

Late in 1913 Lawrence returned to Italy and began work again on *The Sisters*:

The Sisters has quite a new beginning—a new basis altogether. I hope I can get on with it. It is much more interesting in its new form—not so damned flippant. I can feel myself getting ready for my autumn burst of work. [September 4, 1913]

This alone might imply that Lawrence had found the historical vision that is the basis of *The Rainbow,* but a letter five months later indicates that he is still working on the situations that eventually became *Women in Love:*

I agree with you about the Templeman episode. In the scheme of the novel, however, I *must* have Ella get some experience before she meets her Mr. Birkin. I also felt that the character was inclined to fall into two halves—and gradations between them. It came of trying to graft on to the character of Louie [Louise Burrows, his fiancée in 1911] the character, more or less, of Frieda. That I ought not to have done. To your two main criticisms, that the Templeman episode is wrong, and that the character of Ella is incoherent, I agree. Then about the artistic side being in the background. It is that which troubles me most. I have no longer the joy in creating vivid scenes, that I had in *Sons and Lovers.* I don't care much more [sic] about accumulating objects in the powerful light of emotion, and making a scene of them. I have to write differently. I am most anxious about your criticism of this, the second half of the novel, a hundred and fifty pages of which I send you tomorrow. Tell me *very* frankly what you think of it: and if it pleases you, tell me whether you think Ella would be possible, as she now stands, unless she had some experience of love and of men. I think, impossible. Then she must have a love episode, a significant one. But it must not be a Templeman episode.

Then, a paragraph later:

I am going through a transition stage myself. I am a slow writer, really—I only have great outbursts of work. So that I do not much mind if I put all this novel in the fire, because it is the vaguer result of transition. I write with everything vague—plenty of fire underneath, but, like bulbs in the ground, only shadowy flowers that must be beaten and sustained, for another spring. I feel that this second half of *The Sisters* is very beautiful, but it may not be sufficiently incorporated to please you. I do not try to incorporate it very much—I prefer the permeating beauty. It is my transition stage—but I must write to live, and it must produce its flowers, and if they be frail or shadowy, they will be all right if they are true to their hour. It is not so easy for one to be married. In marriage one must become something else. And I am changing, one way or the other. [January 29, 1914]

So much here needs comment that it is perhaps best to take it in order. Templeman is obviously the man who later became Anton Skrebensky in *The Rainbow,* and from what is said of him it can be gathered that some of the later parts of that novel have been written as "an episode." Birkin is in the book, but we do not have a single reference to Ella's sister. Already in an earlier letter Lawrence is contemplating *The Wedding Ring* as a new title, which would imply that the role that became Gudrun Brangwen's is not clear or not even in existence. There is no mention of Gerald Crich either, or of the first two generations of Brangwens. The project is in flux, in transition, vague but, like bulbs, able to produce flowers another spring: "In marriage one must become something else." The implication is that Lawrence is moving uncertainly from an Ella reflective of Frieda's "God Almightiness" toward an Ella that is Ursula and a novel about marriage.

But the transition was not soon over: "Oh, I tried so hard to work, this last year. I began a novel seven times. I have written quite a thousand pages that I shall burn" (April 3, 1914). Draft after draft of the novel was being sent off to Edward Garnett, and each one apparently made him less sympathetic than the last. The strain becomes marked in Lawrence's letter to him of April 22:

You know how willing I am to hear what you have to say, and to take your advice and to act on it when I have taken it. But it is no good unless you will have patience and understand what I *want* to do. I am not after all a child working erratically. All the time, underneath, there is something deep evolving itself out in me. And it is *hard* to express a new thing, in sincerity. And you should understand, and help me to the new thing, not get angry and say it is *common,* and send me back to the tone of the old *Sisters.* In the *Sisters* was the germ of this novel: woman becoming individual, self-responsible, taking her own initiative.

Here at last is the real subject. In many ways this is a more important letter than the famous one two months later that describes the breaking down of the old stable ego of character. In the old *Sisters,* now spoken of deprecatingly, we have Frieda's "God Almightiness"; now we have "woman becoming individual." It is the first hint that Lawrence sees his subject historically. In *The Sisters* Frieda-Ella was clearly individual enough, but in a way that made Lawrence want to jeer or be combative. If the emphasis is placed on the verb in "woman *becoming* individual," then the perspective of history can allow Lawrence to do more than set the woman against himself, to do more than ask if he approves of the woman who has become individual and who takes her own initiative.

We don't know how fully historical the vision had as yet become, but the symbol of the rainbow, which depends on a historical vision of a covenanted family for its power, is mentioned for the first time in the very next letter to Garnett:

> I hope you will really like the novel. You will swear when you see the length. It's a *magnum opus* with a vengeance. I have got about three thousand more words to write—two more days, and then *basta*. Frieda wants the novel to be called *The Rainbow.* It doesn't look it at first sight, but I think it is a good title. I like it better than *The Wedding Ring.* [May 9, 1914]

The Rainbow is a title for a historical novel as the earlier ones are not, but how much of the Brangwen family history is in the version that is being finished here cannot be known. But at any event what we think of as *The Rainbow* is clearly coming into existence, though as yet the magnum opus still includes much that was turned into *Women in Love.*

Shortly thereafter Lawrence and Frieda went to England to be married, and because this led to a sharp decrease in the number of letters written, we know little about what happened to the book. But on December 5, seven months after the last reference, Lawrence wrote to his agent J. B. Pinker that he is writing the novel over, and on January 7, 1915 he announced that he is "going to split the book into two volumes: it was so unwieldy." We don't know just what happened to force this decision, but the most likely explanation is that *The Rainbow* was becoming increasingly a historical novel so that the parts taking place in the historical present began to seem like a sequel rather than part of the same book. For between May and December of 1914 comes the war, the crucial event for Lawrence as for so many others, which made the past feel a very long time ago. He had planned to return to Italy shortly after the wedding, but the outbreak of the war trapped him in England for the next five years, and this led to a sense of being caged, which brought everything that had been both growing and festering inside him to a point of crisis and fruition. The will to dominate and the temptation to careen off into darkness was now being enacted on what seemed a universal scale:

The war makes me depressed, the talk about the war makes me sick, and I have never come so near to hating mankind as I am now. They are fools, and vulgar fools, and cowards who will always make a noise because they are afraid of the silence. I don't even mind if they're killed. But I do mind those who, being sensitive, will receive such a blow from the ghastliness and mechanical, obsolete, hideous stupidity of war, that they will be crippled beings further burdening our sick society. Those that die, let them die. But those that live afterwards— the thought of them makes me sick. [September 21, 1914]

We have seen enough of the Prussian officer in Lawrence to know how dangerous and destructive to his hopes for Love Triumphant are the feelings expressed above. This sounds like Ursula Brangwen at the end of *The Rainbow* or Birkin at the beginning of *Women in Love*; its nausea and despair seek to blot out all other considerations and thereby to endanger everything for which Lawrence had been hoping since he finished *Sons and Lovers* two years earlier.

The Rainbow was finished by March, 1915, and Lawrence wrote relatively little for the next year. The world he moved in was the world of *Women in Love*. We must stop here, thus, to consider *The Rainbow* and to watch its historical vision bring Lawrence and us back down to the searing and frightening world of 1915. To begin at the beginning of the novel is to feel we are moving backward, to the preindustrial England with which it is concerned and to the Lawrence who worked so hard on the novel in the months just before the war. He had begun his novel with Ella and Birkin, in the present, but that did not work. What he needed to find was a sense of history, of woman becoming individual over the course of three generations, for that not only makes *The Rainbow* what it is but allows *Women in Love* to be what it is, a version of *The Sisters* transformed because the present too can now be a part of history, a continuation and a testing of that history. The discovery of history is essential in the making of a heroic Lawrence, for it enables Lawrence to transform his private terrors and joys into a fiction that is not simply a vehicle for ideas but is an enactment of the lives of impassioned and struggling people.

All that precedes *The Rainbow*, thus, can be seen by us as it was by Lawrence, as preparation, and for our purposes *The Rainbow* itself can be considered as preparation for the heroic climax that comes in *Women in Love*. But if we consider it only in that context, we will do considerable injustice to one of the world's great novels, so some of what follows is written simply for the sake of describing its achievement.

– 2 –

One advantage Lawrence enjoys over other formulators of the Myth of Lost Unity is that he knows it to be a myth. Henry Adams, Eliot, and Yeats all point to precisely named periods of history to find their Golden Age, while Lawrence, fully aware that the aim of the myth is only to illuminate the relationship between past and present, is freer and more imaginative than they. He begins with what we ordinarily think of as prehistory, when the world knew no progress and time was only a cycle of season and life:

They felt the rush of the sap in spring, they knew the wave which cannot halt, but every year throws forward the seed to begetting, and, falling back, leaves the young-born on the earth. They knew the intercourse between heaven and earth, sunshine drawn into the breast and bowels, the rain sucked up in the daytime, nakedness that comes under the wind in autumn, showing the birds' nests no longer worth hiding. [*The Rainbow* (Compass ed.), p. 2]

Such full prose, it is a shame that it has been partly victimized by those who always seek to have Lawrence take sides, to be for one thing and therefore against its opposite or complement. Surely is it not necessary to be in favor of "the drowse of blood-intimacy" here, or in favor of what comes next, the first motion of the women away from this life of cycle and participation:

she strained her eyes to see what man had done in fighting outwards to knowledge, she strained to hear how he uttered himself in his conquest, her deepest desire hung on the battle that she heard, far off, being waged on the edge of the unknown. She also wanted to know, and to be of the fighting host. [P. 3]

First one thing, then the next thing; first the living with the cycles of growth and decay, then the women entering the linear motions of time called history and associated with the idea of progress. No judgment is made on the drowsy men or the active women; in a myth it is what *is* that counts.

The women will keep the spotlight most of the time, to be sure, because theirs is the motion that demands watching while the men can be left alone until they offer some countermotion. "About 1840" a canal is built across the Marsh Farm of the Brangwens, collieries are built, and railroads, so towns spring up around the Brangwens, making them seem "pastoral," old-fashioned. The flow of the prose itself expresses the motions of time—gradually, as we emerge from prehistory and into human consciousness, we move from "man" to the Brangwen family, to "the Alfred Brangwen of the period," then to Tom himself, the first important Brangwen man because the first to live strongly under the influence of the Brangwen women and their engagement with "the active scope of man" and "the far-off world of cities and governments." Our focus becomes more specific as we increasingly have a sense of human consciousness to make it more specific, to dwell on acts of choice and will, to move away from the collective blood-intimacy of earlier generations.

Tom Brangwen is the first important character, then, because he is the first to be attentive himself. He cannot lapse into the life of earlier Brangwen men, yet he cannot be the active hero his mother wants him to be, so he is confused:

> There was a life so different from what he knew it. What was there outside his knowledge, how much? What was this that he had touched? What was he in this new influence? What did everything mean? Where was life, in that which he knew or all outside him? [P. 19]

For Tom what is "outside him" is neither the participating universe of his fathers nor the magical civilization of his mothers, so he is individual, a character, because he cannot be fitted into the previously satisfactory category of "Brangwen men."

All this needs stress because we need a constant sense of the context provided by the motion of history expressed in the motion of the writing in order to make that writing at all clear. Here, for instance, is a passage that badly needs its context in order to be intelligible. Tom has seen Lydia Lensky and is suddenly suspended: " 'That's her,' he said involuntarily." One day she appears unexpectedly at his home, and he is dazed:

> In his breast, or in his bowels, somewhere in his body, there had started another activity. It was as if a strong light were burning there, and he was blind within it, unable to know anything, except that this trans-

figuration burned between him and her, connecting them, like a secret power. [P. 33]

To have a "strong light" in Tom's breast or bowels and then to have Tom blinded inside that light is to use prepositions very strangely. Such writing has led many otherwise sympathetic readers to feel Lawrence writes a kind of jargon, and it is certainly true that if we are not very careful with it or if Lawrence is not careful with it, the result is jargon and inarticulate submission or rejection by the reader. We need always to demand of such a passage what we demand of any writing. We cannot allow it to become vague. We must see the kind of sense it makes in order to make any real sense of the novel as it unfolds.

The motions of history have forced Tom to see the outside world as different from himself, but as long as it remains merely "outside," Tom is confused, set off. Lydia is foreign, a Pole, a woman, yet he knows "That's her." He is the vessel into which the knowledge that she will be his wife comes. The knowledge is thus "inside" him. But because it is not a matter of his conscious choosing and is not subject to his control, what is "inside" is also "outside," surrounding and blinding him. This relationship of "inside" to "outside" is insistently paradoxical because Tom is when he is in history: he is not as his ancestors were, so what is within and what is without are not in automatic harmony, but he is not, as his descendants will be, so cut off from the outside and so conscious of being cut off that he must seek to dominate or control his world. That which is foreign and beyond is suddenly inside as well, and so Tom is transfigured. Thus Lawrence can say "Gradually, even without seeing her, he came to know her." He does not know "about" her; he does not know Lydia Lensky; he knows the light that "is" her, that is inside him. "He was nothing. But with her, he would be real," and

But during the long February nights with the ewes in labour, looking out from the shelter into the flashing stars, he knew he did not belong to himself. [P. 35]

Leavis has more than once used this sentence as a sign of the religious basis of Lawrence's writing—see especially the Richmond Lecture attack on C. P. Snow—and in such contexts it begins to seem a slogan, a badge of faith. But it need not be so taken. Without the preceding historical context we would be almost forced to read it as Romantic poetry and to say the ewes and the stars are symbols that make a vital universe known to Tom Brangwen: nature exists to direct human feeling. But the ewes and stars are really only out there just as Lydia is, and they "teach" him nothing. But because Tom has been transfigured, because that which is outside is also burning inside, he can "learn" from the external world the nature of his inner self, namely that he does not belong to himself. He must yield himself up, not to the outside world but to the light and the flame inside him, to his new self.

To read *The Rainbow* one must stop at every murky or mysterious passage and see the kind of sense it makes. Lawrence's unsympathetic readers are often more helpful here than his admirers, because they do ask what he means and demand sensible answers. They will not be put down with a passage from a letter or an essay offered as exegesis as though such passages could serve as substitutes for a passage in the novel. The rule on this point is clear: if the context of the novel does not make a passage clear, then the result is jargon, private language, inferior. There are such passages in *The Rainbow,* a great many even, but very few compared to the number that seem impenetrable when read out of context. To pick up the novel and to begin reading at any place but the beginning is almost necessarily to be baffled and irritated. We know that since the Renaissance our culture no longer has a common visionary language such as was available to Langland or Spenser. We know that our visionary authors since then—Milton, Blake, Shelley, Swinburne—were driven to invent their own language and systems of symbols, and that this meant either greater vagueness or greater cultist insistence, or both, as time went on and the common basis of the visions was diminished. This has led to quarrels between staunch admirers willing to operate inside the fearful symmetries of private visionaries and amused or alarmed detractors who stand outside and insist that all writing make sense. It seems to me that with *The Rainbow* one can stand implicitly with the detractors and still be "inside" the book. It is a strange novel, and as Lawrence cheerfully admitted, it is imperfect because written in a new language its author was struggling hard to learn, but, for me at least, it is clear in ways that Blake or Shelley seldom are when at their most incantatory.

Because the fabric of the vision is a fabric, the book will not have climaxes in the usual sense, but the action does move inexorably forward so by the end of the third chapter we are in a good position to understand where it is going. Tom, settling into his new life with Lydia, Anna, and the new baby, finds himself incomplete, dissatisfied, and restless. Lydia seems to him lapsed:

> He wanted to give her all his love, all his passion, all his essential energy. But it could not be. He must find other things than her, other centres of living. She sat close and impregnable with the child. [P. 78]

So Tom announces one evening that he is going to Cossethay, and Lydia answers, "You do not want to be with me any more." He denies this, while admitting to himself that she is right, and then she stuns him by asking if he wants another woman:

> "Why should you want to find a woman who is more to you than me?" she said.
> The turbulence raged in his breast.
> "I don't," he said.
> "Why do you?" she repeated. "Why do you want to deny me?"
> Suddenly, in a flash, he saw she might be lonely, isolated, unsure. She had seemed to him the utterly certain, satisfied, absolute, excluding him. Could she need anything? [P. 89]

We have looked at enough of what precedes this to see why this last paragraph is crucial, new. Tom has come into his new being seeing Lydia as that which is outside, a woman, his wife. But this is the first time he sees her not as something "outside" him, not as the impregnable fortress he takes her to be, but also as a person whose needs and wants he hitherto had ignored because he had let them be outside, beyond. Suddenly he stands fixed before this stabbing vision of her:

> She was silent for a long time, stitching. He was aware, poignantly, of the round shape of her head, very intimate, compelling. She lifted her head and sighed. [P. 89]

To be aware of the object that is her head is to put it out there, beyond him, but to feel it "very intimate" is to recognize that he is nonetheless close to that which is outside; to feel it "compelling" him is to know the poignant power of its otherness for him.

Thus:

> She was the awful unknown. He bent down to her, suffering, unable to let go, unable to let himself go, yet drawn, driven. She was now the transfigured, she was wonderful, beyond him. [P. 90]

For a moment compare this with an earlier sentence to see all that has happened in the meantime:

> But during the long February nights with the ewes in labour, looking out from the shelter into the flashing stars, he knew he did not belong to himself. [P. 35]

This sentence makes no causal connections, and in order to understand the relations between its objects—ewes, stars, Tom —one needs a context that acknowledges the fragmented quality of Tom's universe and his struggles to pull it together. But in this passage with Lydia we see causal relations among the clauses and sentences, see the relationship come together as the parts of the sentences do: because she is unknown, he suffers, yet because she is unknown he is also driven toward her, and because he is both suffering and driven she is transfigured, wonderful because unknown.

This is what it is to be a visionary writer. It is not a matter of ideas, or of strongly held beliefs. It is a matter of knowing one's created world so completely that the grammar is expressive of the entire vision, and here the grammar is descriptive of a world where the inside and the outside, the known and the beyond, are coming together:

> Blind and destroyed, he pressed forward, nearer, nearer, to receive the consummation of himself, be received within the darkness which should swallow him and yield him up to himself. [P. 90]

The word "nearer" expresses both a physical and a metaphorical coming closer; so too does the "darkness." She is dark, he is lost in her, swallowed up, yet the darkness is only that which is beyond himself as he loses himself, yields himself up, and goes into the unknown that is both "Lydia" and the "beyond." In such a context the really strange next sentence becomes intelligible:

> If he could come really within the blazing kernel of darkness, if really he could be destroyed, burnt away till he lit with her in one consummation, that were supreme, supreme. [Pp. 90–91]

"The blazing kernel of darkness" is literally nonsense. By holding on to the physical scene as best we can we see it as a place inside Lydia—it is where he will come, be destroyed and consummated. It is in the darkness because it is inside her, it is a kernel because it is her and is the seed of her life, it is blazing because they are lighting it. But we need a more fully metaphorical sense of the phrase too. The darkness is the world outside Tom and unknown to him, it is a kernel because it contains the possibilities of new life for him, and it is blazing because such possibilities in darkness are transfiguring, blinding, destroying.

We are still in a particular scene, though the action is not really imaginable in the room where Tom stood before Lydia as she sat sewing, but the characters are being gathered up in a generalized symbolic action as well, one that finally dissolves our sense of time and space:

> Wherever they walked, it was well, the world re-echoed round them in discovery. They went gladly and forgetful. Everything was lost, and everything was found. The new world was discovered, it remained only to be explored. [P. 91]

The "wherever" places the characters in an imperfect tense where they walk and discover generically, so now Tom and Lydia are anywhere and anytime:

> They had passed through the doorway into the further space, where movement was so big, that it contained bonds and constraints and labours, and still was complete liberty. [P. 91]

It is Lawrence's triumph that these paradoxes offer no trouble for any reader, and Tom's and Lydia's accession into new being makes the shift into more specifically religious language perfectly appropriate:

> Now He was declared to Brangwen and to Lydia Brangwen, as they stood together. When at last they had joined hands, the house was finished, and the Lord took up his abode. And they were glad. [P. 92]

People who know no Bible know this is biblical. The motions of standing, joining, and taking up the abode are still historical motions, symbolic though they all are. Tom and Lydia are divided, conscious of themselves and their separateness from each other and the surrounding heavens and earth. When they triumph over these obstacles, when they acknowledge and love the foreignness of each other to each other, then the Lord takes up his abode with them. The motions of history are destructive —by tearing people apart and making them conscious of their apartness—but creative as well—by making or allowing for the

Lord to respond to the coming together of the two separate people. The Lord himself is a historical phenomenon, as a named deity takes the place of the simply participating universe. As Tom chooses Lydia in his transfiguration, so the Lord chooses them, something that in earlier generations would have been inconceivable because unnecessary. Now the Lord comes and transforms not only Tom and Lydia, but the next generation as well:

> Anna's soul was put at peace between them. She looked from one to the other, and she saw them established to her safety, and she was free. She played between the pillar of fire and the pillar of cloud in confidence, having the assurance on her right hand and the assurance on her left. She was no longer called upon to uphold with her childish might the broken end of the arch. Her father and her mother now met to the span of the heavens, and she, the child, was free to play in the space beneath, between. [P. 92]

So far as I know, no one can honestly resist these sentences, but it must be reiterated that their triumph depends on their being clear and their clarity is the result of the context of history. The broken arch becomes the rainbow, and human achievement is once again a universal action; thus the child is free.

The family and the covenant made with the Lord are not the result of the old blood-intimacy of the earlier Brangwens. They are triumphs against the forces at work from the book's opening to separate men and women from one another and from the rest of creation. What Tom and Lydia do, thus, is like the action of modern heroes, but because the Lord is there to respond and the universe can once again be theirs, their world is not a modern world at all. In a generation or two people might look back on them and think family and covenant had always existed, but to think that would be to take what is in fact heroic action and think of it nostalgically. The generations before this one needed no strong sense of marriage or the family because the Lord's abode and their own was the same thing, the whole

universe. The generations after Tom and Lydia will face forces
of disintegration so strong the family cannot stay intact and
the children cannot be free. But at this moment—Lawrence offers no dates, but the period must be around 1870—the family
is a difficult, rare, and powerful achievement, needed, acknowledged by the Lord. Our sense must be that even though the
noisier forces of disintegration, such as the collieries, the railroads, and the schools, are kept in the background, the triumph
of Tom and Lydia is a triumph for the whole civilization, because in Lawrence's vision the most powerful of the separating
forces, the human consciousness, is in the foreground, and here
its power can be both acknowledged and used in a unifying triumph. The person becoming individual can know the unknown outside it, can love the unknown and so gain access to
the world beyond itself. What had been only theory or doctrine
in earlier versions of *The Sisters* and in the *Look! We Have
Come Though!* sequence is here made an action, believable
and wonderful.

Tom and Lydia meet to span the heavens, and though to
speak of such a span is to give the action a sense of firmness and
permanence, the very act of saying Tom and Lydia made it
implies a tenuousness: it may go when they go. Young Anna
Lensky grows up under the arch, and she is secure knowing it
is there, but she did not make it, and the world that she inherits
is necessarily new and different:

These two, her mother and father, held her still in fee. But she was
free of other people, towards whom, on the whole, she took the bene-
volent attitude. She deeply hated ugliness or intrusion or arrogance,
however. As a child, she was as proud and shadowy as a tiger, and as
aloof. She could confer favours, but, save from her mother and father,
she could receive none. She hated people who came too near to her.
Like a wild thing, she wanted her distance. She mistrusted intimacy.
[P. 93]

Lawrence does not say how different are the terms of Anna's
life from those of her parents, but from the beginning Anna's

freedom is associated with her ability to be independent, aloof, apart.

Woman becoming individual—that is the subject, and here is where it begins to take hold in the novel. Anna is able to be herself, free of the implications of the past with its strong sense of shared experience and its participation in the activities of earth and sky. There are immense dangers in such freedom and individuality—farther down the line lies Frieda's "God Almightiness," and grave consequences for the men involved with such free women—farther down that line lie men like Walter Morel and Baxter Dawes. But when Lawrence says Anna is free, we feel a surge of energetic optimism, we feel that a woman is now not just searching for a freedom, an individuality beyond the confines of her present life, but achieving it. Yet we are made to see the consequences, too: shyness, imperiousness, awkwardness, contempt for authority—not so we can judge the freedom but only so we can know what is entailed in its attainment. Lawrence here is aloof from simple judging, and so he never records the past nostalgically or implies despair about the present. For all the turbulence in the life of Anna, Lawrence's writing about her is marvelously even-paced, serene, secure in its historical vision. The moment is the moment of Lawrence's parents' marriage and his own childhood, but he is handling the matter differently now from the manner of *Sons and Lovers.* By comparison with Mrs. Morel Anna is shadowy and imperfectly seen, but the characters in the earlier novel are clear because nothing is imagined larger than the individual characters, each of whom has what Lawrence calls a stable ego. In *The Rainbow* energies are at work which are larger than the individual characters, and so we are always aware of patterns larger than the individual. Time is passing, in minutes, in days and weeks, in whole generations, and the energies running through men and women in time, expressed by them but not dominated by them, animates every sentence and paragraph. Anna Lensky marries Will Brangwen and the two engage in a fierce fight for domination of the other. We see more than this, though. We see that in this middle generation such a struggle is inevitable as a consequence of the free and secure woman, and that the woman will "win," but she wins as Mrs. Morel and the Prussian officer win, by guaranteeing that both will lose.

The terms of the struggle derive from Anna's strong sense of freedom, individuality, and conscious knowing; what is unknown for her is something to be controlled or ridiculed before it controls or ridicules her:

> "It's because you don't know anything" [Anna has been scornful of "that lamb in Church"], he said violently, harshly. "Laugh at what you know, not at what you don't know."
> "What don't I know?"
> "What things mean."
> "And what does it mean?"
> He was reluctant to answer her. He found it difficult.
> "*What* does it mean?" she insisted.
> "It means the triumph of the Resurrection."
> She hesitated, baffled, a fear came upon her. What were these things? Something dark and powerful seemed to extend before her. Was it wonderful after all?
> But no—she refused it.
> "Whatever it may pretend to mean, what it *is* is a silly absurd toy-lamb with a Christmas-tree flag ledged on its paw—and if it wants to mean anything else, it must look different from that." [P. 158]

"But no—she refused it" is Anna's crucial trait; when confronted with the unknown, with the dark and powerful, she refuses, lapses into scorn and irony, which has the effect of making Will more angry, less conscious, "in a state of violent irritation against her."

But now it is a fight, so Anna must win. She has the greater consciousness, the greater self-command, and so she forces Will into black rages and blind sensuality. It is the Prussian officer and the orderly again, but this time Lawrence seems in complete control, knowing himself and placing the most destructive qualities in him at the service of his vision. Lawrence moves here, as he did in the climactic episode with Tom and Lydia, from scene to paradigm:

> She was quite willing to make it up with him when he came home again. He was black and surly, but abated. She had broken a little of something in him. And at length he was glad to forfeit from his soul all his symbols, to have her making love to him. He loved it when she put her head on his knee, and he had not asked her to or wanted her to, he loved her when she put her arms round him and made bold love to him, and he did not make love to her. He felt a strong blood in his limbs again. [Pp.158–159]

The actions are specific—he comes home, she puts her head on his knee, she makes love to him and he is aroused. But the actions are generalized now too—she has broken a little of something in him, and the "at length" stretches out the action of his gladness at his forfeiture,— so that the "when" of "he loved it when she put her head on his knee" becomes what she does "whenever" she breaks a little of something in him.

But Lawrence makes no simple judgment of Anna for her cruelty or of Will for his sullen yielding and willingness to become "strong" in a way she can control. It is awful, this struggle, and "Anna Victrix" is one of the most searing passages in modern literature, but we know the context disallows our making simple judgments. Anna and Will live in the abode of the Lord, so theirs is a violent intensity because the woman in that abode has become more individual, her passions more conscious, her power more a matter of will. If we do not think of both Will and Anna as participants in the flux of history, then we are liable to say strange things of them; Leavis calls Anna a "Magna Mater" and Julian Moynihan says she is "a complacent, fruitful and thoroughly commonplace English mum." One might as well call Emma Woodhouse a bitch or Hamlet a malcontent. Anna is what she is because of the covenant of the rainbow and the passage of history working at this point against each other—the one holds out hope that all is not lost, but the other brings struggle, disintegration, and a mechanical humanity:

> Soon, she felt sure of her husband. She knew his dark face and the extent of its passion. She knew his slim, vigorous body, she said it was hers. Then there was no denying her. She was a rich woman enjoying her riches. [P. 193]

Will is now a thing for her, and she knows him as her prize, her triumphant riches:

> If she were not the wayfarer to the unknown, if she were arrived now, settled in her builded house, a rich woman, still her doors opened under the arch of the rainbow, her threshold reflected the passing of the sun and moon, the great travellers, her house was full of the echo of journeying. [P. 193]

Anna is settled now. But her house is not hers alone, but the abode of the Lord as well, so that the sun and moon are still the travelers over her head and the house is full of the echo of journeying. Anna is made small in her satisfaction, living in her builded house rather than in the house of the Lord, but she is also a door for her child Ursula, who is not free to play because her parents are not the pillars on either hand, but who is nonetheless heir to the covenant of the rainbow as she shades her eyes and seeks her way.

Up to this point the processes of woman becoming individual have been all Lawrence has needed to show of the history of the century of his lifetime. But once Anna has triumphed, once the family has become an arena of struggle, Ursula as the child must in effect leave the house to seek her destiny, and so we are fully introduced to the many human, impersonal, and disintegrating forces that have been lying all around waiting, as it were, for a chance to break in. Town, school, and friends appear for the first time in the novel, as important forces in Ursula's childhood. This is the world of Lawrence's childhood too, and we are slowly coming down to the historical present that Lawrence had found painful to face ever since he began trying to do so in the spring of 1913.

Lawrence does wonderfully at showing how the love of Will and Ursula, even though in many ways more intimate and intense than the love of Tom and Anna, drives the girl away from home. Will, defeated, no longer secure in himself, goes off with a tart one night as part of his effort to dissolve himself in sensuality—his child, thus, grows unable to trust her father's passions. Gradually family, church, and soil are all diminished, and for Ursula their place is taken by dehumanized and brutal schools, the ruins of a religious artisan in her father, the lapsed contentment of her mother sleeping the sleep of motherhood. Ursula has been told of the past of the Brangwens by her grandmother, Lydia, when the two became friends after Tom Brangwen drowns, and the grandmother's sayings and stories "became a sort of Bible to the child":

> Ursula was frightened, hearing these things. Her heart sank, she felt she had no ground under her feet. She clung to her grandmother. Here was peace and security. Here, from her grandmother's peaceful room, the door opened on to the greater space, the past, which was so big, that all it contained seemed tiny, loves and births and deaths, tiny units and features within a vast horizon. That was a great relief, to know the tiny importance of the individual, within the great past. [P. 258]

For Anna the covenant meant freedom because her parents had formed the arch of the rainbow; for Ursula it can only mean the past because her parents have not and could not have secured the future for her. As she faces the future, Lawrence really has little to defend Ursula with except the ancient belief that *his* covenant had been with woman becoming individual and his promise or his hope had been for her a Love Triumphant.

The belief, however, had been at best tenuously held when

first enunciated, and between that time, the winter of 1912–1913, and the completed version of *The Rainbow*, lies the war. It was, as we have seen, a searing experience for Lawrence, and it seemed to release in him all the frustration and anger that had for so long been threatening the belief in Love Triumphant, the promise made to the Brangwens, to Frieda, and to himself. "The War finished me," he wrote to Cynthia Asquith just after he had divided his novel in two and was finishing *The Rainbow*, "it was the spear through the side of all sorrows and hopes" (January 31, 1915). Middleton Murry has a rather terrifying passage about Lawrence's response to the war:

I remember his saying that he would like to kill one million—two million Germans—for letting loose this horror of mechanical death upon the world. And it was not at all a rodomontade with him; one felt that he meant it, that somehow he wanted a terrible revenge. It was mysterious to me, and frightening, as though he hated this War only because it was not war enough, and was in some sort a further frustration of the animal rather than a satiation of it. It was partly in the name of essential war that he repudiated this grim parody of war. [*Between Two Worlds* (New York, 1936), p. 339]

With such feelings inside him, what was to come of the covenant, the hope, the implicit defiance of the disintegrating processes of history whereby the conscious will dominated and the civilization became mechanical, mechanized, and warlike? What did he have left to defy *with*? He had been able thus far to bring his doctrines to full imagined life only as realized by Tom and Lydia, and they were trapped, as it were, in the past.

So Lawrence slowly and at times even pathetically sets Ursula out, independent but not free, a seeker without any knowledge of what she seeks, aided mostly by her knowing she wants to avoid points of rest. Thus when in her first love affair, with Anton Skrebensky, she repeats the "triumph" of her mother and conquers her man, she does not feel at all fulfilled:

But there was a wound of sorrow, she had hurt herself, as if she had bruised herself, in annihilating him. She covered up her two young breasts with her hands, covering them to herself; and covering herself with herself, she crouched in bed, to sleep. [P. 322]

Her one indispensable virtue and weapon is that she cannot deceive herself. Her consciousness has developed to the point that instinctive self-knowledge is possible. It keeps her restless, unwilling to settle unfulfilled, and brave. So she turns from the shadowy Skrebensky, who believes in progress and the greatest good of the greatest number and who is therefore something of a "brick in the whole great social fabric," to the lesbian Winifred Inger, who denounces religion in the name of human aspiration and the man's world in the name of feminism. Miss Inger at least does not lie about history, as Skrebensky in effect does by glossing over its unpleasant truths. But having effectively shown Ursula how mechanized the world of men is, Miss Inger has no alternative but to try to be manlike, dominant, willful. Ursula briefly submits to her but soon knows the relationship is unreal, and she leaves Miss Inger to her logical fate: marriage to a mine manager. By seeking power and thereby submitting to its awful influence, Miss Inger can shift easily from the seduction of Ursula to being seduced by the greater power of the machine.

Ursula is left to a less mechanical but thereby more painful life. Slowly she too is becoming frustrated like her author, and when she takes a job teaching school, she is forced to face the full implications of the horrors of mechanized modern "democratic" civilization and the horrors of her response to it:

The first great task was to reduce sixty children to one state of mind, or being. This state must be produced automatically, through the will of the teacher, and the will of the whole school authority, imposed upon the will of the children. [P. 382]

One of Lawrence's earliest mentors, Ruskin, had been clear on this subject: "You must either make a tool of the creature, or a man of him. You cannot make both." ("The Origins of Goth-ic," *The Stones of Venice*). Ursula is asked to employ her highly developed consciousness and the strong will attendant upon it to make tools out of the children. Caught between school and pupils, between the fascist principal and the unruly children, Ursula is tortured, protected from annihilation only by the consciousness and the will she has come to loathe in herself and in others. Everything becomes a matter of power and control, and inevitably Ursula too gives in to these temptations and seeks to destroy those with less power by controlling them:

> She knew if she let go the boy he would dash to the door. Already he had run home once out of her class. So she snatched her cane from the desk, and brought it down on him. He was writhing and kicking. She saw his face beneath her, white, with eyes like the eyes of a fish, stony, yet full of hate and horrible fear. And she loathed him, the hideous writhing thing that was nearly too much for her. In horror lest he should overcome her, and yet at the heart quite calm, she brought down the cane again and again, whilst he struggled making inarticulate noises, and lunging vicious kicks at her. [P. 398]

It is almost an insult that the serene vision of *The Rainbow* had to come to this, but no one can doubt it had to come to it: "She was isolated now from the life of her childhood, a foreign-er in a new life, of work and mechanical consideration" (p. 406). For all that is shocking and degrading in these scenes in the school, we can see that Lawrence is still in control of his vision and of himself because of it. He may write carelessly, as in the previously quoted phrase that speaks of Skrebensky as a "brick in the whole great social fabric," but of history and the consequences of woman becoming individual, he is as se-cure and supreme as ever.

But where it is to end Ursula certainly cannot see and her author seems at least uncertain. He could know, for instance, that he had been both teacher and pupil in schools similar to the one in which Ursula teaches, and that he had not been destroyed by either experience. But what to make of that, how to translate an instinctive faith that all is not lost into part of his vision, especially at a time when the war was bringing to the surface all his potential violence? After "The Man's World," what forgiveness?

The only weapon still of use in the fight is the same that is also the major instrument of destruction: the girl's consciousness, her knowing herself now to be exiled from the world of her childhood. When Ursula's friend Maggie Schofield says that love is the flower of life and is to be enjoyed for the brief hour of its duration, Ursula knows she is different, a Brangwen, an heiress of the covenant still:

> She was staunch for joy, for happiness, and permanency, in contrast with Maggie, who was for sadness, and the inevitable passing-away of things. Ursula suffered bitterly at the hands of life, Maggie was always single, always withheld, so she went in a heavy brooding sadness that was almost meat to her. [P. 412]

Ursula must suffer bitterly because she must assume that the reality of the past is not simply dead. Yet she is separate, apart, tiny:

> Yet she was always Ursula Brangwen. But what did it mean, Ursula Brangwen? She did not know what she was. Only she was full of rejection, of refusal. Always, always she was spitting out of her mouth the ash and grit of disillusion, of falsity. She could only stiffen in rejection, in rejection. She seemed always negative in her action.
> That which she was, positively, was dark and unrevealed, it could not come forth. It was like a seed buried in dry ash. [P. 437]

Ursula is little here, but only because Lawrence is not for a moment diminishing the scope of his vision in writing about her; it is in the context of the heavens spanned with the rainbow, of the absolute potentiality of individuals, that she is in rejection, unrevealed, buried like a seed in dry ash. These are the terms of Lawrence's heroism: the disaster of modern life, the individual stiffening in rejection and seeking positive

identity, all enacted on a scale large enough to show that what
is at issue is not less than everything:

> This world in which she lived was like a circle lighted by a lamp. This
> lighted area, lit up by man's completest consciousness, she thought
> was all the world: that here all was disclosed for ever. Yet all the time,
> within the darkness she had been aware of points of light, like the
> eyes of wild beasts, gleaming, penetrating, vanishing. [P. 437]

If Lawrence knew anything it was that the light cast by the
completest consciousness described only a circle, and outside
of that was darkness. The darkness that had been Lydia Lensky
was lit for Tom Brangwen by the light of his transfiguring
vision of their life together that could acknowledge and love
the darkness of the unknown; the darkness that had been Will
Brangwen was for Anna something to subdue, so she had
subdued it. But not obliterated it. The darkness was still there,
in him, in his mindless sensuality, and it is still here, outside
the light of Ursula's consciousness:

> But she could see the glimmer of dark movement just out of range,
> she saw the eyes of the wild beast gleaming from the darkness, watch-
> ing the vanity of the camp fire and the sleepers; she felt the strange,
> foolish vanity of the camp, which said "Beyond our light and our
> order there is nothing," turning their faces always inward towards
> the sinking fire of illuminating consciousness . . . [P. 437]

Miss Inger had tried to tell Ursula "Beyond our light and our
order there is nothing" when she announced she was marry-
ing the manager of the mine; the school principal had tried
to say the same when insisting the pupils had to be brought
to heel. But no, the darkness is still there, and in it are the eyes
of the subdued wild beast seeking revenge: Morel, Baxter
Dawes, the would-be suitors of Jessie Chambers in the stories,
the orderly in "The Prussian Officer," Will Brangwen. What
is so wonderful and moving here is the completeness of the
union of Lawrence's personal desires and experience and the
myth of history.

The myth offers Lawrence's profoundest critique of the idea of progress and the developing self-consciousness that so many believed—and believe—would accompany our coming to man's noblest estate. Those in the camp do not see that in developing the individual consciousness civilization has separated itself from everything else:

> Nevertheless the darkness wheeled round about, with grey shadow-shapes of wild beasts, and also with dark shadow-shapes of the angels, whom the light fenced out, as it fenced out the more familiar beasts of darkness. And some, having for a moment seen the darkness, saw it bristling with the tufts of the hyena and the wolf; and some having given up their vanity of the light, having died in their own conceit, saw the gleam in the eyes of the wolf and the hyena, that it was the flash of the sword of angels, flashing at the door to come in, that the angels in the darkness were lordly and terrible and not to be denied, like the flash of fangs. [P. 438]

Without more than four-hundred pages of close textured writing behind it, such a passage could only seem authorial comment rather than the paradigmatic rendering of Ursula's experience. The light of the consciousness thrusts out angel and beast alike, tries to insist they exist no more. But they are there, and now seek their revenge.

In these late visions and in the accompanying cruelty of Ursula's toward Skrebensky, author and heroine seem to have been transformed from victims of war and modern life to avenging animal-angels, seeking blood, as if following the by now well-established pattern of seeking domination and destruction for having been oneself dominated and destroyed. But *The Rainbow* was to have been a book about eternity as well as history, about transcendent human achievement as well as the victimizing power of modern civilization. So we have the end of the novel—the feverish scene with the horses, the miscarriage, the final vision of the rainbow arching over the corrupt earth—which has caused much comment. The book, we know, *should* end with the vision of the rainbow, and not to have so ended it would have been a sentimental yielding to darkness and violence. But to justify the ending on these grounds is to admit that Lawrence has sufficiently lost control of his vision that either ending, Armageddon or the rainbow, seems unsatisfactory to us.

We know another book is to come and that the rainbow must end this one if that other book is to keep any of the promises implicit in this one. But the history of Lawrence and his writing since the completion of *Sons and Lovers* does not really offer much hope that that book could be the book about Ursula and "her Mr. Birkin," about Frieda and Lawrence, that he set out to write in the spring of 1913. It may be true, as Leavis says, that "By 1915 Lawrence . . . was already predominantly the Lawrence of the later novel, though still sufficiently of the 'younger' one to be able to finish it." (*D. H. Lawrence: Novelist* [New York, 1955], p. 110). But what strikes me most about the closing chapters of *The Rainbow* is the jeopardy in which they implicitly place the planned sequel. Lawrence is not simply content to bring his novel down to the present, to balance its horror against its hopes, and to move on to the novel about the present. It takes Lawrence as long to get through the later stages of Ursula's coming of age as it does to get from the beginning of the novel to the wedding of Will and Anna. There is no single thing that is extraneous, but as I read the book through I feel increasingly that Lawrence, having been torn by the world and so tearing it in return, could only shred the pieces over and over. He keeps his promise to Ursula at the end, but it begins to look as though it is really too late to help her, or himself. The rainbow that appears at the end cannot triumph over the history of the world it arches, not really. The heroic impulse is certainly very strong in Lawrence here, but other impulses seem to be becoming stronger.

Nonetheless, *The Rainbow* is a very great book, unique. It has never become fully established in our thinking about modern literature as a separate book, and somehow it is always assumed to be inferior to *Women in Love*. But the reasons for that assumption are far from obvious. After *The Rainbow* Lawrence never again experiments with the modes of characterization and action which express his vision of history on which he had worked for so long. It is his one book in which prophesy is not simplified eventually into propaganda, and his only historical work that really tries to express the passage of time. It is his only major effort to write steadily about a marriage and, as we have seen, Lawrence needs that steadiness of vision to write strangely and tentatively and still be clear. It is his best effort at dealing with two subjects he is often praised for handling well, nature and children. After *The Rainbow* he has a few good moments about children and of course there are magnificent landscapes scattered throughout his work. But nothing else has what *The Rainbow* has, a sense of the life of nature and the living of children. When one tries to isolate moments in *The Rainbow* where nature or childhood enter the vision, the effort fails. The scene with Tom and Anna in the barn the night Lydia has Tom's first baby, the scenes with Will escaping the failed relationship with Anna into the lovely and painful relationship with Ursula—these have great force in the memory but little when read in isolation, without the full context of the novel. In this book Lawrence is so fully possessed by his vision that almost every word is brought to strange and unexcerptible life. He never had the peace or freedom to do this again.

Had something happened to Lawrence in 1915 such that he wrote nothing after *The Rainbow*, we might be able to see the outlines of an aborted heroism but probably no more than that. To this point Lawrence's triumphs seem too much a personal working-out of some of his feelings about his parents to be called heroic. In *The Rainbow* he had set himself free of the paralysis of the present into which *The Sisters* and *The Wedding Ring* had continually fallen, and the history he created there gave him an arena sufficiently large that we can see his personal problems as being paradigmatic of the culture's. But he had not yet seen what reply he could make to that history, what defiance he could offer to its implications, other than the willed ending of *The Rainbow* which insists that the end is not yet. It was extremely important, however, that he could bring his own situation and his culture's into a single focus, because he could then show how the forces that threatened to overtake the one were the same as those that threatened to overtake the other. In Ursula's nagging insistence on her own consciousness, with all its littleness and will to dominate, we can see what was also being insisted upon, in 1915, by the generals and the politicians. The Armageddon that is Ursula's temptation was, we know, theirs as well.

We can call this single focus that expresses the individual and the culture simultaneously a fortuity or an accident, but if we do we must add that it was fortuitous that Shakespeare was writing *Hamlet* when the world "out there" was inventing the need for a single, isolated human consciousness, insistent, destructive, heroic. Perhaps all heroism is the accidental result of an individual bringing his culture into focus as he clarifies the needs of his own life, and that the case of Lawrence is different from that of Shakespeare or the *Beowulf*-poet only because we know so much more about Lawrence's individual case. The trouble is that theories of heroism have a way of staying theoretical, and our concern is Lawrence. We know that whatever heroic actions he will be able to perform will not alter human history—such heroism has not been possible for centuries—and they will, like all other heroic actions, be fraught with great danger. *Women in Love* tells us many stories and truths, not the least of which is that for a modern hero every triumph will be accompanied by the terms or the conditions of his ultimate disaster.

After he was in effect incarcerated in England in the fall of 1914, Lawrence began talking among his friends about a utopian community, later known as Rananim, to be located by them almost anywhere except in Europe. It was the most persistent of all Lawrence's efforts during the war years to nullify or to avoid the devastating ravages of the war on his consciousness. He felt deeply and expressed openly the need to escape, "to Thibet—or Kamschatka—or Tahiti." But he had cut himself off from his old friends of the Nottingham and Croydon years—not only Jessie Chambers, but Helen Corke, George Neville, A. W. McLeod, William Hopkin, even Edward Garnett—and now saw mostly London bohemians or society people associated with the intelligentsia—the Murrys, the Asquiths, Ottoline Morrell, S. S. Koteliansky, Philip Heseltine, Catherine Carswell, Viola Meynell, Aldous Huxley, Dorothy Brett—who were generally more rootless and certainly far less steady than his earlier friends. England was no longer home for Lawrence and he lived among many who had always been temperamentally homeless. Good and kind though many of them were, most were clearly little good for Lawrence during a crisis. They were too mercurial, too willing to dream up or to go along with wild schemes, and they seemed to bring out these qualities in Lawrence and thereby to dissipate much of his capacity for work and common sense. Lawrence himself did not see this, but he did clearly recognize that he was in trouble: "I feel somehow I shall go mad, because there is no place to go."

What was perhaps the decisive blow came in the late fall of 1915. *The Rainbow* was published by Methuen on September 30 and soon a campaign was launched against it, begun by reviewers and completed by police. Methuen was ordered to suppress publication on grounds that the book was obscene, and the publisher not only complied but refused even to defend the book in court. Some insidious malaise seems indeed to have overtaken England in wartime, for almost certainly at any other time the book would have been found only obscure or strident by reviewers and other philistines. Lawrence's response was, characteristically, both forceful and ambiguous: "I am not very much moved: am beyond that by now. I only curse them all, body and soul, root, branch and leaf, to eternal damnation" (November 6, 1915). His friends were sympathetic but helpless when he tried to organize a protest; Philip Morrell asked questions in Parliament, but no one answered. Lawrence had never expected to be popular, but now he was in serious difficulties: he was not only without money but suddenly without hope or prospects. Before *The Rainbow* was published, Lawrence had never had trouble getting his work published, and since 1912 he had lived entirely on what he earned from writing; more than once a single poem, "Snapdragon," published in *Georgian Poetry,* provided him with an unexpected few pounds when he most needed it. Suddenly instead of being "interesting," a "genius," he was obscene, and publishers and editors stopped accepting his work. Three years of immensely hard work on *The Rainbow* had brought him only to this. He was left angry and desperate, bewilderedly hoping for something better, limply receptive to anyone who would champion him or any of his causes.

After living for more than a year in and around London in various borrowed or cheaply rented villas, the Lawrences in December of 1915 accepted the offer of the novelist J. D. Beresford of his house in Cornwall and they moved there shortly after Christmas. It was not a happy place, but they agreed it was better than London where Lawrence never was able to feel settled. In order to work he had to be free of the chance visitor and the admirer who happened to be nearby. The natives were suspicious and later openly hostile to Lawrence, who was draft-exempt, and to Frieda, a German citizen. Lawrence coaxed the Murrys down for a visit, then apparently hounded Murry over the moors with his cravings for a blood-brotherhood. Katherine Mansfield wrote anxious letters to friends in London about fights between Lawrence and Frieda. Nonetheless, Cornwall was less irritating and distracting than London, just remote enough to let Lawrence keep working.

Once reasonably settled, Lawrence began working on his "philosophy," the work that eventually became *Psychoanalysis and the Unconscious*. Meanwhile he had sent off to Germany for the manuscript of the unfinished *Insurrection of Miss Houghton* he had left there on his way from Italy to England in 1913, but given wartime conditions, it was a long time coming. He also was busy preparing both *Twilight in Italy* and *Amores* for publication; Duckworth had agreed to do these some time earlier and could not renege now. So is wasn't until May 1916, that he began to pick up where *The Rainbow* left off:

> I have begun the second half of *The Rainbow*. But already it is beyond all hope of ever being published, because of the things it says. And more than that, it is beyond all possibility even to offer it to a world, a putrescent mankind like ours. I feel I cannot *touch* humanity, even in thought, it is abhorrent to me. [May 1, 1916]

A few months later he wrote the following to Catherine Carswell. I quote it here because it is typical of the tone of the letters of the period in which he was working on *Women in Love*:

> I think, of course, that we are now just curving into the final maelstrom: in a few more months there will *be* no English nation, there will be a vast horde of self-interested mad brutes padding round seeking their own ends: a chaos, a horror. . . . So hurrah for the debacle: let it be soon, for suspense is intolerable. [December 20, 1916]

Given this, the wonder is he tried at all to keep the promises he had made to himself, to Ursula, to Frieda.

But Lawrence's way is not simply the way of other historians of the Myth of Lost Unity, for many of whom 1916 was the year that signalized the end of all the old possibilities. He worked very quickly on *Women in Love* once he began the revision. "It has come rushing out," he tells Catherine Carswell on June 19, "and I feel very triumphant in it." He seems to have taken little more than two months to "finish" the book, though some revisions and additions were made during the fall. We have no way of knowing how much of the competed novel was in earlier versions of *The Sisters–The Rainbow*, but it is clear that the tone, the manner, the line-by-line accent all belong to 1916, and to a Lawrence who had finished *The Rainbow*. He says in the Foreword to the American edition published in 1920:

This novel was written in its first form in the Tyrol, in 1913. It was altogether re-written and finished in Cornwall in 1917 [*sic*]. So that it is a novel which took its final shape in the midst of the period of war, though it does not concern the war itself. I should wish the time to remain unfixed, so that the bitterness of the war may be taken for granted in the characters. [*Women in Love* (Compass ed.), p. vii]

Everything that had been put into the letters—all the rage, despair, boredom, and bitterness with the war—is in the novel too, but the novel has more. It is a searing book, outrageous in many ways, and the urge to destroy which threatened the end of *The Rainbow*, and held off for most of *Women in Love*, finally does overwhelm it. But it is a miracle too, for it is the growing darkness and the sense of curving for the last time into the maelstrom, that make bright the struggle to write the book he still remembered he had to write.

The subject of *Women in Love* is Love Triumphant, and what is needed to fulfill that love, in our dying civilization. When that *is* the subject, the book carries everything before it grandly, making all that might at first glance seem blurry or repetitive in fact be clear and bright and resplendent. The two couples, Birkin and Ursula, Gerald Crich and Gudrun Brangwen, counterpoint each other, the one seeking a new relationship, the other swirling off in a suicidal fulfillment of the urge to dominate implicit in all the old relationships. Gerald and Gudrun have received a disproportionately large amount of the attention given the book, because they fit the Myth of Lost Unity and fulfill the "modern" destiny: living in the land made waste by industrialization, they implicitly accept power as the moving force in human relationships. They are, thus, easy to understand and to bring into the usual censuses of the leading modern citizens. Furthermore, they belong in each such census for they are superbly and carefully created characters, the trophies of Lawrence's cunningly and beautifully controlled hatred. But they shoud not have the major share of the attention, because even when he is working well with them Lawrence cannot avoid a gloating tone that reveals *his* will to dominate and destroy them.

More interesting, really, if not more "powerful" in the conventional sense, are Birkin and Ursula, the hero and heroine, the seekers after the new love amid the ruins of all the old loves, the figures with whom Lawrence had started in the spring of 1913 and with whom he emerges in a battered and incomplete triumph in the completed novel of 1916. But there have been changes along the way. Birkin in *Women in Love* is, far more than is Ursula in the same novel, the heir of Ursula in *The Rainbow*. He is, as she was in the earlier novel, Lawrence's spokesman, his voice of rage and frustration. In Birkin we see the historical vision of *The Rainbow* brought down to the present. He has the Brangwen hope for the new relationship, made wan now, and insistent, because it seems so impossible to attain.

But the triumph of the novel, the sign that the dream can really be designed and even fulfilled in the modern world, is the new Ursula Brangwen of *Women in Love*. In her can be seen the finest of Lawrence's qualities—his eagerness to explore, his honesty, his insistence on clarity in things great and small, his desire for more than anyone imagined possible. If he had let *Women in Love* be a visionary novel in the sense that *The Rainbow* is visionary—an unquestioned rolling out of historical vision—then almost certainly it would have had Birkin for its mouthpiece and the destruction of humanity as its action. But instead Birkin is not allowed to stand secure with the theories or doctrines Lawrence had held for so long. He states the theories right enough, and often, about the end of humanity and the establishment of a new relationship between men and women, but Ursula does not let him get away with mere statements. For she is the fulfillment of "woman becoming individual," and not simply a victim of the historical processes of disintegration. For the instrument of the consciousness has always in Lawrence been seen doubly and paradoxically, as the instrument of separation and the dominant will, but also as the means whereby domination is challenged and defied. She will not be dominated by Birkin's theories. She insists that he, and he and she together, make them actual, and thereby she fulfills Lawrence's promise to women to do his work for them, work "better than the Suffrage." Ursula, the individual, insists on that individuality and thereby makes realities of theory and gives the lie to history.

We must begin with Birkin, the Lawrence of the war years, speaking as Lawrence often does in the letters. Early in the novel, before he knows Ursula well, he and Gerald Crich ride to London together:

' Birkin looked at the land, at the evening, and was thinking: "Well, if mankind is destroyed, if our race is destroyed like Sodom, and there is this beautiful evening with the luminous land and trees, I am satisfied. That which informs it all is there, and can never be lost. After all, what is mankind but just one expression of the incomprehensible. And if mankind passes away, it will only mean that this particular expression is completed and done. . . . Let mankind pass away—time it did. The creative utterances will not cease, they will only be there. Humanity doesn't embody the utterance of the incomprehensible any more. Humanity is a dead letter. There will be a new embodiment, in a new way. Let humanity disappear as quick as possible." [P. 52]

Birkin's position here is similar to Ursula's at the end of *The Rainbow,* so that we can see her continuation in him. But he is more conscious, more intellectual, than she ever is, and we know such a development in consciousness must not be viewed as a total disaster, indeed that heroic opportunities are created precisely by that development.

Just before this reflection, in talking with Gerald, we can see Birkin trying to save himself. He asks Gerald where life centers for him:

"I don't know—that's what I want somebody to tell me. As far as I can make out, it doesn't centre at all. It is artificially held *together* by the social mechanism."
Birkin pondered as if he would crack something.
"I know," he said, "it just doesn't centre. The old ideals are dead as nails—nothing there. It seems to me there remains only this perfect union with a woman—sort of ultimate marriage—and there isn't anything else." [P. 51]

Even without *The Rainbow* behind us we know that anyone who relies on the social mechanism to hold life together is doomed; with that novel in mind we can see in Gerald the heir of Winifred Inger and Anton Skrebensky. But the problem with Birkin is different and more complicated. He knows that mankind once embodied "the utterance of the incomprehensible" as it does at the very beginning of *The Rainbow.* He knows too that "the old ideals are dead as nails," and he has no covenant and vision of the rainbow to sustain hope. He speaks of a "new embodiment" and of a "perfect union with a woman" but he has no way of saying what he means by either "new" or "perfect," and Gerald does not ask. The words are abstract because Birkin has nothing to unite them to or with, and for this reason he is desperate, bent on the destruction of humanity.

If Gerald does not ask Birkin what he means, if Hermione
Roddice, with whom Birkin is ending a disastrous affair, only
mimics Birkin and so earns his repudiation, Ursula does not let
him off so easily. When he first tries out his notions on her and
says "If only man was swept off the face of the earth," she stiffens and mocks him, thus dramatizing Lawrence's last hope:

> He was silent now, feeling she wanted to insult him.
> "And if you don't believe in love, what *do* you believe in?" she
> asked, mocking. "Simply in the end of the world, and grass?"
> He was beginning to feel a fool.
> "I believe in the unseen hosts," he said.
> "And nothing else? You believe in nothing visible, except grass and
> birds? Your world is a poor show." [P. 121]

Ursula's "mother," Anna, had spoken thus to her husband, because Will's ideals frightened her and she felt compelled to
destroy them. Ursula, though, is speaking to one who can easily
defend himself, if he indeed knows what he means. She forces
him to see his ideals for what they still are, personal ideals and
not revealed truths. Both are attracted to the other, both sense
their future lies with the other, but neither yet can use his or
her superbly developed consciousness to gain the terms for their
relationship.

The first climax in their relationship comes in the chapter
called "Mino," where Ursula visits Birkin in his rooms and they
watch Birkin's male cat Mino cuff and subdue a wild female
cat:

> "Oh, it makes me so cross, the assumption of male superiority! And it
> is such a lie! One wouldn't mind if there were any justification for it."
> "The wild cat," said Birkin, "doesn't mind. She perceives that it is
> justified."
> "Does she!" cried Ursula. "And tell it to the Horse Marines."
> "To them also."
> "It is just like Gerald Crich with his horse—a lust for bullying—a
> real Wille zur Macht—so base, so petty." [Pp. 141–142]

The full force of all *The Rainbow* and *Women in Love* lies
behind this. The will to power, the presumption of superiority,

the bullying that is base and petty, all have been the instruments whereby the will has made itself known and modern civilization a reality. Birkin must back off a bit:

> "I agree that the Wille zur Macht is a base and petty thing. But with the Mino, it is the desire to bring this female cat into a pure stable equilibrium, a transcendent and abiding *rapport* with the single male." [P. 142]

It is a doctrine as old as the poems of 1913 in *Look! We Have Come Through!* But it has not really come through yet, and Ursula is having none:

> "Ah——! Sophistries! It's the old Adam."
> "Oh yes. Adam kept Eve in the indestructible paradise, when he kept her single with himself, like a star in its orbit."
> "Yes—yes——" cried Ursula, pointing her finger at him. "There you are—a star in its orbit! A satellite—a satellite of Mars—that's what she is to be! There—there—you've given yourself away." [P. 142]

What is so intelligent and exacting here are not the ideas, which exist as empty abstractions, nor any particularly subtle use of conversational tones, but the action, the drama, the willingness of Lawrence to lay himself open, the implicit acknowledgment of Lawrence's deepest novelistic instincts that life must test ideas by making two people known to each other:

> He stood smiling in frustration and amusement and irritation and admiration and love. She was so quick, and so lambent, like discernible fire, and so vindictive, and so rich in her dangerous flamy sensitiveness. [P. 142]

Lovely, the paradoxes brought to life in acceptance and admiration of another, and lovely too, the way this insures that after the argument makes them both weary, they stay together, the bond there even though neither likes the other's terms to describe it:

> "Say you love me, say 'my love' to me," she pleaded.

He looked back into her eyes, and saw. His face flickered with sardonic comprehension.

"I love you right enough," he said grimly. "But I want it to be something else."

"But why? But why?" she insisted, bending her wonderful luminous face to him. "Why isn't it enough?" [P. 145]

By the new rules of the game, Birkin must concede to her, at least momentarily, because he cannot say why love is not enough: "Let love be enough then. I love you then—I love you. I'm bored by the rest" (p. 146).

But the peace brought about through affectionate weariness cannot be lasting, and so right away we see how love is not enough for either of them even though neither knows what more there is. At the beginning of the next chapter Birkin and Ursula are walking on the Crich estate and suddenly he breaks into a dance:

"I thought you liked the light fantastic."

"Not like that," she said, confused and bewildered, almost affronted. Yet somewhere inside her she was fascinated by the sight of his loose, vibrating body, perfectly abandoned to its own dropping and swinging, and by the pallid, sardonic-smiling face above. . . . And moving in the rapid, stationary dance, he came a little nearer, and reached forward with an incredibly mocking, satiric gleam on his face, and would have kissed her again, had she not started back.

"No, don't!" she cried, really afraid.

"Cordelia after all," he said satirically. [Pp. 160–161]

Birkin is not moving away from Ursula, but is only responding to an instinct that cannot be defined or controlled by the idea of "Let love be enough, then." So Ursula is frightened, and because she is, he mocks her. There is a Birkin out there, beyond her "love."

Later that same day, after Diana Crich dies, Ursula tries to bring Birkin back into a relationship she understands:

"No! I'd rather Diana Crich were dead. Her living somehow was all wrong. As for the young man, poor devil—he'll find his way out quick-

ly instead of slowly. Death is all right—nothing better."
"Yet you don't want to die," she challenged him.
He was silent for a time. Then he said, in a voice that was frightening to her in its change:
"I should like to be through with it—I should like to be through with the death process."
"And aren't you?" asked Ursula nervously.
They walked on for some way in silence, under the trees. Then he said slowly, as if afraid:
"There is life which belongs to death, and there is life which isn't death. One is tired of the life that belongs to death—our kind of life. But whether it is finished, God knows. I want love that is like sleep, like being born again, vulnerable as a baby that just comes into the world." [P. 178]

Of the life that "belongs to death" we have already learned much. We have seen in some characters the urge to use the consciousness to dominate others become insistent and proud: Anna Brangwen is the leading example, but the same feeling animates Miss Inger and the school principal, Ursula when frustrated in her relationship with Skrebensky, Hermione Roddice, Gerald, and Gudrun. But this same desire can lead in others to an implicit self-loathing that seeks destruction of the conscious self in an ecstatic swoon toward darkness: the Prussian officer is the leading example here, but Paul Morel feels such a sequence of feelings, as does Lawrence in the sequence of poems and the letters. We know, furthermore, that these are not really two different groups of characters but characters with very similar feelings at different stages of their development within the individual and within history. The more violent the character or the more violent the moment in history, the more necessary seems the resolution of the swooning death. We are reminded that in this novel everyone is closer to such feelings because "the bitterness of the war may be taken for granted in the characters."

But we still know little of the "life which isn't death" as a possibility of modern life, except that now, scared and tired, Birkin does not see it as the life that comes after the death of humanity but as a life that comes in spite of such death. We glimpse that this scene is to be a paradigm of the whole book, then, as Birkin and Ursula fight toward some understanding, even as the old civilization, the life that belongs to death, passes away. Birkin's commitment to Ursula has moved him from his rodomontade about the death of humanity toward a real questioning of what might be possible for him. In the presence of Diana's death neither he nor Ursula is secure. Birkin's response is to speak softly, vaguely dreaming; Ursula's is to answer death with the life she knows to be life:

> Then suddenly, to show him she was no shallow prude, she stopped and held him tight, hard against her, and covered his face with hard, fierce kisses of passion. In spite of his otherness, the old blood beat up in him. [P. 179]

The Lawrentian word "otherness" is no slogan here. It is still as vague as the "love that is like sleep" and the "life which isn't death," and all are vague because Birkin still knows them only as words. His quietness and his vagueness have no chance, thus, against the powerful passion that Birkin mistrusts but cannot resist:

> "Not this, not this," he whimpered to himself, as the first perfect mood of softness and sleep-loveliness ebbed back away from the rushing of passion that came up to his limbs and over his face as she drew him. And soon he was a perfect hard flame of passionate desire for her. Yet in the small core of the flame was an unyielding anguish of another thing. But this also was lost; he only wanted her, with an extreme desire that seemed inevitable as death, beyond question. [P. 179]

The phrases "rushing of passion," "perfect hard flame," and "extreme desire that seemed inevitable as death"—here are all the old terms of the dying culture, the culture that had seen the old courtly and romantic passions of heroic lovers become the will to power of Gerald Crich, and at the moment they threaten one last time to overwhelm, because set against them is only the vague and pathetic "another thing," Lawrence's and Birkin's wish to defy and be done with the old ways and to be "born again, vulnerable as a baby."

Birkin is not heroic here. The most that can be said for him at this point is that he has held out, that he has the vague wish for "another thing" before the rush of passion sweeps it away leaving only the mereness of the passion. The possibility for his heroism lies in his *only* wanting Ursula now. But we can claim more for Lawrence. On the one hand the passion is so strong that the process of excitement and fulfillment seems as inevitable as death, inevitable because it too is time-worn and time-honored and because its orgasm is a way of dying and of killing the desire for the other thing that is still vague and incomplete. On the other hand Lawrence can keep his writing clear, his sense of other possibilities beside the passionate open, even as he acknowledges the potential completeness of passion. To call clear writing heroic will seem needlessly insistent only if we forget how strong everything within and outside Lawrence was tempting him to blur and give in, to let passion have its seemingly inevitable sway. The cycle of sexual excitement and fulfillment and death is made parallel to the cycle of the will becoming powerful through the consciousness, then triumphant over the darkness of the unknown of others, then itself suicidal in the wish for darkness and oblivion. These rhythms have become the most powerful rhythms of the culture, and if there is to be a new relationship, it must lie outside these cycles. The discovery of such a relation now takes on the dimensions of a heroic victory. As yet, though, Birkin and Lawrence can offer only their anguished hope for "another thing," and the heroism has no triumph.

So:

satisfied and shattered, fulfilled and destroyed, he went home away from her, drifting vaguely through the darkness, lapsed into the old fire of burning passion. Far away, far away, there seemed to be a small lament in the darkness. But what did it matter? What did it matter, what did anything matter save this ultimate and triumphant experience of physical passion, that had blazed up anew like a new spell of life. "I was becoming quite dead-alive, nothing but a wordbag," he said in triumph, scorning his other self. Yet somewhere far off and small, the other hovered. [P. 180]

To be satisfied, fulfilled, and to burn with passion is to drift and to lapse, so there is a sad irony in speaking of "this ultimate and triumphant experience of physical passion." But it is one thing to dramatize the way passion is only part of a process of dying, and quite another to say what else if not desire and fulfillment should take place. Ursula has set Birkin free to be what he wants, but she also has insisted he know what he wants. At least passion keeps Birkin from being nothing but a word bag.

After "Water-Party" both Birkin and Ursula recoil from the emptiness of their fulfilled passion:

And for several days she went about possessed by this exquisite force of hatred against him. It surpassed anything she had ever known before, it seemed to throw her out of the world into some terrible region where nothing of her old life held good. [P. 190]

As for Birkin, "He lay sick and unmoved, in pure opposition to everything. He knew how near to breaking was the vessel that held his life" (pp. 190–191). Birkin's dream of "more" and of "a further conjunction" and Ursula's dream of "love" have carried them out of their old world, away from the civilization dying around them, but only into voids of inaction, hatred, and a drift toward death. Once again the heroic effort to make real a new relationship has fallen back, defeated. At least it cannot be claimed that Lawrence seeks easy victories.

Trying to break free, Birkin goes away, but Ursula finds him one night by Willey Water, muttering to himself: "You can't go away. There *is* no away." But if this is true he can break free only by destroying what holds him, so as he looks at the image of the moon on the water he sees the moon as Cybele, and both as Ursula, and he hurls rock after rock at the pond. Thus, after his longest assault, "Ursula was dazed, her mind was all gone. She felt she had fallen to the ground and was spilled out, like water on the earth" (p. 240). But she is not destroyed, only stunned by the depth of his desire to destroy her, and when she discovers herself to him she accuses him of wanting to kill her because she will not be his servant:

> It was a great effort to him to maintain this conversation, and to press for the thing he wanted from her, the surrender of her spirit.
> "It is different," he said. "The two kinds of service are so different. I serve you in another way—not through *yourself*—somewhere else."
> [P. 242]

And they must fight again because he is not clear and she is suspicious of what seems like a program to have her submit to him, and again she feels she has won:

> "Do you really love me?" she asked.
> He laughed.
> "I call that your war-cry," he replied, amused. [P. 244]

Their wan admission of battle lines is the best they can do, and though Birkin gives in for a moment and the two are peaceful, that leads only to Ursula's being more passionate, so he backs away, and "The next day . . . he felt wistful and yearning." What is so telling about this extended testing is precisely the way the instrument that "saves" them both, which keeps either from giving up or accepting simplifications, is the consciousness. They *know* when Birkin's words are vague, they *know* when they are lapsed, or incomplete, or filled with hate. It is a curse to them, this highly developed consciousness that is civilization's greatest prize, but without it either would be lost.

So Birkin turns around on himself and confronts his desire as a meditative problem. He begins by remembering the West

African fetishes owned by his friend Halliday in London. He finds in the pregnant woman a lapsing of "the desire for creation and productive happiness" and a pursuit of "knowledge in one sort, mindless progressive knowledge through the senses, knowledge arrested and ending in the senses, mystic knowledge in disintegration and dissolution, knowledge such as the beetles have, which live purely within the world of corruption and cold dissolution" (pp. 245–246).

In one sense speculation about such existence is idle. At the beginning of the episode Birkin "knew he did not want a further sensual experience—something deeper, darker, than ordinary life could give," and he knows it again at the end of the daydream. But in another sense this daydreaming is very important. The fetish comes from a culture that had explored mindless sensual experience for thousands of years after it had died mystically, as a culture: "Thousands of years ago, that which was imminent in himself must have taken place in these Africans." Birkin had assumed that there is no way out for Western culture, so that mankind should "pass away—time it did," and since Ursula saw the flash of fangs in the darkness in *The Rainbow* the implication had been that the passing away would be sudden and violent, an Armageddon. But this experience imagined in remembering the fetish is different:

> He realised now that this is a long process—thousands of years it takes, after the death of the creative spirit. He realised that there were great mysteries to be unsealed, sensual, mindless, dreadful mysteries, far beyond the phallic cult. [P. 246]

Birkin's fear of passion must be equivalent to a fear of the phallic and of the rhythm of excitement, climax, and death, and it is almost bound to lead him to speculate about "further sensual experience." It is one way in which the individual sexual desire and the culture's possibility meet, an awful way, Birkin knows, but there, possible. The other obvious way is the destruction of the West in mechanized violence, achieved as the suicidal triumph of the dominant conscious will. But still, Birkin believes "There was another way, the way of freedom." As yet, though, the way is jargon-ridden, the theory of a word bag:

> a lovely state of free proud singleness, which accepted the obligation of the permanent connection with others, and with the other, submits to the yoke and leash of love, but never forfeits its own proud individual singleness, even while it loves and yields. [P. 247]

After a book and a half, the context is so powerful it spits up such a passage as phony and unreal with no trouble. There is not a word in it that is clear, that has been made clear by the unrolling of the vision or the testing of the drama. Ursula would mock it, and so must we.

So Birkin flees again, this time to Gerald. Lawrence's characterization of Gerald as "an incarnation, a great phase of life," as the dominant figure in a culture become so mechanical and permeated with the Wille zur Macht that it is on the verge of destruction, has received so much good critical attention that it hardly seems necessary here to explicate him at length. What we need is what we find in "Gladiatorial," a seeing of the "homosexual" problem that is also a seeing of the problem of historical disintegration and the task of the Love Triumphant:

> He seemed to penetrate into Gerald's more solid, more diffuse bulk, to interfuse his body through the body of the other, as if to bring it subtly into subjection, always seizing with some rapid necromantic foreknowledge every motion of the other flesh, converting and counteracting it, playing upon the limbs and trunk of Gerald like some hard wind. [P. 262]

Here Birkin does what Ursula had accused him of wanting to do with her; we can see that he feels free after he wrestles, and relaxed, because he has dominated Gerald, subjected him, and he can do this because Gerald, unlike Ursula, really seeks to be dominated. "It takes two people to make a murder: a murderer and a murderee," Birkin says to Gerald in their first conversation in the novel. In "Gladiatorial" we see that Birkin is potentially a murderer in his effort to resolve his incomplete relation with Ursula somehow—by throwing rocks at the image of the moon, by speculating about mindless sensual knowledge, by wrestling and conquering Gerald Crich. He is doing what he so despises Hermione Roddice for trying to do: willing one's own victory. The murderee, Gerald, is the "other man" of earlier Lawrence transformed into an industrial magnate. He retains their physical power and attractiveness, he accentuates their unconscious inability or refusal to make their experience truly available to themselves, he adds social position, education, and a sullen will to power: a latter day Baxter Dawes or Will Brangwen.

But here their attraction for each other, the murderer and murderee, is clearly seen for both as escape: from the emptiness of a life that does not center for Gerald, from the challenge of Ursula for Birkin. The aim of the escape, furthermore, is a one-man world; in philosophical terms it is solipsism, and in psychological terms it is narcissism. When domination and subjection are possible, the world becomes simple because otherness and its constant tensions are resolved; in such a world murder is possible. Here we can see the full scope of Lawrence's torment and the measure of his heroism and his greatness in his creating the Ursula of this novel. Birkin is moving, and moving with Ursula, in a tortured way toward some Love Triumphant, but in the act of moving in that direction when the direction is unclear, Birkin and Lawrence are tempted to escape from the frustrations of the search and the implications of the triumphant love into a simple world of destruction and eventual darkness.

Because Birkin has been running from her, in "Moony" and "Gladiatorial," Ursula responds with her most savage attack on him when they meet next. At the beginning of the climactic chapter, "Excurse," the two ride away, to "anywhere," and Birkin gives her three rings, which they both admire. But nothing has really been resolved between them, and soon they are quarreling, about Hermione Roddice and the hold Ursula thinks she still has over Birkin. Ursula is in fact wrong because Hermione has had no real hold on him since he met Ursula, but she is in essence right, and what ails him is what ails Hermione. Ursula delivers her harshest speech:

> "*You!*" she cried. "You! You truth-lover! You purity-monger! It *stinks*, your truth and your purity. It stinks of the offal you feed on, you scavenger dog, you eater of corpses. You are foul, *foul*—and you must know it. Your purity, your candour, your goodness—yes, thank you, we've had some. What you are is a foul, deathly thing, obscene, that's what you are, obscene and perverse. You, and love! You may well say, you don't want love. No, you want *yourself*, and dirt and death—that's what you want. You are so *perverse*, so death-eating. And then——." [P. 299]

She throws the rings in the mud and begins walking up the road. She is right in everything she says, as the previous chapters show, but not right enough. For Birkin is driven by more than the desire for himself and the answering desire for death, however great a hold these have on him and his author:

> He felt tired and weak. Yet also he was relieved. He gave up his old position. He went and sat on the bank. No doubt Ursula was right. [P. 301]

Before, in "Mino," in "Water-Party," and in "Moony," Birkin has softened under her attacks, and sought peace, but as a means of fending off the implications of what she says. Here he takes them on, fully:

> It was true, really, what she said. He knew that his spirituality was concomitant of a process of depravity, a sort of pleasure in self-destruction. There really *was* a certain stimulant in self-destruction, for him—especially when it was translated spiritually. But then he knew it—he knew it, and had done. [P. 301]

Once again it is the consciousness that saves. But likewise it defends, so Birkin moves out, in his thoughts, onto the attack once more:

And was not Ursula's way of emotional intimacy, emotional and physical, was it not just as dangerous as Hermione's abstract spiritual intimacy? Fusion, fusion, this horrible fusion of two beings, which every woman and most men insisted on, was it not nauseous and horrible anyhow, whether it was a fusion of the spirit or of the emotional body? Hermoine saw herself as the perfect Idea, to which all men must come; and Ursula was the perfect Womb, the bath of birth, to which all men must come! And both were horrible. [P. 301]

Unquestionably Birkin is making it rather easy on himself here, and the allegations against Hermione and Ursula are simple and self-indulgent. Furthermore, there is no way to avoid feeling that Lawrence endorses Birkin. But really all that is minor compared to the assurance and the rightness of the motion of Birkin's thoughts. If the consciousness saves, it saves by being alert, alive to the people outside and the instincts within, so the intense revulsion against fusion is the response of that consciousness when it feels threatened with the loss of itself. If man no longer utters the incomprehensible he must acknowledge his apartness, from others and from the mystically apprehended universe. During the long February nights, with the ewes in labor, Tom Brangwen had looked at the stars and known he did not belong to himself. But that was two generations ago, and now Birkin must belong to himself, else all is lost, in passion, in mindless sensuality, in violence:

Why could they not remain individuals, limited by their own limits? Why this dreadful all-comprehensiveness, this hateful tyranny? Why not leave the other being free, why try to absorb, or melt, or merge? One might abandon oneself utterly to the *moments*, but not to any other being. [P. 301]

That last sentence, which is crucial, is vague here, but not for long:

There was a darkness over his mind. The terrible knot of concious-
ness that had persisted there like an obsession was broken, gone, his
life was dissolved in darkness over his limbs and his body. But there
was a point of anxiety in his heart now. He wanted her to come back.
He breathed lightly and regularly like an infant, that breathes innocently, beyond the touch of responsibility. [P. 301]

"He wanted her to come back"—the key sentence in the book,
really, and in Lawrence. Birkin has done with himself as a
taker of positions. The consciousness that has knotted him in
opposition breaks, but not so he can lose himself but only so
he can abandon himself to this moment. Birkin had felt a point
of anxiety in his heart before, at a similar moment, on the
road to Beldover when Ursula passionately kisses him. But the
result is crucially different:

he was a perfect hard flame of passionate desire for her. Yet in the
small core of the flame was an unyielding anguish of another thing.
But this also was lost; he only wanted her, with an extreme desire that
seemed inevitable as death, beyond question. ["Water-Party"]

his life was dissolved in darkness over his limbs and his body. But
there was a point of anxiety in his heart now. He wanted her to come
back. ["Excurse"]

In the first passage the anguish in his heart is for something
vague, so he is powerless against the dissolving rush of passion:
he wanted her. But in the second, the anxiety is not vague:
he wanted her to come back. To want her is to want to take
her so both can dissolve in a desire as inevitable as death. To
want her to come back is to want her to be herself and with
him and to want himself to be abandoned not to her but to
the moment of her coming back.

That the difference is crucial can be seen immediately: "He
breathed lightly and regularly like an infant, that breathes
innocently. . . ." This is exactly what Birkin had said he
wanted in "Water-Party" ("like being born again, vulnerable
as a baby that just comes into the world"), but which was not
possible because he was not willing to abandon himself to

the moment. So here they come together, tired and bored with emotion, knowing the worst there is to know of the other and no longer caring:

> She came up and stood before him, hanging her head.
> "See what a flower I found you," she said, wistfully holding a piece of purple-red bell-heather under his face. He saw the clump of coloured bells, and the tree-like, tiny branch: also her hands, with their over-fine, over-sensitive skin.
> "Pretty!" he said, looking up at her with a smile, taking the flower. [P. 302]

If we ask of Lawrence that Love Triumphant be a doctrine, this lovely passage will probably be disappointing. The "positions" Birkin and Ursula take here are simply positions in space, he sitting and she standing over him, and they are stripped of all the other means they have had of locating themselves and their needs and desires. They are there, in a scene, nothing more—that is what it means to abandon oneself to moments:

> Was it all real? But his eyes were beautiful and soft and immune from stress or excitement, beautiful and smiling lightly to her, smiling with her. She hid her face on his shoulder, hiding before him, because he could see her so completely. She knew he loved her, and she was afraid, she was in a strange element, a new heaven round about her. She wished he were passionate, because in passion she was at home. But this was so still and frail, as space is more frightening than force. [Pp. 302–303]

Almost a thousand pages lie behind that "space is more frightening than force," and we need almost every one to read it rightly; if only to do justice to this scene everyone should read *The Rainbow* before reading *Women in Love*. It is not a matter of connecting this image with the many in *The Rainbow* about the space of the heavens. It is a matter of watching a story unfold; of seeing the human consciousness develop into so powerful an instrument that it denies heaven and finally

seeks death; of watching that instrument become a weapon in
the hands of Gudrun Brangwen and Gerald Crich, and, in
moments of desperation, such an instrument for Ursula and
Birkin too; of watching both Birkin and Ursula save themselves by that consciousness that keeps them separate; of watching the darkness come over Birkin to dissolve the consciousness
that had knotted him in theories and enmity so as to create a
new consciousness and an awareness of Ursula existing, out
there, down the road, beyond him, creating for him, because
she is separate and yet loving, a new sense of space entirely,
beyond power. It terrifies them as space can terrify a child,
for they are children now, and the space is new:

> "Do you love me?" she said quickly, impulsively.
> "Yes," he replied, not heeding her motion, only her stillness.
> She knew it was true. She broke away.
> "So you ought," she said, turning round to look at the road. "Did
> you find the rings?"
> "Yes."
> "Where are they?"
> "In my pocket."
> She put her hand into his pocket and took them out.
> She was restless.
> "Shall we go?" she said.
> "Yes," he answered. And they mounted to the car once more, and
> left behind them this memorable battle-field. [P. 303]

It is the least defeated moment, surely, in modern literature.

The two drive off for tea, and in an inn their dreams are
realized:

> Unconsciously, with her sensitive finger-tips, she was tracing the
> back of his thighs, following some mysterious life-flow there. She had
> discovered something, something more than wonderful, more wonder-
> ful than life itself. It was the strange mystery of his life-motion, there,
> at the back of the thighs, down the flanks. It was a strange reality of
> his being, the very stuff of being, there in the straight downflow of the
> thighs. It was here she discovered him one of the sons of God such as
> were in the beginning of the world, not a man, something other, some-
> thing more. [P. 305]

The sons of God such as were in the beginning of the world—
we know them because Birkin is only and totally for Ursula
"something other, something more," because they are children, born again. But the passage does present difficulties. The
discovery of the "mystery of his life-motion" that is "more
wonderful than life itself" is certainly not clear, nor is the
discovery of him "not a man." We sense that the need to deny
the phallic is strong here, but the most explicit Lawrence is
about what is happening comes in this sentence:

> It was a perfect passing away for both of them, and at the same time
> the most intolerable accession into being, the marvellous fullness of
> immediate gratification, overwhelming, outflooding from the source
> of the deepest life-force, the darkest, deepest, strangest life-source of
> the human body, at the back and base of the loins. [P. 306]

The action is not phallic and "the marvelous fullness of immediate gratification" is stressed as an alternative to the
rhythmic fulfillment of phallic passion that leads from merging
to a swooning death. Birkin has been right to the extent that
we see that something other is possible. We also know this is
not simply a mystic discovery; whatever Ursula discovers "at
the back and base of the loins" must be *there,* though it will
not be simply physical.

There has been a good deal of discussion since the *Lady
Chatterley* case about the explicit qualities of Lawrence's
sexuality, most of which has been carried on in what can only
be described as a spirit of appalling vulgarity. But George
Ford, in *Double Measure,* does a clear and sensitive and
literary analysis of this and other difficult passages in *Women
in Love,* one that can be faulted, it seems to me, only on the
grounds that he misses some important things by not taking
the book, and especially the relationship of Birkin and Ursula,
in order, as it comes in the book, as a story. What Ford shows
is that the more we think of Lawrence as a case, the more this
scene will seem like others with which it should not, really,

be very closely associated.

So we must be very clear. This scene is not, or not explicitly, anal, after the fashion of the euphemistically described celebration of Connie Chatterley's last night with Mellors before she leaves for Venice. Nor is it very close to Cipriano's doctrine of the unfulfilled woman in *The Plumed Serpent*. Nor are its tone and manner at all like that of Gudrun's vision of her potential degradation at the hands of Loerke. It is not even much like Ursula's own acceptance, one night in the Alps, long after this, of shame as part of "the whole round of experience." Birkin and Ursula are fully clothed here, he stands in front of her and she runs her hands down the back of his thighs, "she seemed to touch the quick of the mystery of darkness that was bodily him." The problem here is not finding out what is happening, but what justifies the triumphant and rapturous and finally not fully clear writing:

It was a dark flood of electric passion she released from him, drew into herself. She had established a rich new circuit, a new current of passional electric energy, between the two of them, released from the darkest poles of the body and established in perfect circuit. [Pp. 305–306]

At such a moment it seems to me Lawrence passes away, outside the reach of his own context. The metaphor of electricity seems to me hopelessly muddled. But let that be the complaint, that he becomes shrill when he need not be because he wants to emphasize the value of what is happening more than he knows how to do. His literary instincts fail him.

But as yet the obscurity only threatens to cloud the vision Lawrence worked for four years and a thousand pages to achieve. The writing makes clear that this is a celebration indeed, not a hoax:

They were glad, and they could forget perfectly. They laughed and went to the meal provided. There was a venison pasty, of all things, a large broad-faced cut ham, eggs and cresses and red beetroot, and

medlars and apple-tart, and tea.
  "What *good* things!" she cried with pleasure. "How noble it looks! —shall I pour out the tea?—" [P. 306]

So might a daughter of men speak, born anew, "at her ease, entirely forgetting to have misgivings."

So despite the vagueness and shrillness of the description of the lovemaking, it is a great scene, worthy of allowing still further exploration. Having watched Lawrence achieve this much, we can be tempted into feeling the demons could be laid to rest. The promises made more than a novel earlier have been kept, and the ironist in Ursula and the preacher in Birkin have been waylaid this side of destruction. Everything for which Lawrence had been working since the death of his mother lies behind this scene, lighting it up, making it magical. He had, in effect, taken on the whole civilization, rendered as fully as anyone had the collapse of its old order, and he had found, in the human consciousness pushing itself to the verge of annihilation, a heroic countermotion. But Lawrence had gone as far as he could go. The dangers without and the sicknesses within in fact became too strong. Beyond this point, as some medieval maps phrased it, there be dragons.

Before the end of "Excurse" Lawrence does try to move out once more, as Birkin tells Ursula of his dream for expanding the perfected relation to include "a few other people." This is the project, Rananim, that Lawrence dreamed of often in the years he was writing these books, but it never came to anything beyond discussions with his more abject disciples. Ursula, fortunately, is no follower, and so, at the very end of the novel, the two dramatize Lawrence's implicit admission of defeat:

  "Aren't I enough for you?" she asked.
  "No," he said. "You are enough for me, as far as a woman is concerned. You are all women to me. But I wanted a man friend, as eternal as you and I are eternal." [P. 472]

Ursula calls this desire "an obstinacy, a theory, a perversity," linking beautifully the three great Lawrentian defects. Birkin insists, though:

"You can't have it, because it's false, impossible," she said.
"I don't believe that," he answered. [P. 473]

Lawrence insists on his faith here in the last lines of the novel, but in fact his imagination cannot move beyond Ursula's skepticism.

The relation with a man friend cannot be imagined because the man Birkin wants is Gerald Crich. For Birkin to have wanted *him* limits and defines the nature of that want decisively. Gerald is the monarch of industrial civilization, the final flower on the slag heaps, the figure in whom consciousness has been developed into an instrument for dominating, controlling, and hurting others to the extent that Gerald is seeking subjection, being hurt, and suicide. When life becomes, as it does for Gerald, so much a matter of control and power, it also becomes intolerable and he seeks to relinquish the power, to relinquish it violently and finally. So he is relentlessly hunted down, for which purpose Lawrence has created Gudrun Brangwen, bitter, detached, satirical, fatally attracted to what she hates. When Gerald tortures the Arabian mare, in the first of a series of terrifying scenes involving Gerald and Gudrun, Ursula stands back, "in pure opposition," while "the world reeled and passed into nothingness for Gudrun, she could not know any more." Ursula, thus, really does not care about Gerald, but Gudrun does, Birkin does, and Lawrence does.

For the first two thirds of the novel Gudrun's hunting of Gerald—in "Water-Party," "Rabbit," and "Death and Love," is carefully counterpointed with the struggle of Ursula and Birkin for a new relationship, and this allows us to measure the way the struggle between Gudrun and Gerald is by com-

parison murderous, an embrace of cruelty and slavery. We can
see, too, that Birkin by comparison with Gudrun is a pompous
satirist because he does not really care to take the measure of
the society and she does. But after "Excurse" all this changes,
and at that point Birkin and Ursula cease to dominate or even
to provide much balancing weight against the hunting down of
Gerald. That Gudrun is going to triumph over Gerald and
kill him has been implicit in their relationship from the beginning, but at this point that triumph and death begin to be
the culminating event not just of their story but of the whole
novel. Birkin has no chance for any positive relation with Gerald because, as we have seen in "Gladiatorial," Gerald is for
him a means of controlling someone else and living in a world
dominated by his will. So too with Lawrence. He hates Gerald,
he wants to kill him, but in that hate and want is narcissistic
and homosexual temptation that becomes in the last third of
the book so strong it brushes everything else aside.

So in foreshortened form Western civilization is made to
take the same steps Birkin had imagined West African civilization taking thousands of years earlier. Lawrence lines up various steps on that path to corruption—Gerald, Halliday and
Minette, Loerke—and then he sends Gudrun down that path.
The great phase that is industrial life cuts itself off from creative feelings and so sets out, hunter and hunted becoming increasingly alike, down to where the rats, like Loerke, live,
adrift in the river of corruption. Birkin loathes Loerke but is
fascinated by him; Gerald finds him hateful, but is intensely
jealous of him, too, and wants what Loerke has; Gudrun sees
in him chances to enact "the mystic frictional activities of dia-
bolic reducing down, disintegrating the vital organic body of
life." And Lawrence is committed now to carrying his whole
novel at least as far down that life as he must go to kill Gerald.
He is of Gerald's civilization at last, infected by it so that he
can only express his desire for Gerald and his sick passion by

hunting him and it down, destroying Gerald, passion, and self at once. History finally has become the monolithic and irreversible motion of dissolution, perversion, and death.

If we look at Birkin and Ursula in the last third of the novel we can see that what was creative and hopeful in Lawrence simply became paralyzed. Their triumphant love has been achieved by their making a world out of each other, and Birkin, released from the bored hatred of Hermione and humanity, becomes a kind of Lawrentian Good Angel: powerful but detached, calm, ironic, decent, sensible. Because the Lawrentian Bad Angel, Gerald, had to be tracked down, there is nothing for Birkin and Ursula to do and they become supernumeraries in the spectacle, not needing to comment and unable to act; Lawrence treats them almost casually, like characters created for a short story. To say that Birkin wants Gerald is to say Lawrence wants Gerald and the want is diseased enough to stop everything else for the sake of the want and healthy enough to seek its own destruction. Which is to say that Birkin himself has ceased really to matter.

Looking back we can see that there is much wrong in a local way in *Women in Love*—the gossipy London scenes, and especially the tendency toward repetition that makes "Man to Man" only a preliminary version of "Gladiatorial" and "Threshold" and "Woman to Woman" needless reworkings of "Rabbit" and "Breadalby." But these are local, and what is more seriously wrong is something analysis page-by-page cannot show: the atrophying of the dream for Ursula and Birkin in the wake of the hunt for the trophies of Gerald and Gudrun. Certainly it would be foolish to imagine what they might have or should have done, or Lawrence with them. But no one who can see how important they are and how deeply Lawrence struggled to keep alive his hopes for them can feel anything but defeat at the moment when, imaginatively, they cease to be crucial for Lawrence.

The epilogue need not be lengthy. Having explored heroically as far as he did by the end of 1916, having reached these limits, Lawrence could only wander, and imaginatively he could only repeat himself in the last fourteen years of his life. He reworked the old "Insurrection of Miss Houghton" into *The Lost Girl* and he wrote four other full length novels. Each has some interesting or bizarre moments, but mostly they reveal a Lawrence who has lost sight of his desire to sustain a full-length work with care, and each becomes shrill or repetitive or formulaic before the end. The best work is in the stories, poems, and criticism, small scale things, some very beautiful, where he reworks the sense of life he had gained by 1916. The one major book after *Women in Love* is *Studies in Classic American Literature,* written while he was revising the novel and very much dependent on it. It is funny and profound, an irreplaceable book as it has turned out, the work there was time and energy left over for Birkin to do, as it were.

But for the most part, pleasure in reading the later Lawrence is usually overwhelmed by shock or boredom, the almost inevitable results for an admiring reader of Lawrence's inability or refusal to see what had happened to him. Increasingly large sections of his mind and imagination became cut off from the scrutiny of irony and humor, the talismans with which he had created the Ursula of *Women in Love.* The heroic journey of 1910–1916 becomes effortful wandering, and the hero is visible only in the pale light cast by his willingness to wander, his devotion to work, and his occasional bursts of vitality and cheerfulness.

He had not freed himself from the flash of fangs, but given the intensity with which he saw the fangs, that is not surprising. What is, and what is wonderful and heroic, is the struggle so intense that no matter its outcome it availed, and availeth.

III. *The Achievement of William Empson*

Lawrence was born in 1886, Empson in 1906. Lawrence came of age at a time when singly and often unbeknownst to one another various writers were writing the poems and novels that later seemed the beginning of modern literature; Empson came to his maturity when the modern and the direction given it by the war were in full view to many. I know of nothing Empson has said about his youth or his memories of the war. He was raised in Yorkshire, went to Winchester, then up to Cambridge in 1925, to read mathematics. He was, very obviously, superbly educated or able to educate himself. He gives the impression from his first work of having read everything and having assimilated it completely into his own experience. He not only knew all about Eliot's version of the Myth of Lost Unity, he seems really to have had a unified sensibility. There are fears and even terrors in Empson which become expressed as ideas, and there are apparently dry abstractions that he can make moving and lyric. He seems not to have been crippled by anything like the kind of experience that so maimed Lawrence, yet he saw what only such experience could show Lawrence, the need for something new, for a reply to the motions of history he learned so well and so young.

What he did was to reorganize and rework all that he had learned, all that modern criticism and modern science had taught him about his life. He did this, first, by becoming a historian, for that was the only way the Myth of Lost Unity could be explored. He did it, second, by becoming a historian of pastoral and thereby a historian of the complex idea of literary heroism. He was both supremely endowed and supremely placed to do this work, but it turned out that the work of one man was simply not enough. There was too much else in the air, too thorough an assumption on the part of even the most intelligent that anyone who really understood modern life damned well better had despair, and so Empson's work had to wait a generation before it could be read intelligently.

In one sense, then, Empson is the easiest of my three modern heroes to write about. Lawrence and Tolkien became historians because there was no other way. They did not set out to do this, and they seem even unaware that this is what happened to them. Empson clearly is a historian, a historian of Eliot's Myth, a historian of heroism. But it is never easy to write about Empson, in another sense. He learned much from Eliot, most crucially the passion for indirectness and the reasons for that passion. Empson almost always "says what he means," but almost never in a way that makes it easy for anyone to know what he means. Certainly one cannot simply open a work of Empson's and see that he is a historian, much less see that he is a modern hero. Lawrence, whatever his subtleties and complexities, is almost always direct; he moves with passion and fear and hope straight ahead in almost everything he writes. Empson is always indirect—witty, playful, ingenious, talkative, brilliant—and no one would call him heroic without being given many good reasons for doing so.

So let our path be somewhat indirect too, and let us begin the story of Empson with Eliot.

Eliot does not now and may never again enjoy his former reputation. There are now as many as half a dozen early twentieth-century writers one can easily and safely prefer to him. But until a few years ago he was *the* modern writer as Picasso was *the* modern painter, and he was just beginning to gain this status when Empson came up to Cambridge where Eliot was to enjoy the favor enjoyed by Wordsworth at the same place, a century earlier. James Reeves remembers it this way:

> The stranger who enters an Anglican church at service time is handed two books, *Hymns Ancient and Modern* and *The Book of Common Prayer*. When I went up to Cambridge twenty years ago, I was handed, as it were, in much the same spirit, two little books, the one in prose, the other in verse. They were *The Sacred Wood* and *Poems: 1909–1925*. [*T. S. Eliot: A Symposium,* ed. Richard March and Tambimutti (Chicago, 1949), p. 38]

To this should be added Empson's own testimony:

> I feel, like most other verse writers of my generation, that I do not know for certain how much of my own mind he invented, let alone how much of it is a reaction against him or indeed a consequence of misreading him. He has a very penetrating influence, not unlike an east wind. [*T. S. Eliot: A Symposium,* p. 35]

The presumption of such testimony is that it was Eliot's poetry that had the really strong hold on the Cambridge modern mind, and that the criticism was known mostly for its exciting aperçus: the dissociation of sensibility, the objective correlative, *Hamlet* is an artistic failure, slighting remarks about nineteenth-century poets. But Eliot's criticism was at the same time exerting an influence stronger than the famous *mots,* an influence perhaps even stronger than the poems, though the poems were in themselves critical documents of major importance in effecting the idea of history that is Eliot's greatest contribution.

The great reorientation created by Eliot is about our sense

of the past. Much of what he said he was not the first to say, but his were the telling formulations, and his were the poems that could illustrate the point:

What happens when a new work of art is created is something that happens simultaneously to all the works of art which preceded it.

This certainly had been thought before, and statements rather like it had even been written. But Eliot tells us what it really means to say this.

Put in its simplest form the Eliotic idea is this: the critic learns to read by reading historically, and he learns to read historically by knowing that he stands at a given moment in time and creates his history. Not only judgments but all literary perceptions are relativistic to the extent that because we are when we are we read as we do. Arnold writes about history as though it were "then and then and then," the Elizabethans and then the Augustans and then the Romantics. If he has an idea of history at all it is a simple one of periods of expansion followed by periods of contraction. Eliot knows history is always now, something we make. Everything in *The Sacred Wood* and *Homage to John Dryden* depends for its force on his knowing he is remaking the English literary tradition, establishing Kyd and Marlowe, "placing" Shakespeare and Milton, denigrating Shelley, Tennyson, and Browning, because he is when he is, because he is writing "Gerontion," because the nineteenth century is over. He knows the "tradition" he talks about is not the "tradition" made by Saintsbury or Swinburne, but he also knows and demonstrates that they had made their "tradition" because they lived in Wordsworth's century. Opinions that had come to be accepted as facts—Denham and Waller are the precursors of Augustan verse, Gray and Collins are "pre-Romantics," Tennyson and Browning are great poets—could be shown to be only reflections of the sense of tradition felt by a previous age.

Having put the matter this bluntly, I must add that if ten academic scholars of literature were asked to name the crucial element in the Eliotic revolution, nine would probably answer differently from the above. There might even be some reluctant to talk about the "Eliotic revolution" at all, as though it had not happened. Eliot is still known as a "critic" and he became that at a time when to be a "critic" somehow implicitly meant that one was uninterested in or opposed to "literary history." Eliot was a journalist, a book reviewer, and in an era when "criticism" was fast becoming the "practical criticism" of I. A. Richards. This in turn meant that he was set up in opposition to the likes of Q, H. L. Chadwick, G. G. Coulton, and E. M. W. Tillyard—just to mention those at Cambridge when Richards arrived and Eliot was becoming known there—faded aesthetes or else "scholars." So Eliot was known as a writer of dazzling, irresponsible ideas. No one could accuse him of not knowing enough, he could be as fussily erudite as anyone, but because he was not himself academic, because he spoke as he did of *Hamlet* or Shelley, because he had written *The Waste Land,* Eliot's major contribution was almost inevitably misunderstood. Indeed, his most ardent followers think he still is.

But if one opens up *Selected Essays* and reads until he comes on the first memorable sentence, one finds it is almost always a historical statement, and of a kind few had made before him. This is the kind of thing I mean:

Had Massinger had a nervous system as refined as that of Middleton, Tourneur, Webster, or Ford, his style would be a triumph. But such a nature was not at hand, and Massinger precedes, not another Shakespeare, but Milton. [*Selected Essays* (New York, 1960), p. 187]

Eliot does not mean simply that Massinger wrote before Milton, which is all Arnold could have meant by the phrase, but that in the development of style, manner, and feeling of which

111

both poets are a part, Massinger comes before and could not have come after. It is something more subtle and more allied with the motions of the whole culture than the old-fashioned notion of "influence." Marlowe and then Jonson, Milton and then Dryden, Shelley and Keats and then Tennyson, Browning, and Swinburne—over and over Eliot establishes tradition by insisting that the earlier writer establishes the possibilities for poetic expression in the later writer. First this, and then that, and here is why.

But it was part of Eliot's strategy to deny that he was doing anything differently from the way it had been done before, even though he knew everyone was finding him outrageously new. This means that Eliot's statements about criticism almost never talk about history, and this, in turn, means that his efforts in this line, from "The Function of Criticism" to "The Frontiers of Criticism" are generally unsatisfactory. For instance, in "The Function of Criticism" Eliot reworks the central idea of Arnold's "Literary Influence of the Academies" into the historical assertion that "the French in the year 1600 *had already a more mature prose.*" Had Eliot ever said he was writing literary history he would have been inviting someone to see he had stolen Arnold's idea because Eliot himself is in a tradition as well as making one. Theoretically this had to be so—if "Marlowe and then Jonson," surely "Tennyson and Arnold and then Eliot." But the Possum had to try to conceal that, to conceal that Tennyson was a major force behind his poems and Arnold an equally major force behind his criticism. He had to behave as though we all understood a real break was being made with the immediate past. In fact Eliot was both doing something new and forcing everyone thereby to reread the entire tradition, and developing naturally from the poets and critics of the nineteenth century. But until these truths became clear, it could not be clear that Eliot is the first great modern literary historian.

If we take a look now at the direct successors of Eliot, we can probably then begin to see the nature of Empson's distinction as one whose mind was invented by Eliot but whose genius took him in un-Eliotic directions. Leavis fought for years for something he called "criticism," and he has always been known as a "critic" as opposed to a "scholar" or a "philosopher" or a "historian." But his two important books, *Revaluation* and *The Great Tradition*, give us the terms by which we can know the tradition Eliot made for us. Like Eliot, Leavis believes fully in the Myth of Lost Unity and generally is in despair concerning the conclusions about modern life to which it leads him. It is worth noticing in this context that Leavis's idea of Lawrence's heroism is quite different from mine. He uses Lawrence to prove that despair is really the proper response to history (Lawrence has never had proper recognition, Bloomsbury and the British Council have taken over the instruments of culture, C. P. Snow is a portent) by making Lawrence a stick with which Leavis can beat on the denizens of modern life lying all around. Though in recent years Leavis has attacked Eliot very harshly, making him indeed the prime victim of his stick that is Lawrence, Leavis's best work shows a profound understanding of Eliot and an extremely intelligent working out of Eliot's ideas about tradition and individual talents.

The best current successor to Eliot is the American Hugh Kenner, whose *The Invisible Poet* is much the best work on Eliot and whose work on a whole series of modern authors is the best effort yet made to accept the historians of the Myth of Lost Unity on their terms and to understand the tradition they have made from it. Just as it took a generation for Eliot or Leavis to be understood as major literary historians, so it may take that long for Kenner's magnificent work to be understood as a rethinking of the whole culture on Eliotic lines. To be ignorant or scornful of him, I think, will prove as dangerous in the next few years as scorn of Eliot and Leavis was thirty years ago. What this line—Eliot-Leavis-Kenner—shows is that any criticism that attempts to operate outside or ignorant of history is almost certainly criticism that cannot be fully relevant. Not to see that Eliot is still inventing the best critical minds is to try to sidestep the modern generation out of which we are evolving. Richards has dated, the American New Critics have dated, all but the historical parts of Northrop Frye and C. S. Lewis are quickly dating, while Eliot's "Andrew Marvell" or Leavis on Pope are still wonderfully fresh, and Kenner's *The Counterfeiters* offers more new ideas per page than any recent book of criticism. For the point about history is that it does in fact happen, and once Eliot happened then any writer after him who failed to see what he had done would inevitably resemble the seventeenth-century Spenserians who tried to pretend Shakespeare had never lived.

The best place to begin to see the Empson Eliot had invented is the undergraduate poems of 1928 and 1929, written while Empson was shifting from mathematics to literature and beginning work with Richards. They are not exactly "like" Eliot, but they derive from him a vaguely felt resemblance to Donne, a tendency toward obscurity lined with implicit despair, and a sense that the world's poetry of all ages is breathing in the lines. If there is a poem that earns the label "the twenties, after reading Eliot," it is one like this:

> Ripeness is all; her in her cooling planet
> Revere; do not presume to think her wasted.
> Project her no projectile, plan nor man it;
> Gods cool in turn, by the sun long outlasted.
>
> Our earth alone given no name of god
> Gives, too, no hold for such a leap to aid her;
> Landing, you break some palace and seem odd;
> Bees sting their need, the keeper's queen invader.

["To an Old Lady," *Collected Poems* (New York, 1956), p. 15]

This is youthful work of an aged eagle. Like Eliot and unlike Victorian poets Empson does not see the world as something to be "accepted" or "rejected." The mind, keeping alive by leaping and by diminishing the good to be gained thereby— "Project her no projectile"—distinctively avoids such simplifications. The earth cools but will long outlast her gods; we probably would kill any new gods offered us. That is what the second quatrain here says, but what it does is be nimble, quick, vibrant with a witty fear. Empson is never still, never dreary, never getting closer to silence or "the end" though he says we all inevitably are. The voice of such a poem seems to say to the author of "Gerontion": "Yes, yes, of course, absolutely right, but now I must work this matter all out." Here, at his most derivative, Empson is himself, and we must remember that when testifying about Eliot's influence he said not only "I do not know for certain how much of my own mind he invented" but also "let alone how much of it is a reaction against him." Earlier, though, he wrote something else about Eliot's *The Criterion,* something that applies at least equally well to himself at this time:

Its formula [is that] the artist must, by falling back on the organizing and centralizing intelligence, grasp in some enduring and inclusive mental order those scientific and political novelties by which he is at present overcome. [*Granta,* November 11, 1927, 104]

Eliot would never have said he was "overcome" by "scientific and political novelties," for Eliot would never underrate any danger or mitigate any reason for despair, while Empson here very characteristically shows the witty possibilities to be derived from not overrating such dangers.

Martin Dodsworth in a very interesting essay, "Empson at Cambridge" (*The Review,* June, 1963, pp. 3–13; the issue is devoted to Empson and is all good), says that early critics of Empson's poems "seem to have seen the exultation, which is in the technique, but missed the tragedy." One presumes that Empson made such a splash, and was so overwhelmingly impressive, that his early admirers could see only the exultation in him. But one who was not there does get a quite different impression, that of a very scared young man much in need of some "enduring and inclusive mental order." A poem like "Villanelle" is moving in its evocation of the lover's pain, and "Arachne" is a really frightening poem. Empson's early perception that to live at all in the world one had to live intelligently does not seem to me so much the result of his seeing he was very bright as of his sensing the horrors that would rise up if one did not. He also saw how very intelligent Eliot was and why Eliot had to speak intelligently in order to speak well. If shoring up one's lands against the ruins was not to seem pompous, empty, or Victorian, it had to be done indirectly, even evasively. In the early poems Empson is not evasive about the fact that he is afraid, but he is often very obscure and the obscurity seems as much refuge as necessity.

The poems, however, were only one expression or outlet for his energies. Empson wrote a play, acted in it, wrote book reviews and movie reviews, tried to be a debater. In 1928 *Granta* sent over a man to interview Empson, now in his first year of English study at Magdelene College:

The poet was alone when we entered; lying in a welter of banana skins, mathematical instruments, and abandoned pieces of paper, singing as he worked, and automatically writing with his left hand, he was patiently sucking some beers stains out of the carpet.

It may be safely presumed that not even Empson could sing and suck beer stains out of his carpet at the same time, but one would like to think nonetheless that he was working automatically on *Seven Types of Ambiguity,* that great book of undergraduate sport that is also a great book. In it there is no timidity or shyness, and the tactics of indirection seem more a way of working out fears than a running from them, though that is certainly not the only reason for thinking it much better than the early poems. Even after almost forty years, there is still nothing quite like *Seven Types of Ambiguity*. It is Eliotic in the sense that it is very indirect about its intentions and in the sense that it accepts many of Eliot's perceptions about individual poems and the Myth of Lost Unity as a whole. But to read it right after reading *The Sacred Wood* or Leavis's *Revaluation* is to see that it is a book about ambiguity in order to be a book about history—something one can imagine Eliot approving—and that it is a book about history in order to be a book about Empsonian heroism—something one cannot imagine Eliot comprehending.

In his preface to the second edition, Empson would say this much about the book's origins and the extent to which it is really about ambiguity:

Apart from trailing my coat about minor controversies, I claimed at the start that I would use the term "ambiguity" to mean anything I liked, and repeatedly told the reader that the distinctions between the Seven Types which he was asked to study would not be worth the attention of a profounder thinker. As for the truth of the theory which was to be stated in an irritating manner, I remember saying to Professor I. A. Richards in a "supervision" (he was then my teacher and gave me crucial help and encouragement) that all the possible mistakes along this line ought to be heaped up and published, so that one could sit back and wait to see which were the real mistakes later on. [*Seven Types of Ambiguity*, 3d ed. (New York, 1955), p. viii]

The first of the "possible mistakes along this line" had been made by Robert Graves and Laura Riding in *A Survey of Modernist Poetry* (1922) where they show many of the possible ways of reading an unpunctuated version of Shakespeare's 129th sonnet. Empson's saying that he intended only to heap up "all the possible mistakes" is clearly mock modesty, for he goes on to say that "Sixteen years later I find myself prepared to stand by nearly the whole heap."

The book is not a heap, really, but Empson should have

been believed when he said it was not a book about ambiguity; it is no more a book of quasi-philosophical accuracy than it is a book of mistakes. It is a book like *The Sacred Wood,* designed to outrage Empson's elders and betters (one of whom would be Eliot) by apparently agreeing with them. How, for instance, was either Eliot or Sir Arthur Quiller-Couch to reply to something like this:

> unexplained beauty arouses an irritation in me, a sense that this would be a good place to scratch; the reasons that make a line of verse likely to give pleasure, I believe, are like the reasons for anything else; one can reason about them; and while it may be true that the roots of beauty ought not to be violated, it seems to me very arrogant of the appreciative critic to think that he could do this, if he chose, by a little scratching. [P. 13]

On the one hand, a writer like Q is made into an arrogant appreciative critic, while on the other a writer like Eliot is presumed to be too modern and thus forgetful that there are indeed roots of beauty. Their response, if either ever read the book, is not recorded, but E. M. W. Tillyard's is:

> In 1930 Empson published his *Seven Types of Ambiguity,* a book which pushed the fierce and minute scrutiny of short texts very far and which showed that the new type of criticism had matured with surprising speed. Anyone quick to distinguish the rotten from the ripe and to sniff the taint of incipient corruption might now have guessed that an impulse had attained its maximum strength and that henceforward a decline or coarsening might be expected. [*The Muse Unchained* (London, 1958), p. 130]

Tillyard could gain his revenge on Empson, as it were, by embedding in his comment an ambiguity of the first type: "the comparison of two things which does not say in virtue of what they are to be compared." Thus *Seven Types of Ambiguity* might be for Tillyard "rotten," or it might be "ripe," it might be filled with the taint of incipient corruption," or it might show "an impulse had attained its maximum strength." If this was the direction practical criticism was taking, Tillyard wanted to write on Milton. It is characteristic of almost all the commentary made on the early Empson. People are of course impressed—as who could not be?—but unsettled, worried, and driven to issue shrill warnings. There is a lot about Empson in the early issues of *Scrutiny,* all of it admiring as long as it can be presumed Empson is on "our side," but all of it uneasy, too. Which is as it should be, though no one back then seems to have seen why.

Empson shows very early in *Seven Types of Ambiguity* that he has learned Eliot's "tradition" very well:

> This belief [in Atmosphere somehow unavailable to literary analysis] may in part explain the badness of much nineteenth-century poetry, and how it came to be written by critically sensitive people. They admired the poetry of previous generations, very rightly, for the taste it left in the head, and, failing to realize that the process of putting such a taste into a reader's head involves a great deal of work which does not feel like a taste in the head while it is being done, attempting, therefore, to conceive a taste in the head and put it straight on to their paper, they produced tastes in the head which were in fact blurred, complacent, and unpleasing. [P. 22]

He later buttresses this with some neat remarks about Peacock's "War Song"—Peacock "makes a cradle and rocks himself in it"—and with a psychological theory to explain it:

> Almost all of them [nineteenth-century poets], therefore, exploited a sort of tap-root into the world of their childhood, where they were able to conceive things poetically, and whatever they might be writing about they would suck up from this limited and perverted world an unvarying sap which was their poetical inspiration. [P. 25]

This comes before Empson is more than halfway through the opening chapter. It shows not only that Empson had seen how Eliot read nineteenth-century poetry, not only that Empson could adopt strategies as indirect as any of Eliot's—for the fact that this chapter is about nineteenth-century poetry has been concealed to this day—but also that Empson's manner is not Eliotic. Kenner has called Eliot's critical tone "a close and knowing mimicry of the respectable." This might be said of Empson too, but there are significant differences. Eliot had to learn the style of the knowing, anonymous "Englishman," that not being his native calling, while Empson had the public school and university tone in his bones. Empson mimics the High Table, Eliot the *TLS*. But Empson, one notices, is always writing about fears, terrors, complexes, and infinite sadness, while Eliot, even when the poetry he describes expresses such things, never discusses these matters. When Empson says something like "Wordsworth frankly had no inspiration other than his use, when a boy, of the mountains as a totem or father-substitute," we are supposed to be worldly and educated and "know" this about Wordsworth already. We are even supposed to "know" what is in fact not true at all, that Wordsworth "frankly" confessed his use of mountains as totems and father-substitutes. The Eliotic tactic is to divide and conquer by never being openly ironic, which leaves his audience unsure of how to read rightly; Eliot is cold, insidious, and finally contemptuous of his audience. The Empsonian tactic is warm and boyish, openly outrageous. He makes and enlarges the community of his fellow men: you, me, Wordsworth, we are really in full agreement about these apparently private matters.

The top layer of *Seven Types of Ambiguity*, then, is the badinage about ambiguity and its types, and the middle layer is the Eliotic subversive layer that uses the public school or High Table manner to disturb established reputations and received "facts." But the bottom layer is something else again, something we can glimpse in the sentence about Wordsworth but can see in full splendor in the following stunning paragraphs about two simple and very un-nineteenth-century lines of Arthur Waley's:

> Swiftly the years, beyond recall.
> Solemn the stillness of this spring morning.

The quotation must be long, but it is worth it:

> The human mind has two main scales on which to measure time. The large one takes the length of a human life as its unit, so that there is nothing to be done about life, it is of an animal dignity and simplicity, and must be regarded from a peaceable and fatalistic point of view. The small one takes as its unit the conscious moment, and it is from this that you consider the neighbouring space, an activity of the will, delicacies of social tone, and your personality. The scales are so far apart as almost to give the effect of defining two dimensions; they do not come into contact because what is too large to be conceived by the one is still too small to be conceived by the other. Thus, taking the units as a century and the quarter of a second, their ratio is ten to the tenth and their mean is the standard working day; or taking the smaller one as five minutes, their mean is the whole of summer. The repose and self-command given by the use of the first are contrasted with the speed at which it shows the years to be passing from you, and therefore with the fear of death; the fever and multiplicity of life, as known by the use of the second, are contrasted with the calm of the external space of which it gives consciousness, with the absolute or extra-temporal value attached to the brief moments of self-knowledge with which it is concerned, and with a sense of security in that it makes death so far off.
>
> Both these time-scales and their contrasts are included by these two lines in a single act of apprehension, because of the words *swift* and *still*. Being contradictory as they stand, they demand to be conceived in different ways; we are enabled, therefore, to meet the open skies with an answering stability of self-knowledge; to meet the brevity of human life with an ironical sense that it is morning and springtime, that there is a whole summer before winter, a whole day before night. [Pp. 29–30]

Eliot has nothing like this; Lawrence has comparable moments only early in *The Rainbow*. This was written in a world that was trying hard to make *A Farewell to Arms* and *Point Counter Point* into masterpieces. The modernist world could never learn how to feel comfortable with Empson when he writes this way.

We hear of two time scales and then are reminded that considered one way "there is nothing to be done about life, it is of an animal dignity and simplicity, and must be regarded from a peaceable and fatalistic point of view." This is an implicit assault, not only on Eliot but on the whole dramatic idea of life which dominates our literature from Shakespeare on. When life must be seen from a peaceable and fatalistic point of view it is not dramatic, and that point of view reminds us that the other, the dramatic scale of time, which "takes as its unit the conscious moment," from which "you consider the neighbouring space, an activity of the will, delicacies of social tone, and your personality," is not life but only a way of thinking about life, something valuable only for "the brief moments of self-knowledge with which it is concerned." So much, and no more, we can give *Hamlet, King Lear,* and the great novels. Nothing is denigrated, but much is diminished.

Lest it seem that this or Empson's commentary takes us far from Waley's lines, let me quote them again to see how resonant Empson has made them; the quotation that follows is Empson's paragraph immediately after the ones quoted above:

> Swiftly the years, beyond recall.
> Solemn the stillness of this spring morning.

> I call *swift* and *still* here ambiguous, though each is meant to be referred to one particular time-scale, because between them they put two time-scales into the reader's mind in a single act of apprehension. But these scales, being both present, are in some degree used for each adjective, so that the words are ambiguous in a more direct sense; the *years* of a man's life seem *swift* even on the small scale, like the mist from the mountains which "gathers a moment, then scatters"; the *morning* seems *still* even on the large scale, so that this moment is apocalyptic and a type of heaven. [P. 30]

At twenty-four Empson is already one of the great literary moralists, for here we are released from the tortured consciousness in which we, especially if we are not Birkin or Ursula, live, and we rise to some human but seemingly seraphic state where life is as it has always been, but replete with forgotten possibilities. Waley is there, Empson is there, we are there, a community.

Eliot had locked himself into a reaction against the nineteenth century and so had developed its cult of consciousness only one step further, rather after the manner of Rupert Birkin before he meets Ursula. For all its rich impersonality, the voice of *The Waste Land* is exactly what Leavis says it is—"the unity . . . is that of an inclusive consciousness"—unified because tortured, tortured because conscious and unable to release itself from awareness of itself. Empson sees this, all of it, the nineteenth century and Eliot, and replies. We could call his way defiant were it not so serene and triumphant. *This* moment, because it is Waley's moment too, and ours, *is* apocalyptic, and a type of heaven.

For Empson tradition is not only the result of looking at the past in the light of the way we live now but also a bringing of the past and the present into harmonious vision where the critic expresses "himself" by expressing the vision of his author. Eliot does not do this because he works to establish distances between himself and his authors so he can subvert those who want vulgarly to identify with the past and smother it in some Swinburnian marshmallow. His work is therefore of necessity austere, lonely, mocking, and the authors of whom he writes— Dante, Shakespeare, Donne, Marvell, Dryden—all are so placed as to seem ages and ages ago. Empson, though his mind is invented by this criticism and the poetry behind it, is too young, too frightened perhaps and so in need of community, too clear about the implications of the waste land for him, to let the matter go at that. Here, expressed for the first time in the passage about Waley, we see how he addresses the human condition so that the apparently overwhelming implications of the Myth of Lost Unity do not overwhelm him. He places and accepts Eliot, he brings his own voice into harmony with Waley's, he reestablishes those truths that not only must be true if we are to live in our time but which, quite simply, are true.

We must pause now to consider three separate but finally

related matters before we can bring everything together again
in the heroic moment with Herbert and Jesus at the end of the
book, so let it be said that that moment is like this one—Empson expresses himself by making Herbert express the root values of his and our culture. We will see there the ways Empson's
heroism is like Lawrence's, so here it can be said that there are
differences too. Lawrence becomes a hero in his defiance of
those personal dragons that chase him; his sense of history is
the result of his brilliant intuitions about the way he is a historical figure even in his most private agonies. Empson's heroism is much more the direct result of his confrontation of history. Here, with Waley, he seems to step outside history to
achieve his community; with Herbert he will achieve the same
results but he will be staring right down the gun barrel, as it
were, of the culture and its implications for him.

The three separate but related matters that must precede
consideration of the last chapter are Empson's misquotations,
his handling of poets of the English culture who are not central
to the Eliotic tradition, and something I tentatively call his
fears for his own sanity.

Empson has always been unrepentantly scandalous about his
misquotations. The first edition of *Seven Types of Ambiguity*
has as many passages wrong as right, and despite corrections
made in both the second and third editions, many of these remain. Empson rather ostentatiously quotes from facsimiles of
original Shakespearean printed texts as though they had some
mystic validity, then proceeds to misspell, give wrong line num-
bers, punctuate capriciously, and, in one instance, transpose
phrases. He leaves out a line from "The Canonization" which
might jar with his reading, and he punctuates Eliot's "Whis-
pers of Immortality" so he can read the poem as readers of Eliot
cannot. He makes a quatrain of Housman's *A Shropshire Lad*,
xlviii, in which he makes eight copying mistakes, one of the
Last Poems. He has "can I see" where Hood has "there can be,"

"shuddering" where Pope writes "shivering," "when he frowns" for Jonson's "if he frown," "pray" for Chaucer's "help," and as many more. As late as 1968 Empson was replying to complaints along this line:

I was keen on explaining why they [short lyrics] were so beautiful, and of course I was not interested in faking the text; almost any other form of our mortal frailty would then have tempted me more. And what I had written about the text did not apply to the erroneous version which had got printed. For years I have sometimes looked up the facts about these accusations, and they would always seem to me such obvious lies that I need not refute them. [*Hudson Review,* XX (1967–68), 534]

The above list of mistakes is not full of "obvious lies," but neither does it traduce Empson's character or ability as a critic as some have tried to claim. The misquotations have the negative virtue of not being right—Empson does not treat quotations as though he were copying something dead and interred. Respect for the past which converts the historian into a copyist is less than full respect. Misquoting is a telling sign of someone whose sense of the literary past is in his head, not in his books on shelves. We need not make it into a positive virtue in order to see this. The few misquotations of Empson's which are not irrelevant to the argument do not seem to have happened because Empson looked at the text, winced at what he saw, and rewrote. They seem, rather, the result of mulling over lines and trying to read them rightly, in the course of which the memory fades and lines become set, sometimes wrongly.

This way with authors, working them over and over, getting them so they and one's words about them come into harmony, which leads to sloppy quoting and occasional deception, is the hallmark of *Seven Types of Ambiguity.* The famous "verbal analyses" occupy most of the pages of the book, but in emphasizing them it has been possible to overlook other things Empson does with poems. The analyses are always witty and ingenious, they all imply great love of the material, and some are wonderful and some very strained. The work with Shakespearean sonnets is generally inferior, and the first part of the book to be published—the analysis of the sixteenth sonnet—seems only an undergraduate's first attempt to work like Graves and Riding. Many other readings, notably those of Chaucer and the famous one of the central passage of "Tintern Abbey," raise far more problems than they settle. In dealing with obviously minor literature and snippets—Hood, Peacock, *Zuleika Dobson*—he is always wonderful. One or two of the detailed analyses—Shakespeare's uses of "the *a* and *b* of *c*," Donne's "Valediction, of Weeping," the eighteenth-century pun—develop splendid intuitions with tact and ease, making one feel one has never read carefully enough before, but that in the future one will.

Most of the analyses are of authors who lie firmly within the boundaries of Eliot's tradition, and what is really more striking is Empson's writing about writers who, like Waley, tend to lie outside and not to lend themselves to verbal pyrotechnics. Here is an example from Pope, and the passage that follows from Empson has the "analysis" deleted from it:

> Another age shall see the golden ear
> Embrown the slope, and nod on the parterre,
> Deep harvest bury all his pride has planned,
> And laughing Ceres reassume the land.
> [*Moral Essay IV*]

These lines seem to me to convey what is called an intuitive intimacy with nature; one is made to see a cornfield as something superb and as old as humanity, and breaking down dykes irresistably, like the sea . . . there is some sense of the immensity of harvest through a whole country . . . the relief with which the cripple for a moment identifies himself with something so strong and generous gives these two couplets an extraordinary scale. [P. 146]

The omitted analysis is excellent but, one sees, not really needed. The intoning of his vision of Pope and England moves with lovely ease from the quotation and lets us keep hearing Pope's lines as a chord in the mind long after the notes themselves have stopped being heard.

The Augustans, though, were beginning to be read again intelligently by others in the years Empson was growing up. Where and how he found out about Spenser is nigh unfathomable. For three centuries Spenser had been imitated, admired, and ignored by turns, never well, yet Empson could read *The Faerie Queene,* the wrongest of poems for the modern and Eliotic spirit, and write of the Spenserian stanza:

> The size, the possible variety, and the fixity of this unit give something of the blankness that comes from fixing your eyes on a bright spot; you have to yield yourself to it very completely to take in the variety of its movement, and, at the same time, there is no need to concentrate the elements of the situation into a judgment as if for action. As a result of this, when there are ambiguities of idea, it is whole civilisations rather than details of the moment which are their elements; he can pour into the even dreamwork of his fairyland Christian, classical, and chivalrous materials with an air, not of ignoring their differences, but of holding all their systems of values floating as if at a distance, so as not to interfere with one another, in the prolonged and diffused energies of his mind. [Pp. 41–42]

Standard prejudices surrounded Empson so soon after this book was published that even now many Spenserians do not know this passage exists. But it is one of those utterances—like Eliot on Marvell, or Arnold on Byron, Dr. Johnson on *Clarissa* —that we must know and appreciate, or else argue ourselves unknown on the subject. One can go to the books on these authors and check the index. If there is no acknowledgment of such decisive statements, the author is almost certainly wide of the mark. We simply are not good enough to get along without them. In a lifetime's work C. S. Lewis wrote nothing on Spenser as good as this of Empson's, which is almost an aside, and Lewis was easily the finest Spenserian of his generation.

Here once again Empson has gone where the Eliotic tradition told him not to go and he has found there a stabilizing knowledge. Taking *Seven Types of Ambiguity* as a whole, Eliot's tradition is not ignored at all. On page after page are analyses that accept the reorientation which allied Shakespeare with Donne and the metaphysicals, which found its culture full and rich then and thin in the nineteenth century. But Empson's generosity leads him to go farther for his sense of locating himself in his culture—it is his acceptance of the Spenserian stanza on Spenser's terms, his appreciation of Sidney's "Double Sestine" for the beautiful and monotonous thing it is, his admiration for Hood's limericks as the invigorating things they are, that takes him beyond "analysis" and what it can show about poems in the Eliotic tradition.

He needs that generosity and the balance it offers, too. In recognizing Spenser's "prolonged and diffused energies," or the relief of the crippled Pope as he contemplates England's harvest, or the way the scenery in Sidney is "enlisted into sorrow and beats as a single passion of the mind," Empson discovers truths beyond the Myth of Lost Unity, beyond any individual's dramatic anguish, beyond his own "To an Old Lady," and thereby is enabled or emboldened to face some of the strongest and potentially most horrible matters in our culture without losing control.

I spoke earlier of Empson's fears for his own sanity, but I do not know if such a term is really appropriate; as Martin Dodsworth says, it is often easy when taken up in the excitement of Empson's excitement to ignore the fears and sadness implicit in almost everything he says. The early poems offer strong evidence here. In 1963, in an interview with Christopher Ricks, Empson said this of the early poems:

The first book, you see, is about the young man feeling frightened, frightened of women, frightened of jobs, frightened of everything, not knowing what he could possibly do. [*The Review*, June 1963, p. 29]

The poems are much more open about these fears than is the

criticism. Their key rhyme is "old" and "cold"; their central image is Arachne, the deadly female spider; their tone expressed most fully in "It is the pain, it is the pain, endures." There is a strong sense of the coldness and emptiness of space, and of the barely human qualities that men share as much with reptiles and stars as they do with other men. Everywhere he turns what is human is scary, inscrutable, nightmarish: "Twixt devil and deep sea, man hacks his caves"; "There is a Supreme God in the ethnological section; A hollow toad shape, faced with a blank shield."

What is difficult to grasp about these fears is their possible depths. We often do not know if what we are reading is someone talking about being afraid because that is a modish thing to do in the late twenties, or if the fears are very great indeed, and we are allowed only to glimpse them because before they reach us Empson has modified or modulated them with his insistent jauntiness and apparent ease. This much is certain: Empson finds his solace and his wisdom in what I have called communities, points at which the critic's self and voice are submerged into those of someone else. So much of what I want to say about Empson is about the creation of these communities that nothing lengthy need be said about them here, beyond noting that all involve a submerging of the ego and of our claims for the ego. How the creation of communities is a heroic act is not easy to see, for the obvious reason that most heroes state the greatest possible claims that can be made for the ego, the solitary individual self. But I think that if we begin to acknowledge the need for a way out of fear and isolation and despair, we can begin to see that someone who shows us the way out might be performing a heroic act.

Seven Types of Ambiguity is never as naked about its author's fears as are the poems, but its strategy is to move increasingly toward a position where the fears are fully felt, expressed, and mysteriously surmounted. Early in the book Empson says about the opening lines of Macbeth's "If it were done, when 'tis done" soliloquy:

words hissed in the passage where servants were passing, which must be swaddled with darkness, loaded as it were in themselves with fearful powers, and not made too naked even to his own mind. . . . The meanings cannot all be remembered at once, however often you read it; it remains the incantation of a murderer, dishevelled and fumbling among the powers of darkness. [Pp. 59–60]

Just as Waley and Sidney and Spenser are the presiding voices in the opening chapter, so in a way Macbeth's is the presiding voice in the second chapter, the prime instance of one who did not go gentle into that not good night, but about whom all one can say, so Empson claims, is that that trip is obscure, dark, awful. At this point in the book, Empson insistently alternates his work with the likes of Macbeth with work by poets like Chaucer and Dr. Johnson and Hood who express the grounds for fear and despair but then seek to muffle or modify or understand them. Late in the book, though, the impulses that are like Macbeth's are brought out into the open more fully, and faced, at least as well as Empson knows how to do so. Near the end are a few sentences that have been ridiculed more than once, which may help to show us what is involved:

one should try to prevent people from having to analyse their reactions, with all the tact at one's disposal. . . . The object of life, after all, is not to understand things, but to maintain one's defences and equilibrium and live as well as one can; it is not only maiden aunts who are placed like this. [P. 279]

With this in mind one can see how so much in the book and almost everything in the idea of ambiguity works toward balance and equilibrium. Empson assumes that impulses are contradictory, that desire is usually antithetical to fact, that poetry often gains its beauty and power from being able to express feelings that would be intolerable if left unexpressed. It is for that reason that the seventh type of ambiguity, which concerns collisions of opposing feelings, is left for last and is given the climactic position. Coming on it we can see that arranging the ambiguities along a scale of increasing logical disorder has the effect of preparing both author and reader to examine the balances possible and necessary when the poet is touching the deepest human nerves.

The chapter opens with what Empson calls some "mild" examples, becomes thicker in an exhaustive analysis of Ophelia's madness and an exposure of all that is most bizarre in the "Ode on Melancholy," then comes to its real subject, Christianity. Here, and especially in the seventeenth-century treatments of the Crucifixion, Empson finds terms for a vision that is not an alternative to the Myth of Lost Unity but combines the feelings engendered by the Myth with a reply to them. First Crashaw:

> Hee'l have his Teat e're long (a bloody one)
> The Mother then must suck the Son.

This allows Empson to lay out the inherent potential horror of Christianity and the Sacrifice:

The sacrificial idea is aligned with incest, the infantile pleasures, and cannibalism; we contemplate the god with a sort of savage chuckle; he is made to flower, a monstrous hermaphrodite deity, in the glare of a short-circuiting of the human order. [P. 250]

However horrible or strange one finds the Christian God, his acceptance of the sacrificial blood corresponds to a deep human fascination that only someone like Crashaw would bring so fully into the open. The closer we come to understanding ourselves, the closer we recognize the devil and deep sea on either side of where we hack our caves, the closer we come to facing the possibility that the Crucifixion, which is the central act of our culture, brings into focus the paradox of a satisfying horror. In order for *this* vision to be confident and serene like Waley's or Spenser's it must acknowledge and even express the horrors of human potentiality.

Eliot, Yeats, Henry Adams, and Lawrence all make their

myths out of a posited time of unity followed by a process of increasing disintegration. Empson accepts the results of these formulations and in his lyrics he sometimes seems to give in to their implications as completely as did Gerontion or Christopher Tietjens. He also finds balancing counterstatements in imagining the serenity of Waley, Spenser, and others. But as long as the balanced visions remain discrete so the horror of the lyrics is left on one side and the undramatic and serene visions on the other, then Empson is at least open to the charge that for him the horror is a kind of game. Yet in working with the seventh type and with Christianity, the visions are brought together in a single act of apprehension. Empson goes where Eliot went, to the early seventeenth century, and he finds there what Eliot had described, a unified sensibility. But Empson finds more than Eliot did, enough to enable him to act in full defiance of Eliot's nostalgia and despair. The Empsonian vision here conquers history heroically, so that while the "when" of Herbert's "The Sacrifice" is the year of the Crucifixion (A.D. 29), the year the poem was written (ca. 1630), and the year of *Seven Types of Ambiguity* (1930), each moment separate and separated from the others vastly by time, yet all are also together in one moment.

Herbert's poem ends with this stanza:

> But now I die; Now, all is finished.
> My woe, man's weal; and now I bow my head:
> Only let others say, when I am dead,
>   Never was grief like mine.

Empson's comment is as follows:

He may wish that his own grief may never be exceeded among the humanity he pities, "After the death of Christ, may there never be a grief like Christ's"; he may, incidentally, wish that they may *say* this, that he may be sure of recognition, and of a church that will be a sounding-board to his agony; or he may mean *mine* as a quotation from the *others*, "Only let there *be* a retribution, only let my torturers say never was grief like theirs, in the day when my agony shall be ex-

ceeded." (Better were it for that man if he had never been born.)
[P. 258]

This is the only double meaning in the poem that needs the
kind of analysis Empson is famous for. By itself it would not be
enough to carry great weight, though as Empson says, "after
you have felt this last clash as a sound, you will never be able to
read the poem without remembering that it is a possibility."
But Empson does not need or want ambiguities in that sense—
which is why, having exposed a brilliant one in Hopkins' "The
Windhover," he immediately tosses it off—because what he
seeks is a doubleness implicit in Christian doctrine: Jesus as
judge, Jesus as redeemer, Jesus as human sufferer, Jesus as
divine savior. As a human figure Jesus wishes for a horrible retribution: "only let my torturers say never was grief like theirs,"
as redeemer he asks that his torturers be forgiven and that they
never be made to suffer as he is suffering.

For the Sacrifice on any terms will be filled with doctrine,
with Jesus' divinity, and all Herbert need do to create the doubleness is to have the doctrine stated as a human lament:

> Oh all ye who pass by, behold and see;
> Man stole the fruit, but I must climb the tree,
> The tree of life, to all but only me.
> Was ever grief like mine?

The first line now at last, with an effect of apotheosis, gives the
complete quotation from Jeremiah. He climbs the tree to repay what
was stolen, as if he was putting the apple back; but the phrase in itself
implies rather that he is doing the stealing, that so far from sinless he
is Prometheus and the criminal. Either he stole on behalf of man (it
is he who appeared to be sinful, and was caught up the tree) or he is
climbing upwards, like Jack on the Beanstalk, and taking his people
with him back to Heaven. The phrase has an odd humility which
makes us see him as the son of the house; possibly Herbert is drawing
on the medieval tradition that the Cross was made of the wood of the
forbidden trees. [P. 262]

Years later, under Rosemond Tuve's attack, Empson said some
of this passage represents undergraduate excess, but insisted the

central point was right nonetheless (see *Kenyon Review,* XII
[1950], 51–75, 735–738). Empson was determined to make Jesus
active and aggressive as well as a Savior, and he probably would
have been better off simply maintaining that he is vindictive as
well as humble. Unquestionably "Man stole the fruit, but I
must climb the tree" is a curious and puzzling line, one that
remains so long after one accepts Rosemond Tuve's placing of
it within earlier Christian tradition. The "but" there almost
forces upon us a sense of Jesus' embitterment at being forced to
pay for something he did not do, and in such a way that the
other sense of the line, that this is the Lamb of God taking away
the sins of the world, is there only in the background. Furthermore, Jesus chooses to climb the tree as the result of previous
acts by both God and man, so the line carries a strong sense that
Jesus has been forced into the Crucifixion and a much weaker
sense that in so doing he is achieving a visionary triumph. He
is alone, outcast by both man and God—"The tree of life to all,
but only me."

Once Empson has shown that he is doing no more here than
stressing the way Herbert exploits the humanity of Jesus, he
then can reveal to us his heroic Jesus:

> Lo here I hang, charged with a world of sin
> The greater world of the two . . .

as the complete Christ; scapegoat and tragic hero; loved because hated;
hated because godlike; freeing from torture because tortured; tortur-
ing his torturers because all-merciful; source of all strength to men
because by accepting he exaggerates their weakness; and, because outcast, creating the possibility of society. [P. 263]

Charged by both man and God with a world of sin, Jesus accepts, forgives, and underlines the cruelty of both. By accepting
the torture of man he becomes divine, and by accepting the
torture of God he becomes Prometheus and human hero.

Empson's heroic act is to see this and thereby to create for us
the possibility of our society. History had, like the Pharisees,

cast out greatness, rendered man pathetic, whimpering, tired, and fearful. But history has more cunning passages than that. Empson—who misquotes because poetry is not a sacred relic but lines in his head, and alive, who balances his fears and his sense of being overwhelmed by modern life with imaginative reapprehensions of serene visions, who sees ambiguity not as a verbal trick but as a secret of the heart—intones his sense of wonder of Herbert and Jesus, and makes his, and the possibility of our, society out of his link with them. Jesus performs the ancient heroic act—his courage and wisdom are placed at the service of an insensitive and unseeing mankind so that it might be saved. Herbert writes at the moment in history when the year 29 and the year 1929 could be both understood or anticipated, and so he sings the heroic elegiac lay. Empson sees what each has done before him and defines modern heroism as those acts that serve in despite of history to recognize that in the exaggeration of our weakness we can see also the source of all strength.

Knowing this, we can look back on the heroic journey of Lawrence and remember that his key sentence also exaggerates weakness and so finds strength, also are the words of an outcast creating the possibility of society: "He wanted her to come back." We might even look ahead to Tolkien and say the key sentence there is similar: Master Sam sees Frodo and Sméagol, deadly enemies, by the Emyn Muil: "Yet the two were in some way akin and not alien: they could reach one another's minds." Outcasts all, creating the possibility of their society and allowing us to glimpse the possibilities for ours.

– 2 –

How much of this was known to Empson at the time cannot be determined. Certainly *Seven Types of Ambiguity* is best described as a book in the process of becoming a book about heroic deeds, and not as a book with that as its subject. Even now, with the major outlines of his career clear to him, Empson might resist the idea that the shape his book finally takes is the shape of a heroic journey, and indeed to say that at all renders much of the book an apparent digression. We are better off saying that whatever it is about, it becomes a heroic journey as it goes along and is not clearly any one thing from the beginning. But having reached the end and the grand heroic moment with Herbert and Jesus, Empson did set out to write more directly about heroes and the Myth of Lost Unity. He left England in 1931 to teach in Japan, and while there he published a number of essays—on *Troilus and Cressida*, Sonnet 94, "The Garden" and proletarian literature—which make very strange and difficult reading without the context these essays need and which Empson gave them the year he returned to England, 1934, and *Some Versions of Pastoral* was published.

It was and is an unsettling book because though on the one hand it is much tighter in organization and much more in need of a reader who is willing constantly to work and make strange and wondrous connections, on the other its manner is even more superficially casual than that of *Seven Types of Ambiguity*, so that the reader it most needs is the one it least seems to ask for. There may be telling personal reasons for this, but an outsider can only speculate that Empson's ideas, once he discovered his métier in the first book, came almost too quickly for him. Everything is controlled in *Some Versions of Pastoral*, beautifully so, but one has to work hard and attune oneself to Empson's mind to see this. Empson in the years after *Seven Types of Ambiguity* lost none of his zest and excitement about literature, but he added a subject of great richness and potential subtlety, and this meant a book not easy to understand. A version of Empson's idea of pastoral is now vulgarly established as part of modern critical machinery, and anthologies of criticism take their Empson material from this book. The book has eluded almost everyone, nonetheless.

"In the following essays," Empson says at the end of the opening chapter, in what is really his only statement of explanation,

I shall try to show, roughly in historical order, the ways in which the pastoral process of putting the complex into the simple (in itself a great help to the concentration needed for poetry) and the resulting social ideas have been used in English literature. [*Some Versions of Pastoral* (Norfolk, Conn., 1960), p. 23]

H. A. Mason reviewed the book for *Scrutiny* and took Empson's statement that the essays work "roughly in historical order" much too lightly and so failed to see how the book is put together. Kenneth Burke reviewed the book for *Accent* and took the phrase "resulting social ideas" to mean that Empson was a Marxist sociologist. Of the two errors, Burke's is the much less damaging, but it must be said for Mason—and he did a better job of tackling the book than many have since— that Empson's sentence does not make clear how much he is claiming for his province or his method. "Certainly it is not a solid piece of sociology," Empson says at the end of the same paragraph, but by that he seems to mean only that he will not employ the jargon of sociologists and not that what interests sociologists does not concern him. He ends up: "But I should claim that the same trick of thought, taking very different forms, is followed through a historical series." The claim is there, and clear enough in its way, yet somehow we are not invited to take it very seriously: it is only a "trick of thought" we are dealing with, something apparently not deserving of systematic study by the big intellectual guns. Thus the emphasis on "historical series" is almost lost, and with it goes the chances of many for seeing what the book does. People know about it, but seldom read it through—students are baffled by it, and teachers seem not to know or care enough to help out.

Having said this much by way of implying that Empson asked for the readings he has received, I would like to state my claims for the book as a way of beginning to show why the habit of indirection here is not an Eliotic device or a nervous tic but essential to its greatness. *Some Versions of Pastoral* is Empson's best book, and if it is not a "solid piece of sociology," it is in its way a hugely solid work on English history. Empson moves from the many works he brings into view to his historical and moral vision of the culture with no bruising of the particulars of the work. He keeps—for all his apparent wayward-ness—his eye much more on the object than he does in his first book. He builds up details with grace and subtlety until one begins to hear the large chords of its orchestration and even the seemingly most irrelevant aside makes its point. Then for a little while it does what only the greatest books do: it seems like the only book ever written. Its subject is the collapse of the old pastoral relation of the swain-hero to the sheep-people and the consequences of that collapse in the period between the end of the sixteenth and the end of the nineteenth century. Not just the closing scene and odd moments are heroic, but the whole book is about heroism and told by one seeking ways to reply to the history he tells, so that on every page we are aware of both the prices that have been paid for the loss of the magical relation of hero and people and the grand possibilities that remain.

The opening chapter is in many ways the most curious, so if we can see its intentions, we should be able then to move into the brambles and thickets that follow. It is called "Proletarian Literature," and its point about proletarian literature is that it cannot possibly be very good. But it makes that point—one obviously more worth making in 1934 than it would be now—by beginning with Gray's "Elegy," a fact that should alert us to the way Empson has more in mind than some problems raised by Marxist literature and criticism:

> Gray's *Elegy* is an odd case of poetry with latent political ideas:
>
>> Full many a gem of purest ray serene
>> The dark, unfathomed caves of ocean bear;
>> Full many a flower is born to blush unseen
>> And waste its sweetness on the desert air.
>
> What this means, as the context makes clear, is that eighteenth-century England had no scholarship system or *carrière ouverte aux talents.* [P. 4]

Of course no one before Empson thought the lines had anything to do with a scholarship system, but the next stanza is about the mute inglorious Milton and the interpretation does hold, especially given Empson's continuation:

> This is stated as pathetic, but the reader is put into a mood in which one would not try to alter it. . . . By comparing the social arrangement to Nature he makes it seem inevitable, which it was not, and gives it a dignity which was undeserved.

This shows why we do not think of the lines as expressing a political commitment and why it is essential to Gray that we do not. But it cannot be said that Empson is simply expressing a counterbias when he says the dignity of the social arrangement was undeserved. No one thinks the flower "deserves" to waste its sweetness, and "waste" is Gray's word, not Empson's. Then:

> The tone of melancholy claims that the poet understands the considerations opposed to aristocracy, though he judges against them; the truism of the reflections in the churchyard, the universality and impersonality this gives to the style, claim as if by comparison that we ought to accept the injustice of society as we do the inevitability of death. [P. 4]

This is a positive whirlpool of implication, yet we can notice that Empson is not here, as he is at similar moments in *Seven*

Types of Ambiguity, working hard to be impressive. We can object to the idea that a truism gives universality to a style only by being insensitive to Gray's. That Empson is not is best shown in the apparently offhand but singularly precise phrase "as if by comparison." It shows that the poem does not make the comparison between social injustice and death, and also that Gray does make the lot of the poor seem as inevitable as dying. Built into the tone that implies that Gray understands the arguments against aristocracy is an evenness that implies such melancholy is unchanging and unchangeable.

At this point Empson moves off for a moment to discuss objections people of different political persuasions from Gray have made to the poem, so that his largest generalization has the effect of bringing us back, as though there were no difficulty in doing so, to long neglected mother earth:

> And yet what is said is one of the permanent truths; it is only in degree that any improvement of society could prevent wastage of human powers; the waste even in a fortunate life, the isolation even of a life rich in intimacy, cannot but be felt deeply, and is the central feeling of tragedy. And anything of value must accept this because it must not prostitute itself; its strength is to be prepared to waste itself, if it does not get its opportunity. A statement of this is certainly nonpolitical because it is true in any society, and yet nearly all the great poetic statements of it are in a way "bourgeois," like this one; they suggest to many readers, though they do not say, that for the poor man things cannot be improved even in degree. [P. 5]

"And yet what is said is one of the permanent truths"—the beautiful, the telltale mark of Empson. The tone is just impudent enough to keep it from seeming like Arnold, yet defiant of history in a way that keeps it from sounding like any other twentieth-century writer. Lawrence, when he seeks to announce the permanent truths, implicitly accepts the notion he will be ignored and so he shouts. No one else among the century's major writers would talk about "permanent truths" at all. It is especially daring of Empson to use the phrase just after apparently exhausting himself in a series of fireworks that, among other things, expose the trickery of Gray's method. The truths themselves—the waste even in a fortunate life, the isolation of a life rich in intimacy—*are* permanent, not so much nonpolitical as antipolitical, and so do have an air of truism. Yet in their statement the flower and the poor farmer continue to be honored as part of "the central feeling of tragedy." After this, no proletarian literature has much of a chance, and the implications of pastoral can begin to be felt.

It is another of those moments that create a community: Gray, Empson, flower, farmer, and reader are all together in an existence that must recognize "any improvement of society could prevent wastage of human powers" only in degree. But whereas such moments in *Seven Types of Ambiguity* are occasional, in *Some Versions of Pastoral* they are not only more common, but they also are the subject of the book. We become, in effect, "the people," the sheep of the pastoral shepherd, the community or the nation of the hero. We live in a world where the magical relation of hero to people has been lost so that the people have become a mob and the hero painfully alienated—*that* is the story the history tells, the Myth of the Lost Unity and of lost heroism. But we still are the people, here as readers of the book—*that* is the heroic reply that Empson forces upon us because the relation of author to reader is ideally a new enactment of the relation of hero to people.

Perhaps now we can face more directly Empson's indirectness, his refusal to "say what he means." The paradox of seeing ourselves as both lost and found is, when stated, only a paradox, flashy and empty. But if it can be enacted, if in the act of writing the history that shows us our lostness Empson can also discover for us our foundness, then the paradox is no longer a statement but an urgently needed action of acknowledgment and reply. It must be an action, though, something we do, as we are lost and then found in his work. Empson cannot simply say "Dear reader, you are here but not here." He comes as close as he dares to speaking out when he says "what is said is one of the permanent truths." If they are permanent, they are true in despite of history, and just maybe our discovery of them in a context that shows all is slowly being lost, can become more to us than the consoling wisdom of a writer like Gray.

As a result Empson is always tempting us in this book to say "*There* is what he means by pastoral," and always implicitly showing us why we must not yield to the temptation but read on instead. For instance, as we read on in the first chapter, we find the following ideas about "pastoral," usually without any clarifying context:

pastoral literature looks proletarian but isn't.

Pastoral is "about," but neither "by" nor "for" the people.

Pastoral is a queerer business than proletarian literature, more permanent and less dependent on a system of class exploitation.

T. F. Powys writes pastoral; his characters are both artificial and a great distance from their author, yet they are wiser about God and death than the cultivated.

Grierson's film *Drifters* gives a pastoral feeling about the dignity of men who live by catching fish.

Spaniards who enact a ballet as they dance to tread out sherry grapes bring off something like a pastoral feeling.

Hemingway's stoical simple characters have a touch of pastoral insofar as they imply "the fool seems true."

The essential trick of the old pastoral implies a beautiful relation between rich and poor by making simple people express strong feelings in learned and fashionable language.

When shepherds in pastoral become rulers of sheep they become like the hero, who also is a symbol for a society.

Mock-pastoral exploits the clash between simple people and cultivated language, and this could flourish as long as the upper and lower class could be allied against the middle.

Pastoral is always artificial; the praise of simplicity is often accompanied by flattery of a patron.

The simple man may be a fool yet also better than the cultivated man because closer to nature.

Realistic pastoral is good for creating a sense of social injustice; when the poor man is poor enough he is outside society, like the artist and Christ, and so able to become its critic.

Empson does not try to relate these ideas to one another or to offer an idea about pastoral at odds with received notions. By comparison I have been in this book totally straightforward about my use of the term "heroism." All Empson tries to do is to summon our usual and not very interesting ideas about pastoral: it is about the simple life, shepherds, and rustics, and written by people living complex lives; it is useful as a means of satirizing cities and courts, as in Virgil and Spenser. Then, having filtered these received ideas through his remarks on proletarian literature so as to indicate that the class consciousness promoted in proletarian literature is thin material for literature compared to the class consciousness involved in pastoral, Empson begins to bring these ideas together with his earlier statements about Gray so as to put them all in a new light:

> The poetic statements of human waste and limitation, whose function is to give strength to see life clearly and so to adopt a fuller attitude to it, usually bring in, or leave room for the reader to bring in, the whole set of pastoral ideas. [P. 19]

This may seem more than we had bargained for, as it certainly is not part of our ordinary sense of pastoral that it involves "the poetic statements of human waste and limitation." But:

143

They [the whole set of pastoral ideas] assume that it is sometimes a good thing to stand apart from your society so far as you can. They assume that some people are more delicate and complex than others, and that if such people can keep this distinction from doing harm it is a good thing, though a small thing by comparison with our common humanity. [P. 20]

For even in our usual ideas about pastoral, the swain is potentially a complex figure. He can be a hero because he has power over his world; he can be a judge because he stands outside society and, knowingly or unknowingly, foolishly or wittily, comments upon it. Such a figure obviously is or can be "more delicate and complex" than other people, yet this power also implicitly expresses "our common humanity" because the swain is simple, does not put on airs, maintains his relations with "the people." He is especially impressive in our culture because he is always potentially a type of Christ, the shepherd and fisher of men who judged us by taking away the sins of the world and who joined us in our common humanity because there never was grief like his.

But just saying this much puts Empson in a position where he can do much more than had ever been done before with the idea of pastoral. The other twentieth-century mythographers of the Myth, of the One and the subsequent Many, had imagined a specific time in the past, 1150, or 1450, or the lifetime of Donne, when life could be seen steadily and whole. Lawrence sidestepped or transcended the problem by moving back into an imagined prehistory and down into the nineteenth century without having to give dates until quite close to the present. But the others got into trouble because later writers came along and pointed out that in 1150, or 1450, or the lifetime of Donne there was much chaos and many dissociated sensibilities. Empson saw that this literalism about history was not really necessary, and that what was involved was a nostalgia for a Golden Age that would be better off not having to stand up directly to close scrutiny, especially by unsympathetic professional historians who did not like their territory being invaded by the likes of Eliot, Yeats, and Pound. So Empson puts his unifying figure in the background, a metaphoric hero-swain-Christ, and then begins at the end of the sixteenth century and tells his stories of those swains, heroes, and Christ figures who are only *versions* of the old pastoral figures because the distintegrating motions of history prevented their being more than this. On the one hand, then, the old pastoral characters are used as a backdrop against which we can measure the stature and scope of those who seek to gain or recapture the magical relation of swain to sheep, and on the other these characters bring in "the poetic statements of human waste and limitation" which are permanent truths, not subject to historical disintegration. This double perspective allows Empson to do in the succeeding chapters of the book what he does with Herbert at the end of his first book: make him and us members of a community. This time, however, that community will be achieved against the narrative motion of the book which insists that as we come down to the twentieth century the possibilities for such community are diminishing.

But, maddeningly, Empson never says this or anything like this, and does not even within each chapter explain his often apparently random and sudden shifts in subject. Probably one who is not deceived by the casual air of "Proletarian Literature" and keeps the bearings it offers about "the whole set of pastoral ideas" could hear echoes of it as he reads through the next chapter, "Double Plots," but even then many readings are needed before anything coherent takes shape. The rule is that nothing is irrelevant in *Some Versions of Pastoral*, but only one very familiar with it could formulate such a rule. "Double Plots" is divided into three sections, which begin as follows:

> The mode of action of a double plot is the sort of thing critics are liable to neglect; it does not depend on being noticed for its

operation, so is neither an easy nor an obviously useful thing to notice. [P. 25]

I shall add here some remarks about irony and dramatic ambiguity, arising out of the double plots, and only connected with pastoral so far as they describe a process of putting the complex into the simple. [P. 51]

One of my assumptions about double plots was that they invoked certain magical ideas, and I had best give another line of evidence from the thought of the period. [P. 67]

Given such casual appearances, it is hard to believe that more is happening than the chatter of an intellectual raconteur.

In the first of the three sections we are indeed concerned with the double plot, but its relation to pastoral is seldom mentioned and never strenuously enforced. We have, in order, discussions about *The Second Shepherd's Play* (with asides about Falstaff, Tamburlaine, and Middleton on clowns), *Friar Bacon and Friar Bunguy, Troilus and Cressida, 1 Henry IV, Marriage à la Mode,* and *The Changeling,* and all a reader or critic can do is begin where Empson does and try to gain his bearings. In *The Second Shepherd's Play* the parallel is made between the sheep and the Christ child:

The Logos enters humanity from above as this sheep does from below, or takes on the animal nature of man which is like a man becoming a sheep, or sustains all nature and its laws so that in one sense it is as truly present in the sheep as the man. [P. 26]

The "plots" really are not double in this play, written well before the Renaissance, because they are unified in the pastoral as it once was: Christ becomes hero and swain magically as he "becomes" man and man "becomes" sheep; the possible destructive irony of the joke is subsumed in the beautiful relation of all created things existing in easy and hierarchical harmony.

But the parallel between sheep and Christ child is obviously one capable of exploiting the implicit irony, and the Elizabethan subplot does just this: Falstaff takes the role of the people-sheep and parodies the king-hero. The relation of king and people is no longer describable as an instance where the Many are contained in and expressed by the One; the pastoral unity is under a strain. Now, coming into the heart of the section, we can see a pattern repeated in each of Empson's major examples: *Friar Bacon, Troilus,* and *The Changeling.* In each a goddess—Margaret, Cressida, Beatrice—is created or controlled by a conjuror who makes her become like him— Bacon, Pandarus, DeFlores. The goddess is a pastoral figure in her ability to express herself and her world simultaneously, which is a kind of magic, but increasingly as we move from 1590 to 1600 to 1620 the "world" she expresses is not in easy and hierarchical harmony but strained and chaotic. Margaret of Fressingfield in Greene's play is a pastoral figure in all our usual senses of the term. She is made parallel in the other plot to Friar Bacon because her beauty, like his magic, can be dark as well as white, dangerous as well as saving. Thus Greene invents a subplot where this parallel can be exploited. Margaret kills her suitors Lambert and Serlsby by her beauty and Bacon kills their sons by his magic, thereby showing that the powers available to goddess and conjuror are capable of getting out of their control: "they are well-meaning, but their powers are fatal."

Troilus and Cressida offers a much more complicated version of the same pattern:

the whole Pelion of theory ranged through the speeches of Ulysses, is piled by mere juxtaposition onto Cressida; her case has to be taken as seriously as the whole war because it involves the same sanctions and occupies an equal position in the play. [P. 34]

This fact, that in effect love and war are alike and made of equal importance, is the source of many dark ironies. First, Troilus is isolated from and made ignorant of the world of

the play as known by all the others: he fights for the honor of
a Helen who exists only as a symbol; he makes love to a Cressida who is certainly "better" than Helen but who never pretends to be the figure Troilus imagines. The result is something
quite unexpected, given the general mood of the play:

> People complain that the play is "bitter"; it is not to be praised for
> bitterness but for a far-reaching and exhausting generosity, which
> is piled up onto the pathos of Cressida. [P. 35]

Ulysses' speeches about order, virtue, and reward are victimized by his clear-eyed awareness of the military and political
situation in which there is little order and virtue is a plaything.
So too Cressida is a victim, not to be condemned for being
false, but seen pathetically as a symbol of all her world. When
Troilus sees Cressida with Diomedes, the two plots come so
close together as to be interchangeable; his great speech—"The
bonds of heaven are slipped, dissolved, and loosed"—contra-
dicts Ulysses' speech on degree, and

> at once there is the universal break-up of the last scenes; only the
> Colossus Pandarus is left standing, a thundercloud over the wreckage
> of the camps, to rain down his bone-ache in answer to the prayers
> of Thersites. [P. 40]

The more the plots converge, the more Cressida can symbolize
everything in the play and be a version of the pastoral shep-
herdess. But her world, though she can in these final scenes
and in this sense unify it, shows us this power can be given her
only because all is war and lechery, the argument of a cuckold
and a whore, as the choral ("the people") Pandarus and
Thersites tell us. Still, the machinery of the double plot *is* a
pastoral device here just as surely as is the pun with the sheep
and Christ child in *The Second Shepherd's Play*, only now we
see what happens to the magical unity when it is threatened
and the devices still contain most of their old potency.

When we come to *The Changeling*, we can see how strongly

and fearfully "the people," now comically present as the madmen, continue the role given Falstaff and Pandarus and express the truth about the goddess Beatrice and the conjurer DeFlores. We begin with a simple enough parallel between love and madness, and then do terrible things with it by bringing in the idea of the changeling: an ugly child is substituted by the fairies for a beautiful one. The obvious changeling is Antonio in the subplot, but the way the plots are made parallel allows the image to be carried over into the main plot. DeFlores is a changeling, the substituted ugly lover for the real beautiful lover Alsemero, and Beatrice is herself a changeling as she is transformed from beautiful to ugly: "I am that of your blood was taken from you," she tells her father. The unity that is left is the ugly passion of madmen and lovers—when DeFlores tells Alsemero that he coupled with Beatrice at barley-break and so "now we are left in hell," Alsemero answers, "We are all there, it circumscribes us here," and Empson comments:

We have heard about barley-break before. "Catch there, catch the last couple in hell" scream the lunatics in the darkness at the back of the stage, when Antonio discloses his plot to Isabella; the two parts are united, and they are all there together. [P. 50]

The power of the old magical relationship is still there, but now it is in the service of the pandar and the parasite who become magicians because they hold the power to make the goddess. The double plot inherently contains a tension in which two things or ideas or people are made parallel but never identical, so that it both functions as a metaphor and measures shifts in the relations of the two things compared. If Cressida "is a symbol of the Trojan War," she is not that throughout the play as a static "permanent" fact. Her magical ability to express her world is made shaky and destructive because the two plots keep shifting their relationship to each other. The "whole set of pastoral ideas" is a group of permanent relationships, but the Elizabethan drama that takes over these ideas is active, restless, so that the same power that can make a character express his or her whole world is the same power by which everyone can be jeopardized and even destroyed if the power is not controlled. This also means that the relationship between hero or heroine and "the people" is changing. As the hero moves out of his unifying relationship with his world, he becomes isolated and his magic destructive; in the wake of that the people increasingly become a mob, an army of tatters, a group of sycophants or madmen.

Such are the statements Empson allows us to make or to say he is making, but perhaps nowhere in all his work is he more elusive and indirect than here. We go into the second and third sections of the chapter and he offers us almost no sense of direction, and the best we can do is to begin as before, by simply listing the items discussed: in the second part, *The Atheist's Tragedy,* Christopher Smart, *Aureng-zebe,* A. E. Housman, Rupert Brooke, Swift, Ernest Jones on *Hamlet,* Verrall's Euripides, with smaller references to Sidney, Swinburne, Fielding, Poe, Pope; in the third part, Raleigh, *Doctor Faustus,* and Donne, with passing references to Wordsworth, Crashaw, Carew, and Herrick. What such listing makes clear is as Empson talks about irony in the second section he is also talking about periods later than the Renaissance, but when he is talking about kinds of deification he comes back to the earlier period. A good deal of the irony he discusses in the second section is the result of a joke or a horror arising from the same kind of material focused earlier by the double plot: language once used for one subject—God, courtly love—now used to describe ones more trivial or more offensive—sex, fish, bodily functions. What the double plots hold in dangerous tension (the power of beauty is like the power of magic, love and war are alike, lovers are madmen) become jokes when the tension is no longer possible, so that what Smart renders ambiguous and funny is rendered ambiguous and disgusting by Swift.

Finally, when we come to Verrall's ideas about Euripides, we have two whole audiences, one that sees the irony and one that does not. And Empson makes a distinction that in effect divides the kind of irony inherent in the double plot from the later ironists:

> The fundamental impulse of irony is to score off both the arguments that have been puzzling you, both sets of sympathies in your mind, both sorts of fool who will hear you; a plague on both their houses. It is because of the strength given by this antagonism that it seems to get so safely outside the situation it assumes, to decide so easily about the doubt which it in fact accepts. This may seem a disagreeable pleasure in the ironist but he gives the same pleasure more or less secretly to his audience, and the process brings to mind the whole body of their difficulty with so much sharpness and freshness that it may give the strength to escape from it. [P. 60]

This will not do as a definition to cover all irony or ironists. But if we remember for a moment *The Second Shepherd's Play* and *Troilus and Cressida,* we can see that scoring "off both the arguments that have been puzzling you, both sets of sympathies in your mind" works well as a description of the earlier play and that the presumed resultant tone from this scoring off—a plague on both houses, antagonism, disagreeable pleasure in the ironist, secret pleasure for the audience—is more apt to the later. What this does is to make the process of both plays more like each other so we do not, as we did in the first section, think of their differences.

This is exactly what Empson wants because he then goes on to talk about a later moment in history compared to which the medieval and the Renaissance play seem indeed alike:

> It is when the ironist himself begins to doubt . . . that the far-reaching ironies appear; and by then the thing is like a dramatic appeal to an audience, because both parties in the audience could swallow it. [Pp. 60–61]

Of course, this describes Shakespeare better than the Wakefield master, but it describes Swift's *The Mechanical Operation of the Spirit,* Ernest Jones, and Verrall much better than it does *Troilus and Cressida.* Though the statement as written is not historical at all, the only way we can read it is as though it were, and the history shows the pastoral unity breaking down, first in the tension of the double plot then in the horror and joking of later ironists, who are writers much more isolated and doubting, more disagreeable and secretive, than any Elizabethan dramatist.

With this we can come to the end of the section and see that the distinction made there is really historical too:

> a poetical ambiguity depends on the reader's weighting the possible meanings according to their probability, while a dramatic ambiguity depends on the audience's having the possible reactions in the right proportions, but the distinction is only a practical one. Once you break into the godlike unity of the appreciator you find a microcosm of which the theatre is the macrocosm; the mind is complex and ill-connected like an audience, and it is as surprising in the one case as the other that a sort of unity can be produced by a play. [P. 66]

The stated distinction here is between readers and audiences, but the rest of the chapter to this point shows that "readers" come historically later than "audiences." The audience of an Elizabethan play can be assumed to weigh the possible meanings instinctively, while watching, and the reader, coming later, must pause, judge, remain uncertain of ironies because he is—like the macrocosmic reading public of these later periods—complex and ill connected, because his relation with his author is uncertain, because the author is less certain himself, both of his material and his audience. Behind such a passage lie our common ideas about community, the rise of the reading public and its eventual decline, each stage forcing upon a writer more complex and less certain ironies.

From this point we go back again in the third section, and find that having taken a brief look at what was lost after the

Renaissance, we now can see much richness in the nondramatic deifications in that period. We are "readers," to be sure, but an "audience" as well, because when we feel the richness we can have "the possible reactions in the right proportions." The trick of Empson's structure makes us aware of history in the second section and then in the third allows us momentarily to transcend it. First we have Raleigh, who is deft indeed as he compares his own true love to Our Lady of Walsingham, saying on the one hand that she is "as the heavens fair," yet on the other that his is only

> the love of woman-kind
> Or the word, love, abused,
> Under which many childish desires
> And conceits are excused.

Though love is a durable fire, ever burning in the mind, the love is inspired both by fickle women, though "Love likes not the falling fruit," and divine beings, "as the heavens fair." So, says Empson,

The fundamental idea of the poem is a clash of styles and indeed of historical periods which sets her up in direct rivalry to the Queen of Heaven, and in the last verse it is not clear that true love is to be found in either of them. [P. 69]

So Raleigh does what Shakespeare does in *Troilus,* places the religious and the courtly love conventions under a strain without saying he is doing so. But the ironies, if that is even the name for them, are not fearful, disruptive, isolating, or frightening; not yet. In Donne, however, just a few years later, the clash between earthly and divine claims can be felt as a genuine clash in both the love poetry and the holy sonnets. Donne himself is like the magician in the Elizabethan plays conjuring goddesses and whole worlds to mock and to submit to, to satirize and lament. Empson takes the sonnet "I am a little world made cunningly," and contrasts two passages, one from the octet and the other from the sestet:

> You which beyond that heaven which was most high
> Have found new sphears, and of new lands can write,
> Powre new seas in my eyes, that so I might
> Drowne my world with my weeping earnestly,   [5–8]

>   Let their flames retire,
> And burne me o Lord, with a fiery zeale
> Of thee and thy house, which doth in eating heale.   [12–14]

Then he comments:

The symbolism of the use of fire as a punishment for heresy could not but work on a man exposed to it as it was meant to do; it produced a sort of belief. The reader is now safely recalled from the interplanetary spaces, baffled among the cramped, inverted, cannibal, appallingly tangled impulses that are his home upon the world. [P. 74]

The only noun in the second sentence available for "his home" to refer to is "reader," and the irony of "safely recalled" is secured. Donne imagines God's great power to make new worlds and seas of tears by which to get there, but returns, fiercely and "penitently," to the doctrines of heresy and punishment of "his home," our home, the earth. The Renaissance turns out expansively into the world, converts its deities into creators of new geographies, only to see that deity burning its worshipers for that very heresy of expansiveness.

We are far removed from pastoral here, because Donne is too. He finds only in torture a means of bringing himself home, to and with his God. Donne and God work as a kind of double plot, with Donne taking the position of "the people," submitting ironically to the awfulness of his God by means of a bitter attack on His ways. If this seems fearful, if the fear of fire is an awful thing, yet we can say, in the light of the trivia of Smart and Brooke and the disgusted ironies of Swift discussed in the previous section, "How grand and powerful are these tensions, how fully and frankly felt are the clashes, how close is Donne to the whole universe when we compare him to the later ironists who are left only to play with words." What we saw at the end of *Seven Types of Ambiguity* we see again at the end of "Double Plots": the hero is a type of Christ when he is tragic, yet a rebel too because he is proud rather than humble and seeks self-realization rather than self-denial. That is what the Renaissance is: a full acceptance and working out of both the harmonious and the discordant relations of the individual man with his inherited universe.

I have tried to spell out the implications of this long chapter because it seems essential at least once to show the tensions, strategies, and resolutions that underlie the casual and even chatty manner of the book. "Double Plots" has no moment of community like the one with Gray's "Elegy" at the beginning of the book, but only because the works in question deny that possibility. Once they are at ease with each other Empson and his reader can range easily over the material, but they can join with the Renaissance figures only in moments of pathos, as with Cressida, or awed terror, as with DeFlores and Donne. It is essential to our understanding of the period that we feel the almost warlike fierceness of the pastoral ideas as they first break up, because only that way can we guess the power and magic they once had when they were in harmony with one another.

But Empson also withholds the soaring prose of heroism from this chapter because hs is reserving that for the next chapter on Shakespeare, who in "Double Plots" is only another participant in the historical moment, like Greene, Middleton, and Donne. If he is the great figure we take him to be, that greatness will be expressed in the completeness with which he can dramatize and define his historical moment and will be the best place for us to find these powerful early versions of pastoral. The chapter devoted to him, "They That Have Power," is much less of a mountain than "Double Plots" out of which we must mine the ore, though compared to most writing it is Empsonian enough in its fastidious waywardness. One can plot its curve best by showing the three paraphrases it offers of the 94th sonnet, one at the beginning of the chapter, one at the end of the first section, one at the close. The first paraphrase is relatively straightforward, "literary analysis":

> "The best people are indifferent to temptation and detached from the world; nor is this state selfish, because they do good by unconscious influence, like the flower. You must be like them; you are quite like them already. But even the best people must be continually on their guard, because they become the worst, just as the pure and detached lily smells worst, once they fall from their perfection." [P. 85]

This is sensible enough, what Empson calls "a coherent enough Confucian sentiment, and there is no very clear hint as to irony in the words." Let me quote the sonnet first:

> They that have power to hurt, and will do none,
> That do not do the thing they most do show,
> Who moving others, are themselves as stone,
> Unmoved, cold, and to temptation slow;
> They rightly do inherit heaven's graces,
> And husband nature's riches from expense;
> They are the lords and owners of their faces,
> Others but stewards of their excellence.
> The summer's flower is to the summer sweet,
> Though to itself it only live and die:
> But if that flower with base infection meet,
> The basest weed outbraves his dignity.
>   For sweetest things turn sourest by their deeds,
>   Lilies that fester smell far worse than weeds.

From his opening paraphrase Empson goes on to say why the kind of verbal analysis he does in *Seven Types of Ambiguity* is not well suited to Shakespeare's sonnets, thereby finding himself the best reason for the relative inferiority of his analysis of the sonnets in the earlier book:

The vague and generalised language of the descriptions, which might be talking about so many sorts of people as well as feeling so many things about them, somehow makes a unity like a crossroads, which analysis does not deal with by exploring down the roads; makes a solid flute on which you can play a multitude of tunes, whose solidity no list of all possible tunes would go far to explain. [P. 86]

Empson then takes ten pages working up what verbal analysis is possible, exploiting nuances of phrases rather than building up anything like alternative readings. "That do not do the thing they most do show" operates in apposition to "They that have power to hurt, and will do none," but "show" hints at a veiling that is made even darker by "Who moving others, are themselves as stone." The second quatrain begins "They rightly do inherit heaven's graces":

Either "inherit, they alone, by right" or "inherit what all men inherit and use it rightly"; these correspond to the opposed views of W. H. as aristocrat and vulgar careerist. . . . Clearly this gives plenty of room for irony in the statement that the cold people, with their fine claims, do well all round; it also conveys "I am seeing you as a whole; I am seeing these things as necessary rather than as your fault." [Pp. 88–89]

Then when we come to the sestet, Empson shows how it works like a double plot, so that "The summer's flower is to the summer sweet" is parallel to, contradictory of, and ironic about they that have power. The trick makes the political hero into a natural object—like the flower, whose faults are therefore natural—and indicates the strain of doing so—like the flower, and therefore narcissistic, and liable to corruption. The pastoral idea of the hero being at one with nature is simultaneously accepted, making the hero great and important; exploited, condemning the hero; denied, so as to isolate the hero from protection and to make his position dangerous.

Having done this, Empson makes his second paraphrase of the whole sonnet, this one much richer than the first:

"I am praising to you the contemptible things you admire, you little plotter; this is how the others try to betray you through flattery; yet it is your little generosity, though it show only as lewdness, which will betray you; for it is wise to be cold, both because you are too inflammable and because I have been so much hurt by you who are heartless; yet I can the better forgive you through that argument from our common isolation; I must praise to you your very faults, especially your selfishness, because you can only now be safe by cultivating them further; yet this is the most dangerous of necessities; people are greedy for your fall as for that of any of the great; indeed no one can rise above common life, as you have done so fully, without in the same degree sinking below it; you have made this advice real to me, because I cannot despise it for your sake; I am only sure that you are valuable and in danger." [Pp. 96–97]

This brings us back to the truth of "Double Plots": the precariousness of those powerful people whose stability depends on their right relation with "the people" and with nature, and who now seem cut off from such stabilizing influence. Empson seems deliberately to have made his tone rather flashy, in order to show the lyric urgency that wells up in this poem the moment we begin to read it hard. Ths second paraphrase makes Shakespeare the magician of the double plot, the Bacon, Pandarus, or DeFlores, and makes him also the determined and baffled lyric poet, like the Donne of "I am a little world made cunningly."

Only at this point does Empson begin to move beyond the positions he laid out about the Renaissance in "Double Plots," and he does this by glancing down those separate roads in Shakespeare's plays which seem to lead to this crossroad at the 94th sonnet. There are other older man–younger man relationships in *The Merchant of Venice, Henry IV,* and *Measure for Measure*; there are young men, plotters, valuable and in danger, like Claudio in *Much Ado about Nothing* and Orsino, who are rescued by their dramatist from moments of caddishness and cruelty; there is Henry V, moving others though himself as stone, the summer flower that is sweet to the summer that is England, the festered lily that has banished plump Jack and so all the world. These plays all belong to the late nineties, and serve, better than does any other evidence, to date the sonnet. Empson looks only at Hal and Angelo to show some of Shakespeare's variations on a theme that was so important to him personally, so crucial in his development as a writer, and so important to Empson as Shakespeare's way of expressing the central concern of his life, his age, and Empson. How to deal with this man—Hal, Angelo, W. H.—when he is genuinely isolated, will be the subject of the tragedies. Here, in the plays of the late nineties, he is in the process of *becoming* isolated:

> The issue indeed is more general than the sexual one; it is "liberty, my Lucio, liberty," as Claudio makes clear at once; which runs through pastoral and is at the heart of the clowns. [P. 109]

For in the 94th sonnet, and unlike many of the other sonnets, the sexual issue is not important, nor is the personal relationship of Shakespeare and W. H. "Liberty" is not, in the sonnet or in *Measure for Measure,* a matter of license or licentiousness, but a matter of independence, standing free of the society and its codes, free of the harmony of nature from which the society derives its codes. It is a matter of raising the question of whether a man belongs to himself or to nature, raised now because society may not be able properly to be "natural":

> "Nature in general is a cheat, and all those who think themselves owners are pathetic." Yet we seem here to transfer to Nature the tone of bitter complaisance taken up towards W. H. when he seemed an owner; she now, as he was, must be given the benefit of the doubt inseparable from these shifting phrases; she too must be let rob you by tricks and still be worshipped. [P. 109]

The transference of "the tone of bitter complaisance" from W. H. to nature is inevitably the consequence of feeling the loss of the magical tie with nature. For instance, Falstaff's magnificent speech in praise of sherris-sack in *2 Henry IV* insists, and without irony too, that drinking is the way to maintain the magical tie, and that they that have power should always be heavy drinkers. Yet we are forced to read the speech ironically because it ends with Falstaff's mistaken assurance that Hal agrees with him on this matter. Shakespeare sees and makes us see that not only Hal but Falstaff is isolated. The praise of sherris is wonderful but it deceives, and we have the sense that those who do maintain the tie with nature are all old men, foolishly out of step with history and the world it creates around them.

In order to place the matter in final focus and to see what attitudes we can have about these apparently bitter facts, Empson first gives us a moment with Bassanio: "more than any other suitor he is an arriviste loved only for success and seeming; his one merit, and it is enough, is to recognise this truth with Christian humility" (p. 110). The Christian humility of Henry V is something of a sham, and that of Angelo is part of his icy puritanism, but Bassanio's easy and rather sloppy openness is the best we seem to have when we seek for humility in our great men as our and their safeguard against becoming the festered lily. With this last emphasis on humility, Empson then moves off for his third paraphrase:

"Man is so placed that the sort of thing you do is in degree all that any one can do; success does not come from mere virtue, and without some external success a virtue is not real even to itself. One must not look elsewhere; success of the same nature as yours is all that the dignity, whether of life or poetry, can be based on." [P. 110]

The ironic tone of the second paraphrase is gone now, released into acceptance that sees the young man not only as special, valuable, and in danger, but as a type of everyman, doing well what all men must do in one way or another in the world where men are becoming isolated from nature. "Success" is now the ideal "natural background" because it enables a hero's virtue to seem real to him—a strange transformation of the pastoral, but inevitable given the historical circumstances:

> The feeling that life is essentially inadequate to the human spirit, and yet that a good life must avoid saying so, is naturally at home with most versions of pastoral; in pastoral you take a limited life and pretend it is the full and normal one, and a suggestion that one must do this with all life, because the normal is itself limited, is easily put into the trick though not necessary to its power. [Pp. 110–111]

Here is perhaps the supreme instance of the Empsonian miracle. We need, first, to hear the Shakespearean poetry of the nineties reverberate in the sentence: the rain it raineth every day, hour by hour we ripe and ripe and hour by hour we rot and rot and thereby hangs a tale. We need also to compare with this all that comes earlier in *Some Versions of Pastoral*: the waste even in a fortunate life, some people are more complex than others and to keep that distinction is a good thing though a small thing by comparison with our common humanity. Thus we create our history by seeing Shakespeare as the master ironist and double plotter who comes to accept his roles with full generosity toward the limited hero who is now all of us. We take his acceptance as a version of pastoral and in so doing see life inadequate to his and to the human spirit, then, now, always. We see Empson at once insisting upon Shakespeare's historical moment and releasing us from the bondage of his living then and our living now. History is like life, itself inadequate, and our becoming aware of this is our way of understanding that Shakespeare, Empson, and we ourselves are together, with history as our equivalent of the pastoral landscape. We are at one with history, locked into our moments in time and so creatures doomed to historical existences determined for us. Yet this landscape, like any and all others of whatever beautiful and ancient making, *is* inadequate, to us, to our spirit, to our knowing ourselves and others in heroic despite of history, and with clear and generous acceptance.

I have laid out these first three chapters of *Some Versions of Pastoral* at what might seem like excessive length because they are the hardest in the book and once they are explained, the later chapters are much easier. A good deal of misunderstanding of the meaning, intent, and emphasis in the last four chapters—which have received almost all the attention that has been paid the book—can be avoided by their being seen as continuations of the history here begun. The later chapters are much more self-contained than the first three, but that does not at all make them truly independent of the context of the book. No one interested in finding out about Empson on Marvell is going to be pleased to learn he must first read more than a hundred pages of very strange prose, but if he tries to read "Marvell's Garden" independently, he probably will conclude that he needs more to understand the chapter than the chapter by itself offers, or else that Empson is at best a brilliant eccentric who is always straying from "the subject." But "the subject" is not simply "The Garden" or *Paradise Lost* or *The Beggar's Opera* or *Alice in Wonderland*; it is also the history that can be made by considering the works in sequence. I hope that by working through the first three chapters I have set up enough so that someone baffled by certain paragraphs in the later chapters can see how to solve their puzzle and see their implication. The rule, to repeat it now when it may have some chance of being accepted, is that there are no irrelevant side trails, and Empson writes so as to place his ideas within a context where they can create, in a manner appropriate to each subject, a community of author or character, Empson, and reader.

The post-Renaissance versions of pastoral reveal a gradual narrowing of the sphere or power, influence, and understanding of the hero or swain, plus an increasing emphasis on the necessity of the individual consciousness to explore its own possibilities now that the magical relation with the world is disappearing. It is the story of the first two chapters of my book all over again. Empson must make each hero matter so that the heroism does not seem trifling or pathetic, yet he cannot act as though much were not being lost and that any world of any size is large enough. If nostalgia is the dangerous result of seeing the past as being so large that the present seems small, dreary, or a prison, complacency is the dangerous result of not insisting that versions of pastoral are only versions and that each one is more limited than the one before it.

Marvell creates his pastoral hero by substituting wit for action. What happens in "The Garden" is magnificent, grand, and hugely impressive, but also something that strictly imagined could happen only in a poem:

> The chief point of the poem is to contrast and reconcile conscious and unconscious states, intuitive and intellectual modes of apprehension; and yet that distinction is never made, perhaps could not have been made. [P. 113]

In the garden we cannot say if the mind knows with rich intuitiveness how to experience the whole world, or if the mind consciously knows the whole world and chooses the life of the garden. To annihilate all that's made to a green thought in a green shade is to bring in the outside world and transform it into a green thought; it also is to consider the outside world and find it of little value compared to green thoughts. To annihilate the world into green thoughts is to be an ocean where each kind does straight its own resemblance find—it is an intuitive knowing of the world; to annihilate the world by comparing it to green thoughts is to create, transcending these, far other worlds and other seas—it is a conscious act of comparison and creation. We cannot fathom the two actions taking place at once except in words. Marvell's equipoise depends on his full understanding of this and therefore on his never stating the distinction:

> Society is all but rude
> To this delicious solitude.

Again the trick of language works, and we can on the one hand
be dazzled with the wit and on the other be aware that outside
the poem what the two readings describe cannot happen simultaneously. Society is all but rude to the man in the garden, and
the man knows this just by being in the garden; society is rude
when compared to the quiet of the man, and the man knows
this by having lived in both places:

in this ideal case, so the wit of the thing claims, the power to have been
a general is already satisfied in the garden. "Unemployment" is too
painful and normal even in the fullest life for such a theme to be
trivial. [P. 117]

And we are back with the major theme of Empson's book—
except in "The Garden" the isolation of a life rich in intimacy
is wittily stated as achievement rather than as the painful human condition—the central feeling of tragedy. The terror, the
bitter complaisance, and the unwanted acceptance of earlier
Renaissance heroes is gone, and is replaced by something apparently larger than they; all life can be found in the garden,
and Marvell is a god. Yet "The Garden" is only a poem, and
there is no garden there in fact, and the magical trick of language acknowledges in the very act of creating such possibilities
that they are no longer possible in the world, but only in poems.

Milton's titanic energy abjures such equipoise and faces more
squarely the problem of all that has been lost. Eden too is a
garden, and all is possible there too. Adam and Eve are full
pastoral and heroic figures—but the ones who can know this are
Satan, the exile from heaven, and Milton, the exile from paradise: "what we are to feel here is the ruined generosity of Satan
and the greatness of the fate of man" (p. 161). Empson uses
Bentley and Pearce, Milton's eighteenth-century editors, as a
kind of bridge back to the poem. On the one hand they belong

to a later age and so they insist on rationality replacing many of Milton's large clashing Elizabethan effects, but on the other hand Bentley and Pearce are really much closer to Milton than we are and so show up the real clashes that are there and that we have tried to ignore.

What the strategy is designed to reveal is the many ways in which "the human creature is essentially out of place in the world and needed no fall in time to make him so" (p. 178). Satan is one kind of pastoral figure, the judge of Creation by virtue of his position outside it, and Adam and Eve are another kind, the central figures of a harmonious and unifying paradise. As the two kinds meet and clash, they show what man needs and can never have is the two together, the correctly judging detachment and the harmonious centrality. All positions then assume a beautiful precariousness in the face of the fact of God, the Creator and Supreme Judge who seems determined to push man out of his pastoral Eden. Just as Marvell could create his garden only in a poem, so Milton at the same moment in history but working with a totally different temperament, could create his garden only as something from which we are eternally exiled and to imagine which is possible only as a reminder of our loss.

After the seventeenth century, no such largeness was again available and if Milton and Marvell must settle for less than was possible for Shakespeare, Gay and Lewis Carroll seem small indeed compared to Milton and Marvell. To pursue the history of pastoral in *The Beggar's Opera*, and *Alice in Wonderland*, furthermore, is to indicate that only in popular literature, defined as literature for the less cultivated, can we find the vitality that once had existed in the literature of the whole culture. Empson ends his chapter on Milton by pointing out that after the Restoration the country became "two nations," and no writer, not even Wordsworth who tried so hard, could make them one again: "the mockery of Gay's Pastorals leave him obviously more at home with a labourer than the love of Shelley"

(p. 181). If so, the argument runs, we must turn to what the pretentious would call subliterature or entertainment for anything at all expressive of "the people."

The "people" in *The Beggar's Opera,* it turns out, are the women who love Macheath and also seek his death. I would like here to quote a fairly lengthy passage, more than is perhaps necessary to show where the chapter "fits" in the book and the history of pastoral, because it shows also the direction Empson was to take in his work after this book. He has shown, just before the passage I quote, the sexual pleasure Polly and Lucy derive from contemplating Macheath's being hanged:

> Only the unyielding courage of Macheath, who keeps the thing firmly on the level of the obvious, gives one the strength to take it as comedy or even to feel the pathos of the appeal of Polly.
>
> *Lucy.* Hadst thou been hanged five months ago, I had been happy.
> *Polly.* And I too. If you had been kind to me till death, it would not have vexed me—and that's no very unreasonable request (though from a wife) to a man who hath not above seven or eight days to live.
>
> He takes so completely for granted their state of self-centredness tempered by blood-lust that the main overtone of her speech is that so often important to the play—"we have all very few days to live, and must live with spirit." The selfishness of her remarks reconciles us to his selfish treatment of her, and the idea behind their pathos to his way of life. [P. 218]

"Man is so placed that the sort of thing you do is in degree all that any one can do," is what Empson had Shakespeare say of W. H., and it is true here as well. But by now isolation of a man from all men is assumed to be a necessary human condition and the struggle is not to regain the lost relation of oneness or to rebuke those who deny its possibility, but to make the best of things by assuming selfishness and seeking the virtues that can be found in independence:

> So that to follow up the ideas of "love-betrayal-death," the sacred delight in the tragedy of the hero, is to reach those of "pathetic right to selfishness," the ideal of Independence. This comes out more

clearly in the grand betrayal scene of the second act, of Macheath by
the prostitutes. The climax is one of the double ironies.

> *Jenny.* These are the tools of a man of honour. Cards and dice are
> only fit for cowardly cheats, who prey on their friends. (She takes up
> the pistol; Tawdry takes up the other.)

(First laugh; the great are like the rogues but more despicable.) Having got his pistols she calls in the police. (Second laugh; the rogues are
after all as despicable as the great.) But this is not merely a trick of
surprise because she means it; "we are better than the others only because we know the truth about all human beings"; the characters are
always making this generalisation. "Of all beasts of prey," remarks
Lockit, "mankind is the only sociable one." The play only defends its
characters by making them seem the norm of mankind and its most
informed critics. [Pp. 218–219]

We still have a "unified world" here, but only in the shared
assumptions about bestiality and betrayal. Macheath is like all
the others and so can express them as a kind of pastoral hero,
yet in such a world the hero, the "man of honor" reflecting and
parodying aristocratic values, is the scapegoat, the mark, the
type of Christ. "At the tree I shall suffer with pleasure," says
Macheath, echoing both the agony of Jesus and the pleasure his
women take in seeing him hang. But it is hardly a gesture of
grandeur—"My pleasure, sir" is what he says to Peachum—and
Macheath's heartiness is really all that is left of the heroic
magic. Yet the play expresses its age because its ways of being
hearty and polite show us so much about the narrowness out of
which the Augustans had to make their triumphant "civilization."

By the time of Alice, however, "the people" have none of the
breezy integrity of Jenny Diver. They are the White Rabbit
and the Caterpillar, the Queen of Hearts and the Duchess with
her flamingoes, all instruments for making Alice isolated,
scared, irritated, well behaved, prissy. Empson has said at the
beginning of the book that when the upper and lower classes
lost their pastoral solidarity—and that much, however ironically, is clearly maintained in *The Beggar's Opera* and still

sought in Gray's "Elegy"—then "the pastoral tricks of thought take refuge in child-cult." We may remember also the paragraphs at the beginning of *Seven Types of Ambiguity* about the taproot to childhood that was the lone source of inspiration for nineteenth-century poets. The poets, however, worked and wrote best from positions of isolation and achieved independence, while in *Alice in Wonderland* we see the child moving as our best representative in our "adult" world of nightmare where to be isolated is not so much to be free as to be a potential victim.

This chapter is the most highly praised thing in all Empson's works, but often for its use of "Freudian" techniques, which are flashy but rather a joke, or for its bringing in of so much about Victorian England not apparently related to *Alice,* which is a trait common to all Empson's work. What is really wonderful is the collocation of the fear of growing up, the fear of sex, and the fear of dying, as they are experienced by Alice herself. The cult of the child is a refuge indeed for Lewis Carroll, and Alice shows what courtesy and intellect can do when they exist independently from the terrors of adult life and so are able to judge them—and also how little they can ever do when not supported by the magic of commonly shared experience. In the great scene with the White Queen in *Through the Looking-Glass* Alice becomes very lonely in the wood and begins to cry:

"Oh, don't go on like that," cried the poor Queen, wringing her hands in despair. "Consider what a great girl you are. Consider what a long way you've come to-day. Consider what o'clock it is. Consider anything, only don't cry!"

It is the perfect speech with which to end Empson's book, and in its pathetic phrases is the clearest statement of where we come out:

Alice could not help laughing at this, even in the midst of her tears. "Can you keep from crying by considering things?" she asked.
"That's the way it's done," the Queen said with great decision;

"nobody can do two things at once, you know. Let's consider your age to begin with—how old are you?"

We do not have to have Empson build long bridges to have us feel members of the same community with the Queen and Alice. After the strange and wondrous versions of pastoral in the Renaissance, after the witty and valiant efforts of Marvell and Milton, after the tough-minded retrenchment of Gay, these voices seem almost echoes of our own:

The helplessness of the intellect, which claims to rule so much, is granted under cover of the counter-claim that since it makes you impersonal you can forget pain with it. [P. 279]

This leads easily into mention of the class assumptions supported by this way of thinking about thinking:

Indeed about all the rationalism of Alice and her acquaintances there hangs a suggestion that there are after all questions of pure thought, academic thought whose altruism is recognised and paid for, thought meant only for the upper classes to whom the conventions are in any case natural habit; like that suggestion that the scientist is sure to be a gentleman and has plenty of space which is the fascination of Kew Gardens. [P. 279]

Independence has led to the divorce of mind from life and to the divorce of one class from another simultaneously; magic has become an often desperate snobbery. From here we move to the final statement:

This talk about the snobbery of the Alices may seem a mere attack, but a little acid may help to remove the slime with which they have been encrusted. The two main ideas behind the snobbery, that virtue and intelligence are alike lonely, and that good manners are therefore important though an absurd confession of human limitations, do not depend on a local class system; they would be recognised in a degree by any tolerable society. [P. 281]

So we must speak the permanent truths not just to recognize others of other ages but also to recognize ourselves.

Over these phrases in the last paragraph of the book one can intone all the large generalizations of the book: the waste even in a fortunate life, the isolation of a life rich in intimacy, the delicacy and complexity of some people is important but trivial compared to our common humanity, the inadequacy of life to the human spirit, and one I have not quoted before because it seemed best to save it for now:

> The value of these moments made it fitting to pretend they were eternal; and yet the lightness of his expression of their sense of power is more intelligent, and so more convincing, than Wordsworth's solemnity on the same theme, because it does not forget the opposing forces. [P. 125]

Empson says this of Marvell, but it should also be said of Empson; with Alice as his means of bringing us down to our own time, he makes of this last moment the final claim for civilized values inherent in thinking: we must think because the unity has been lost, and we are no longer magically at one with one another and the universe. The intellect can at least show us what we do have, how much we have lost, and perhaps where we can go. Birkin and Empson are at one on this point and heroic both.

The value of such moments for us, indeed the value of such books, makes it fitting to pretend that they are eternal, though Empson's power, like Marvell's, is based on a lightness of expression that enables him and us to recognize the forces at work to keep such moments from actually being eternal. Next to Alice, Shakespeare and Marvell and Milton seem almost godlike, and the communities we can make with them seem too big for us. Yet our community with Alice—we can add "of course," and so concede the history that makes our world so small and scattered and lonely—is only a benign and cheerful version of the world we live in every day. But it is a community, and one can forget pain with it, so the Queen is right: "That's the way it is done."

Having claimed so much for *Some Versions of Pastoral,* having taken so long and been able to say only those things that seemed most in need of being said, I must try to step back and see what objections can be made to such a lofty estimate of its achievement. After all, no such claims have been made for it before this. I have stressed the unfolding unity of the whole because no single paragraph or chapter seems truly coherent without the context of the entire book, but that does not mean that some chapters are not better than others. "Double Plots," especially, and also "They That Have Power" and "Milton and Bentley" are huge and wonderful, though easy to get lost in, because they adopt tactics that they do not explain; they leave their perceptions scattered; they seem designed so subtly that Empson never questions the worth of the net he uses to catch his fish, so interested is he in the catching. By comparison, "Marvell's Garden" is small-scale work; it is not only much the shortest of the chapters, but the least wide-ranging, the most competent, the least powerful. The last two really are the best, especially considered as detachable essays.

If Empson does anything better than anyone has ever done before, it is uncovering hidden sources of power in works that submerge their strengths in flat statements. One can look at sentences in *The Beggar's Opera* or *Alice in Wonderland* as Empson quotes them and feel confident that no one could pull rabbits out of such empty hats—then, time after time, Empson produces his miracle. These essays range widely, too, and hide their organization in casual camouflage, but they do not require, as "Double Plots" does, that the reader remember every little item in the chapter all the time.

But these reservations do not face squarely any real anti-Empsonian position. The most obvious charge to be made against him is that he is obscure and that the game of reading him is not worth the candle of seeing what he lights up. I have indicated along the way how I think it is always possible to find

one's way in *Some Versions of Pastoral,* but unquestionably it
is hard going, especially on the first few readings which are
bound to be crucial for most readers. More than once I have
confessed to a class of students that what I was about to say
only developed some ideas of Empson's, and have heard the
reply that unless someone explained what Empson was doing
he would remain ununderstood, and once after a whole course
devoted to Empson's criticism, I saw that only half the students
felt that reading him was worth the immense effort. But two
possible grounds for rejecting him on the charge of obscurity
can be rejected at once.

First, Empson is not obscure because he is a cultist or has a
system. He is not an in-group writer at all. In this respect he
is unlike the later Joyce, or Charles Williams, or much of
Wallace Stevens. The reader of Empson does not have to learn
a special series of signs or signals, he does not have to undergo
the torture of learning "symbols," and for that matter he does
not have to be especially learned or to have mastered quite a
few foreign languages. Empson is elliptical but not as much
as is sometimes claimed. If the reader reads Empson's works
from beginning to end, and carefully, he will find there are
very few really difficult leaps and a great many offhand and
unemphasized reminders of things Empson has said earlier. He
does not say what he is doing a good deal of the time, but that
is not the same thing as being obscure. I suspect that his
casualness is a good deal easier for his fellow countrymen to
follow than it is for Americans.

Second, he is not obscure because he is sloppy or fuzzy, the
way Browning or Shelley or Hardy sometimes is. He does not
approach his ideas sideways as a means of avoiding having to
ask himself exactly what it is he does mean, but as a rhetorical
device for placing his ideas so that at key moments they suddenly can have the impact for his readers that they have for
Empson. Even more pervasive is his assumption that his readers

have really read the works he writes about so that as he proceeds he can make side remarks about parts of the work not
directly under consideration and still have his reader's attention secure. But this is not a sloppiness in Empson at all, only
a reminder of original sin for his readers, who generally do not
have the work in question as firmly in their minds as Empson
does in his. All writing about literature faces the thorny question of how much exposition is necessary for courteous relations between writer and reader, and of Empson at least it can
be said that most works he writes about are relatively short or
else very well known. If someone has forgotten *Alice in Wonderland* it only takes an hour or so to reread it, and quite often
during that rereading the relevance of the references in Empson
to Darwin or Wordsworth or Herbert Spencer become clear to
the reader without fuss. Empson can be associational in his
thinking, but seldom in a way that really obscures his point.
For instance, this from the chapter on *The Beggar's Opera*:

> One cause of the range of *Don Quixote*, the skyline beyond skyline of
> its irony, is that though mock-heroic it is straight pastoral; only at the
> second level, rather as the heroic becomes genuine, does the pastoral
> become mock. Most of the story ("oh basilisk of our mountains")
> might be taking place in Sydney's *Arcadia,* and as Quixote himself
> points out (I. IV. xxiii.; in favour of the boy who was on graceful
> terms with his goat) the two conventions are alike, so that the book
> puzzles us between them; we cannot think one fatuous and not the
> other. [*Pastoral,* pp. 188–189]

Unquestionably there are leaps in these two sentences, and
this time the two works mentioned are very long. The point of
bringing in the *Arcadia* is simply to insist that we see enough
of a resemblance to it in *Don Quixote* to recognize the "conventions" at work in Cervantes. They do not seem like conventions there very often, which is why the episode with the
boy is mentioned, and the moment we look up the episode we
can see easily enough how mock-heroic and straight pastoral
are allied.

So it is not, to repeat, in the motion of sentence to sentence
that Empson is unclear, but in the way that once having made
his point about the relation of, for instance, mock-heroic to
pastoral he will expect his reader to have it firmly enough in
mind so that even a sideways reference to it later will have its
point. Empson does not, any more than does Cervantes, say
what he means by "conventions" or "mock-heroic" or "pastoral," but to see what he means all one needs is the episode in
Don Quixote and, of course, *The Beggar's Opera,* and if one
is not going to look at them there is not much point in looking
at Empson either.

To say this will not convince everyone who does not like
the obscurity in Empson, and such readers will certainly not
be convinced by my restating something I said earlier, namely
that Empson is a hero who seeks to create with his readers a
community such as those created earlier in the culture by pastoral literature. But it can be said that Empson does seek a
curious, fugitive, but secure relation among intellectual classes,
and he does this by being elegant, sophisticated no end, as
"modern" in the eyes of the vulgar as Eliot himself, yet by
writing mostly about popular literature and by using as his
central ideas very worldly and very commonplace truths. He
means to be a pastoral hero and to have as his ideal audience
a well-read but formally uneducated reader who will forgive
him his obscurity because he knows that is the only way Empson can be profound, moral, intelligent but not snobbishly
intellectual, able to point up the differences in class forced
upon the world by formal education but only to denigrate
such differences when faced with our common humanity. Perhaps this is what Philip Hobsbaum was trying to say when he
compared Leavis with Empson this way:

Leavis will always remain the critic for the educated man, in the
best sense of the word: the man who wants to see literature whole.
But Empson is likely to stay, thumbed and rumpled, at the bedside of

the erratic and irreverent creative artist. [*The Review*, June 1963, p. 20]

My vision of Empson's ideal audience would certainly include "the creative artist," but would also include the man from Hollywood, Florida, who wrote to me on the occasion of an article on Empson I had published in a literary quarterly, and told me how pleased he was that someone in the academic world, who wrote for the *Hudson Review*, had finally tried to outline the ways in which Empson is such an important writer for everyone. The writer who elicits such a response is not easily convicted on the charge of obscurity.

But there is a more fundamental way to make this objection which needs to be answered in a different way. Shortly after the publication of *Seven Types of Ambiguity*, Leavis wrote of Empson that, in comparison with Auden, he lacked "a profound inner disturbance; a turbid pressure of emotions from below; a tension of impulsive life too urgent and shifting to permit him the sense of intellectual mastery" (*Scrutiny*, III [1934], 78). Twenty years later, in reviewing *The Structure of Complex Words*, Hugh Kenner said that Empson exemplifies the idea that style is "a kind of pathetic elegance in manipulating the inconsequential" (*Gnomon* [New York, 1956], p. 260; it is perhaps the best attack on Empson yet written). If I understand the point rightly, the sin is complacence enforced by a snobbish intellectual slackness and covered over with gestures of nervous intensity that are designed to conceal the absence of genuinely disturbed feelings.

It is not easy to reply. One knows what Leavis means, for instance, when in another context he says Arnold Bennett was not sufficiently disturbed by life to be a great novelist, and one can assent to this as a stricture to the extent that one knows Bennett himself could assent to it too. But to say that Empson's air of intellectual mastery by itself reveals a lack of inner disturbance seems to me to ask of Empson that he be Leavis, and one suspects personal or Cambridge reasons lurking behind Leavis's phrase and the feinting and thrusting he and Empson have done at each other over the years. Yet such a retort may ignore the truth, and as a way of facing it, let me quote a criticism of Alfred North Whitehead made by a colleague of Leavis's, James Smith:

> Here, surely, there is sufficient evidence for a judgment upon the fineness of his feelings. To write the above sentences it is impossible he should realize what tragedy is, what an end is, what the bitterness can be which results from disappointment of an end. He must be ignorant of the nature of change, which brings with it the possibility of tragedy and disappointment. [*Scrutiny,* III (1934), 21]

Smith's strictures against Whitehead certainly could be used to construct an argument against Empson that would go like this: Empson is not really impressed by anything and his ability to turn one thing into another bespeaks a shallowness of perception and a fancifulness of mind. He knows about modern despair in a fashionable way and capitalizes on it. He is cheerful, amiable, witty, and courteous but not at bottom serious because he is more interested in seeing what he can do with a work of literature than in seeing what it is. He does not understand how the greatest writers seek to be truly intelligible about the deepest human concerns, and he substitutes for such understanding sympathetic gestures and an air that assumes everything is intelligible if given a little thought. He does not understand modern life, or the history that made that life as it is. He is a Victorian eccentric being worldly and impressive about matters either not worthy of sustained attention or else not easily subdued by Empsonian tactics.

The extent to which anyone is convinced by such an argument is dependent on the extent to which he believes the tragic sense of life is necessary for the fullest apprehension of literature. Empson's sense of life is not in Leavis's or Smith's sense tragic but pastoral. I do not think, however, he is "ignorant of the nature of change, which brings with it the possibility of tragedy," even though his sense of the relation of change to permanence is different from Smith's or Leavis's or Eliot's. To say that the central feeling of tragedy is the waste even in a fortunate life, the isolation of a life rich in intimacy, is to seek confirmation for a pastoral sense of existence which stresses our common humanity and seeks to avoid an emphasis on a tragic hero which ignores that humanity.

The individual standing alone, the supreme example being the tragic hero, is expressed in our age by Gerontion, Hugh Selwyn Mauberley, Christopher Tietjens. We can avoid their fate by submerging the individual into a community of past-present-permanent truths. The pastoral tricks still work, says the heroic Empson, though we must acknowledge our place in history by calling them only tricks. He is an extraordinary critic because he seeks to participate in the most extraordinary and greatest human acts. He is not himself crushed, crippled, or incapacitated, or at least not yet. He is deeply cognizant of the history that diminishes, but he is not intimidated by it. I see no reason why such a state of mind should necessarily betray shallowness or complacence, and Empson's way of discovering our common humanity seems as often a rebuke to self-assurance as it is to despair. The communities he creates in his great passages fully acknowledge sorrow as our lot and joy in creation as our possibility, and his way of expressing the inadequacy of life to the human spirit is as able to celebrate the greatness of our greatest writers as it is able to withstand the temptation to belittle us for our common littleness.

– 4 –

To tell the story of Lawrence from *Sons and Lovers* to *Women in Love* obviates the necessity of being detailed about his later work. That is not really possible with Empson, though in many ways his later work and career parallel Lawrence's. *Some Versions of Pastoral* seems to me pure, a triumph that carries with it no necessary suggestion of what was to happen next. Looking only at Empson's work up to 1935, the most that can be alleged is that having found a way to express his heroic pastoralism as fully as he had, he had then no clear place to go. By their very nature pastoral insights achieve moments of community, of rest, that need not seek a further journeying, and for a man not yet thirty to have done fully and exhaustively such major work is perhaps to put him in the position of being able only to repeat and rework his ideas. For most of us, after all, there is no compulsion to discover new ways of exploring the world's literature every time we start. We often change, "develop," refine, get better or worse, but we seldom feel obliged to go at literature from radically different directions, and usually feel that it is better for us to go on using what we have rather than looking for ways of being strikingly new. Leavis, for instance, turned from modern poetry *(New Bearings in English Verse)* to traditional poetry *(Revaluation)* to the novel *(The Great Tradition)* to hero worship *(D. H. Lawrence: Novelist)* without once incurring any penalties for never altering his basic critical bearings and techniques. What the example of Empson shows, however, is that the hero must pay a price for his heroism, one that will probably not be exacted of those who work more in tune with the motions of their own time. There are many ways to be a lonely writer, a misunderstood one, without being a hero, but almost certainly the heroic writer will feel uncertain about where he is, who is listening, and what he should do about the fact that no one seems to be listening, such that the heroism cannot be sustained.

Writing about Empson a number of years ago I said that after *Some Versions of Pastoral* "Empson evidently felt he had to go back and write the same history over again from a different point of view." That is true enough, but I do not think I saw then all that this rewriting implied. Even before *Pastoral* was published, Empson seems to have been working on a new history, this time from the perspective of what he calls "complex words." Before he left to teach at Peking University in 1937 Empson had published essays on *Measure for Measure, Othello, Timon of Athens,* on the words "honest" and "dog" which he found crucial in these last two plays, and on feelings and statements in words. For Empson a "complex word" is one that expresses, often in casual and obscure ways, a relation between a speaker or author and an audience that almost never is expressed in "serious" or "official" language. Empson's fullest statement of his method comes at the end of a fine essay on "The English Dog":

> It is surely a striking reflection that a great deal of the thought of a man like Dr. Johnson, and probably the parts of his thought which are by this time most seriously and rightly admired, were not carried on his official verbal machinery but on colloquial phrases like the one about dogs; phrases that he would have refused to analyse on grounds of dignity, even if he had been able to. No doubt you need to know a great many other things before you can understand the working of a society; but there is a claim to be made for the branch of study I am touching on here. You need to know, as well as the serious opinions of a man in the society, how much weight he would allow, when making a practical decision, to some odd little class of joke phrases, such as excite, he would feel, sentiments obvious to any agreeable person, and yet such as carry doctrines more really complex than the whole structure of his official view of the world. [*The Structure of Complex Words* (Norfolk, Conn., n.d.), p. 174]

What is most striking here is the shift in Empson's main point of interest from literature as an expression of history, beauty, and wisdom, to literature as an expression of "the workings of a society" and "doctrines." There were many reasons for this shift, but one, almost certainly, was Empson's desire to respond to the literary and academic world around him. In the thirties many scholars attempted to retrench what they took to be the incursions of Eliot, Richards, Empson, Leavis, and others they identified as "critics," a term usually used to mean "thin," "brilliant," and "unreliable." C. S. Lewis, E. M. W. Tillyard, John Dover Wilson, Basil Willey, A. O. Lovejoy, to offer some of the obvious names, were producing The Allegory of Love, the Elizabethan World Picture, the Seventeenth Century Background, the Great Chain of Being, and in so doing were reducing most of the great English writers to pallid chroniclers of some official doctrine. What was important about a writer was his "ideas," especially when those ideas could be made to square with the ideas of his third- and fourth-rate contemporaries. The result claimed to place the great writers into their "traditions," but what was meant by "tradition" was almost a parody of what Eliot had meant by the term.

In his first two books, as we have seen, Empson states his relation to the work of his elders and presumed betters by employing a kind of mimicry of public school and High Table language, and Empson must have known that if he was taken seriously he would also seem outrageous. His way of turning one thing into another—of making Marvell's "Insnar'd with Flow'rs, I fall on Grass" a parody of Adam's Fall, of making the caucus race in *Alice* be "about" Darwinism and democracy—necessarily has the intention of getting someone to reply that this will never do. There is great danger in this technique because it can easily become something to enjoy for its own sake, and the sillier the opposition the greater the temptation to play the game. After *Some Versions of Pastoral*, Empson shows many signs of giving in to that temptation. Here are two examples from his essay on *Othello*:

Many of the audience were old soldiers disbanded without pension; they would dislike Cassio as the new type of officer, the boy who can displace men of experience merely because he knows enough mathematics to work the new guns. [*Complex Words*, p. 229]
But I suppose Iago greatly resented the high-class affectation of pur-

ity in the presumable adulteress; and perhaps resented it even more when he suspected that she did *not* go to bed with Cassio; these people, he feels, can get advantages from their "charm" (very obscenely) without doing anything you can lay your hands on. (*Complex Words*, p. 247)

Empson is relaxed here, implying he can do anything, including taking a census of the Globe's audience and being inside the "mind" of Iago. His implied antagonists were usually stiff and insistent on strict rules for interpreting, and Empson can anger and annoy them by being cheerfully old-fashioned, by calling A. C. Bradley (whom they admire but Empson is not supposed to like at all) the Master, by seeming never far away from the girlhood of Shakespeare's heroines or the number of Lady Macbeth's children. His opponents would have been less horrified had Empson kept on being what he was alleged to be, fearfully up-to-date.

All this must have been fun for Empson. Sentence-by-sentence these essays are much easier to read than his earlier ones. For the first time Empson begins to crack jokes, and unquestionably he can be a very funny man. But it is hard not to feel he has also suffered from a considerable diminution of care and effort. Empson is not here seeking ways of creating a tension with the past and then overcoming that tension by creating a community. Rather, he assumes that he is in the past, that the Shakespearean plays can blandly be brought down in time about two centuries and he can be moved back about one century so they are nineteenth-century novels and he their novelist. It is a witty ploy, but there is seldom any hard work behind the wit. This is not the fault of either Empson's subject or the method, as can be seen from the opening of his brilliant essay on "sense" in *Measure for Measure*:

There are only about ten uses of the word in the play, but I think almost all of them carry forward a puzzle which is essential to its thought. It is not denied that the word then covered (1) "sensuality" and (2) "sensibility," and I maintain that it also covered (3) "sensibleness," though in a less direct way. . . . Clearly the equations between these three could carry very relevant ironies, though the effect is not so much a covert assertion as something best translated into questions. Are Puritans hard? (Is not-one not-two?) Are they liable to have crazy outbreaks? (Is not-one not-three?) Is mere justice enough? (Is three two?) [*Complex Words,* p. 270]

It matters little whether Shakespeare can be said to sanction or invite Empson's questions. What is important is that the questions raise the play's key problems, and in the order the play raises them. Empson is ready to crack the play wide open. The uses of "Sense" not only show "an examination of sanity itself" in the specter of Angelo's fall, but also lead right into all the problems raised by the Duke after he begins to tighten the reins in Act III. The idea of the complex word is not in itself, thus, the least defective, though it is not perhaps as broad and flexible an idea as that of pastoral, and really is of use only with writers who are phenomenally responsive to the spoken language, like Shakespeare and Pope. But still, the idea carries with it an implied antagonism that says, in effect: "Yes, doctrines are important, the structure of a man's opinions is important, but you people are all looking in the wrong place when you try to find these things in Ulysses on Degree or the Bishop of Carlisle on the overthrow of annointed kings; look instead at how much contempt or snobbery is conveyed when Othello calls Iago 'honest' or at the 'idea of Puritanism' that lies behind Angelo's being trapped by punning uses of the word 'sense.' " Empson can say a lot this way, he can be funny and free, but he also has a tendency to become irresponsible, to make his antagonism or his jokes his primary concern, to make his broad and flexible tolerance itself into a doctrine with which to flail the more obviously doctrinaire.

At this point we can only speculate. Empson himself has said that he went to China in 1937 for the same reason he went to

Japan in 1931: he was offered a job. But it is hard to believe that the desire for simple employment was all that was involved. He may well have felt that teaching was the one job for which he was fitted, but he almost certainly felt too that he did not want to be an English academic if he could help it. This much is certain, at least if the public record is indicative: after he left for China in 1937, Empson wrote almost no criticism for the next ten years. Almost as soon as he arrived in Peking, the university was forced to evacuate to avoid the invading Japanese, and Empson apparently moved with it as it tried to keep going while retreating. In 1939 he went back to England, and during the war he worked on Chinese language broadcasts for the B.B.C., and shortly after the war he was back in China. In 1951 he left, so he has said, because Mao would no longer allow him to import books, and he came back to England once again, and accepted the post as Professor of English at the University of Sheffield. It is very hard to avoid feeling that he found himself, now in his mid-forties, boxed into the very life he sought so hard to avoid.

The Structure of Complex Words appeared in 1951, the year of Empson's return to England. It is much the longest of Empson's books, and while by ordinary standards it is not easy reading, it certainly is less challenging than the first two. A great deal of it is prewar material, and there is no sign that between 1937 and 1951 Empson had really modified or deepened his idea of the complex word, though the best chapter in the book, on "fool" in *Lear,* is postwar work, and shows that he had by no means found himself stuck printing old material and desperately or idly adding on some later work. The whole enterprise, however, represents a considerable retreat from any effort to achieve the centrality, the heroic triumph, of the first two books; the tension between present and past simply is not there. In his review of the book, Kenner saw in it an Empson very much like Empson's own version of Lewis Carroll's White

Knight: "without self-seeking, without sensuality, without claiming any but a fragment of knowledge, he goes on labouring at his absurd but fruitful conceptions." Kenner is right, I think, though his rightness is hard to demonstrate by quoting. In his first two books, Empson's casual manner is deceptive; in *Complex Words,* it is not.

In this book, though, we only begin to see the implications of the return to England. Behind the antagonism toward standard academic doctrines lay something more disturbing and radical, though it took the return to bring it out. The most hateful forms of academic life for Empson were those he could identify as neo-Christian, because neo-Christians willingly licked the feet of that most hateful of creatures, the Christian God. In his early work it is the heroism of Jesus that is stressed, but increasingly in the last twenty years that has given way to its corollary: God was wicked to accept his son as fit sacrifice. The shift, furthermore, has at times seemed almost fatal, because in finding way after way to express his hatred of the Christian God Empson has often become very much like the later Lawrence: a dogmatic and even hysterical partisan who insists that the world has everything all wrong, that we are all going into the darkness, that night is coming, perhaps has come. With both Lawrence and Empson the battle against the implications of the Myth of Lost Unity is one that could be most fully engaged early. It is won, then apparently lost, and after that comes a retreat into the comforts of knowing oneself right and the world hideously wrong.

There are shades and shades of this bleak event, and anyone interested in Empson must be careful to make the necessary distinctions. It is true that most of Empson's writing in the last twenty years is more ideological than literary and is therefore embattled, with a tendency toward the simplistic the way the embattled often are. But how one takes this is often a matter of how much one admires Empson's doctrine, and even one who

dislikes the doctrine intensely can find a good deal in the later
Empson to applaud and even quite a bit to admire. To say that
Empson is expressing a doctrine is not always the same thing
as saying he is narrow-minded or wrong, though it is to say that
he has given up the desire to create those communities of author, critic, and reader, in which beliefs or doctrines will be
submerged, as the celebration of the extraordinariness of an
author is made into a sign of our common humanity. It simply
is not possible to create such communities when one is interested in choosing up sides. Furthermore, when the beliefs, the
opinions, the doctrines are what is being stressed—be they those
of author or critic or reader—what all three most obviously have
in common, the author's verse, is almost certainly going to be
ignored or even subverted. It happened to many of those Empson was fighting, and it happened to Empson too.

We can see this at work in a rather pleasant way in the following, from *Milton's God,* about Book VIII of *Paradise Lost:*

> The eighth Book, with great poignancy just before the Fall, shows us
> both Raphael and God in a uniquely matey relation to Adam; he re-
> counts in it his talk with God immediately after his creation, and ends
> it by making Raphael blush. We are made to feel that he regards God
> not as an absolute lawgiver but as a human father; as when God an-
> swers the petition of Adam by saying, in effect: "What d'you want a
> woman for, hey? *I* don't want a woman." Adam says he then "used
> freedom" in defending his petition; the words as he reports them
> seem very tactful, but at any rate God said he was pleased (VIII. 440).
> He is bound to think of God as a jovial though pompous old buffer
> here; the incident is pointless unless translated like that, though the
> language retains its grandeur. [*Milton's God* (Norfolk, Conn., 1961),
> p. 184]

There are those who are offended by Empson's levity, but I find
it here very charming. "Matey" is hardly the first word that
leaps to mind when reading Milton's passage, but this is certainly the moment in the poem when the word "conversation"
is perfectly allowable to describe the relations between God

and Adam. Furthermore, the phrase "jovial though pompous old buffer" is not altogether wrong as a description of God, who says in response to Adam's request for a companion:

> 'What think'st thou then of me, and this my state?
> Seem I to thee sufficiently possessed
> Of happiness, or not, who am alone
> From all eternity? for none I know
> Second to me or like, equal much less.'   [VIII, 403–407]

But it is one thing to say that God seems like a "pompous old buffer" here, and quite another to say that is what Adam sees, as the following show:

> "He ceased. I lowly answered: 'To attain
> The height and depth of thy eternal ways
> All human thoughts come short, Supreme of Things!'
>   [VIII, 412–414]

> "He ended, or I heard no more; for now
> My earthly, by his heavenly overpowered,
> Which it had long stood under, strained to the height
> In that celestial colloquy sublime,
> As with an object that excels the sense,
> Dazzled and spent, sunk down, and sought repair
> Of sleep . . ."   [VIII, 452–458]

One sees what Empson wants. If Adam does see God as a kind of human father, then when he forsakes his father and clings to his wife in Book IX, he will only be doing, says Empson, what he thought his father told him to do. But this will not do, and to say that the incident is pointless unless translated as Empson wants, to add "though the language retains its grandeur," is to subvert all attention to the verse, and willfully, because Empson thereby implies "I know what Adam means here, and do not be misled by all those big words." Over and over Empson takes the verse and reduces it to some doctrine or position or stance, and in this book the antagonism against academic critics and neo-Christians is overt. Anyone who is put off by a lot of the cheapness in C. S. Lewis's *Preface to Paradise Lost,* anyone who has suffered with a great many academic Miltonists, is bound rather to like *Milton's God* because its dogma is less familiar and the jokes are sometimes very good. But it is a dogma Empson is promulgating, and anyone who reads through his works in chronological order will come to this one with a great sense of diminution and loss.

When Douglas Bush said, in reviewing *Milton's God*, that Empson is "squarely abreast of the early nineteenth century," he was being oversecure in his own reading of Milton, but the point has its validity. For Empson *has* retreated, and the signs of this are everywhere. In *Milton's God* and in many of his shorter essays of recent years, Empson will say that when he was young, or in school, he was raised to accept this or to believe that or to know the other thing, and he will add that he assumed everyone agreed with him until he found the neo-Christians (Eliot implicitly, C. S. Lewis and Hugh Kenner more explicitly) had been preaching such lies that he was driven to say in his middle age that what he learned when young was right: Donne is attacking Christianity in his love poems; the Whig interpretation of history is the correct one; a quatrain of Swinburne's "is what most of the Romantics had been aiming at, finally getting into focus"; the Christian God "is the wickedest thing yet invented by the black heart of man"; poems and poets have doctrines; Imagism is nonsense. Along with this goes an increased willingness to settle into public school jargon: "manly," "wicked," "quite," "absurd," "tidy," "bully," "toady," "cozy," "advanced" to describe a kind of thinking. The air is that of a sensible Englishman, liberal, tolerant, wise, admittedly a little stodgy, who implies there is nothing that cannot be brought into his orbit. It is a kind of intellectual imperialism, really, a triumph of worldly casualness, all of which is certainly consonant with a deep concern with horror, terror, and the fear of being punished.

There is no need to carry the argument further, because whatever the precise nature of Empson's personal case, it only begins to assume major proportions after Empson's major work was done, and when, to repeat, Empson was forced by his return to England to confront a great deal he had tried hard simply to avoid. He has said that he stopped writing poems in the late thirties because the poems he was writing struck him as being quite bad, and it may well be that he practically stopped writing criticism at the same time for similar reasons. Empson is an extraordinarily intelligent man, after all, and there is no reason to believe he did not see what was happening. But, back in England, faced with the practical necessity of providing for his family and with what he has called "the sordidity of Eng. Lit.," he seems to have felt forced to take up the cudgels of his increasingly Victorian morality and wisdom, and to fight by preaching. The result was criticism generally inferior to his prewar work, but the case of Lawrence shows us that such dogmatism is what we might expect in the later work of a faded hero. And it must be remembered that many people sympathize with Empson's beliefs, and admire the breezy tone that accompanies them. He is perhaps the only English poet and critic of the period between the wars whose stock in England has risen since World War II. When it came time to modify the enormous influence of Leavis, and the lesser but still considerable influence of C. S. Lewis, when it seemed that American criticism had become enervated under the weight of its academic machine, there was Empson, who seemed to have been fighting the good fight all along. This was an illusion, because Empson in that sense did not begin fighting until the fifties, when he was being discovered by a new generation, but understandably it would take some time for the mistake to be sorted out.

And some of the later Empson is very good indeed. I have already mentioned "Fool in *Lear*," and would add "Donne and the Rhetorical Tradition" *(Kenyon Review*, 1949), "Wit in the 'Essay on Criticism'" *(Hudson Review*, 1950; in *Complex Words)*, "The Ancient Mariner" *(Critical Quarterly*, 1966), and, best of all, *"Tom Jones" (Kenyon Review,* 1958). This last is wonderful precisely because *Tom Jones* is exactly what Empson's interests and biases would like it to be: a book that preaches a broad and generous doctrine, that is thoroughly worldly without being complacent, that is extremely subtle in its surface manner and massively simple in its outlook on life, that is, by a man Empson can openly and rightly admire. Fielding can be saved, thus, from the slighting remarks of Leavis and the respectful neglect of most people by making him rather like Empson but in a way that makes him no less Fielding. By comparison, his two recent essays on *Volpone* and *The Alchemist,* by an author rather like Fielding, stop short of being really illuminating because those works demand a sustained careful verbal analysis which Empson simply has not done in many years, and so what we get instead is perfectly good things about what is wrong with the stern moralistic readings of Jonson.

Empson is still prolific, astringent but cheerful, a lonely and determined writer who seems convinced there may be no one who can hear what he is saying. He is a man with a cause, and he uses his learning and his subtlety to work out all sorts of wiles and strategies for confronting a hostile world. He was more generous, more accepting, more wise, forty years ago, and he may well know this himself, but he sees the fights that must be fought and he goes on fighting them, although it is doubtful if he ever engages the interest or even the antagonism of those he wants to warn and to convert. He tries to preach with some persuasiveness, but he was much more persuasive when he was not trying to preach at all.

In an interview with Christopher Ricks a number of years years ago, Empson offered this perspective about the possibilities of his future:

In a way, you see, as you approach middle age, though in fact you're a seething pit of scorpions, you don't recognise them in that form. You're getting things tidy: "Can I get the boy to college?" and things like that are what you are thinking about. So it doesn't appear to you in this direct way, as an unresolved conflict which you need to express in a poem. You often do feel it again when you're old, when you're seriously old, when you've been forced to retire and the pressure of making actual decisions in the world is no longer what you ought to be thinking about. The idea that you write old and young fits in with the idea of poetry as the expression of an unresolved conflict. [*The Review,* June 1963, pp. 34–35]

One determinedly opposed to Empson can find in this only a hasty effort to cheer himself up. A better and more sympathetic person would say that Empson had best be done now with the practical considerations that have dominated his criticism, and would then add that an Empson retired, and "seriously old" (lovely phrase), might very well once again write poetry that expressed those conflicts left unresolved in his early poems and resolved heroically in his early criticism. There is great good energy in the man, and the end, thankfully, is not yet.

Whatever work is still to be done, though, it will not be like the heroic work of the thirties, and because that work is what is crucial to the argument offered in this book, we must return there to attempt a final judgment. "Aubade" is one of Empson's very best poems. It was written during the years he was writing *Some Versions of Pastoral* and achieves in miniature the heroic action of that book. It concerns two lovers in the Far East who are awakened by an earthquake and who come to see it as a sign of impending war. Two lines—"It seemed the best thing to be up and go" and "The heart of standing is you cannot fly"—serve as a refrain of sorts. Early in the poem the two lines seem to jar against each other and the other lines:

> Then the long pause and then the bigger shake.
> It seemed the best thing to be up and go.

> And far too large for my feet to step by.
> I hoped that various buildings were brought low.
> The heart of standing is you cannot fly.

As the refrain lines are repeated, however, they begin to serve as the "truth," which in the course of the poem seeks a home, or a way to be seen as the truth. In the last stanza the lines are brought together:

> But as to risings, I can tell you why.
> It is on contradiction that they grow.
> It seemed the best thing to be up and go.
> Up was the heartening and the strong reply.
> The heart of standing is we cannot fly.

As in *Some Versions of Pastoral* the details finally fuse; the lovers in the foreground and the impending violence in the background become part of a single landscape. There are two "risings": the speaker came to the East in flight from the pains of life in Europe only to discover in Japan "the same war on a stronger toe." Outbursts are everywhere, men rise up and fight. Because they do, lovers must rise too, and no place is left for love, men flee and become caught in the violence, which is why it is on contradictions that the risings grow.

"Up was the heartening and the strong reply," then, is a generous acknowledgment by the lover to the revolutionaries that theirs is a heartening as well as a necessary response to the war that is coming as inevitably as did the earthquake. It is also the accepting response of the lover to his girl; there is no place for us here, we must not quarrel with ourselves or with those who part us. "The heart of standing is we cannot fly"; going and coming become the same, and the wry voice that accepts this, that acknowledges the power of history and circumstances, wonderfully finds release in seeing the situation as a matter of physics: we cannot fly. In this final community the "we" is, first, the lovers, unable to flee together; it is, second, all those caught in the great tumult that would become the second war; it is, finally, all of us, always, in constant need of asking what is the best thing, in constant awareness that we are here and now, unable to fly, with only our selves and our pasts as guides. Empson's wan wisdom is once again made into heroic achievement. There are morals aplenty to be drawn from this lovely and moving poem, but here we can rest by saying that it brings us out where Empson lives most grandly.

IV. *Tolkien and Frodo Baggins*

With Tolkien we are back to the catacylsm of World War I, though his reply to the war was different from Lawrence's and was long delayed in taking its crucial shape. Tolkien was born in 1892, so that, though he was only seven years younger than Lawrence, he was still in college when the war started. His experience of the war, while much more immediate than Lawrence's, seems to have been essentially a schoolboy's experience, as Lawrence's certainly was not. Tolkien had been orphaned in 1910 while a student at King Edward's School. He then went to Exeter College, Oxford, from which he was graduated in 1915, just in time, as it were, to join the Lancashire Fusiliers and serve in the trenches around Baupame, where there were very heavy casualties. When the war was over and Tolkien was recovering in a hospital bed in England, he discovered he had only one friend left alive. He has never said much about his wartime experience or his life—the best available information can be found in William Ready's *The Tolkien Relation* (1968) and Henry Resnick's article in *The Saturday Evening Post* for July 2, 1966—but we can gather that in its external details Tolkien's life in wartime France resembled that described by Robert Graves in *Goodbye to All That*. But he said one thing later that seems to me crucial for an understanding of what happened and what kind of man he is: "A real taste for fairy-stories was wakened by philology on the threshold of manhood, and quickened to full life by war." It is not an easy sentence to understand, but it has long seemed to me that no one need pursue his inquiry into Tolkien's life any further than he needs to do in order to understand it.

The sentence itself was not written until 1938, and it may well be that it took Tolkien a full twenty years to realize what had happened to him. He seems to have withdrawn from the wounds and terrors of the war and all we think of as modern life. First, and as a prior condition to everything else, he became that most withdrawn of citizens, a philologist—he was an assistant on the revision of the *Oxford English Dictionary*, reader and then professor of philology at Reading, a fellow of Pembroke College, Oxford, and finally Merton Professor of English Literature there—which means that when Tolkien became a writer of fairy tales he was reflecting or expressing his deep absorption in words and older languages. In some sense withdrawing is integral to the life of a philologist, and it is doubtful if very many have ever become philologists without a need to withdraw or flee. He finds, and makes, orders, symbols, systems, traditions he can nurture so they in turn can nourish him. The lore, myth, and magic that surround ancient words can easily be made into a fortress against the modern world, where there is only tumid apathy with no concentration, men and bits of paper.

In *The Tolkien Relation* William Ready offers a portrait of Tolkien in the twenties and thirties which he compiled from the comments of former students and colleagues. As a lecturer, Tolkien's great virtue was as an enunciator of *Beowulf*; as a tutor his strength lay in giving his students ideas he never claimed title to himself; as a scholar his only serious published work before 1936 is an edition of *Sir Gawain and the Green Knight*. He seems, thus, to have been devising ways of living such that he could carry on his relations with the outside world at one remove. What he was, or knew, or cared for, could not be discerned directly, and no one except friends and close admirers need have had any sense of him other than as the figure he obviously offered, of a diffident and learned professor. Nothing that we can see about his life before 1936, at any rate, gives a clue to what he meant when he said, two years later, that his love of fairy tales had been quickened to full life by war.

But beginning in 1936 Tolkien began to show the world some of the fruit of his years of withdrawal. Within two years he delivered his Israel Gollancz Lecture on *Beowulf* to the British Academy, his Andrew Lang Lecture on fairy stories, and published the book he had been reading to his son, *The Hobbit*. Each one of these gives us a different hint of what Tolkien had been doing all those years and of the great work to come. "*Beowulf*: The Monsters and the Critics," which has since become the single best known essay on Old English literature, begins with an attack on philologists and historians who treat the poem as a quarry for their own specialized interests and so ignore the poem itself and the central fact of its monsters. *Beowulf,* he insists, is a poem about war, and we praise Beowulf for fighting long and bravely, though inevitably he will lose in the end. For Tolkien the poem is as much elegy as epic, and thus no Christian overlay, no mention of God or heaven, is strong enough to dispel the sense that the main task of the *scop* is to lament the death of the fallen hero. He superbly evokes the dimly lit and struggling world of Beowulf and Hrothgar, the imminence of Grendel, the inevitability of the dragon's coming, the sternness of the poet's wisdom, and as he does so he makes clear that we can never say of him that he is only a philologist. He speaks as one immersed in the lore and the atmosphere of old Germanic things, as one who has not just withdrawn from the modern world but gone somewhere else as well.

At first glance *The Hobbit* seems worlds removed from *Beowulf* and Tolkien's meditation on it. Like *The Wind in the Willows* and the Pooh books, which were also written by upper-middle-class Englishmen to read aloud to their sons, *The Hobbit* is episodic and cozy, anything but stern and austere. It begins this way:

> In a hole in the ground there lived a hobbit. Not a nasty, dirty, wet hole, filled with the ends of worms and an oozy smell, nor yet a dry, bare, sandy hole with nothing in it to sit down on or to eat: it was a hobbit-hole, and that means comfort. [*The Hobbit* (Boston, 1938), p. 11]

Though the hobbit-hole may seem far away from Hroth-gar's mead hall, in fact it takes little effort to get from one to the other. All that is required is the mastery of two different tones, both of which are distinctly literary and distinctly not modern. The author of both the lecture and the children's book is very obviously a reader about things long past, an imaginer of worlds free of the strain or despair of the modern-ist, worlds of lore and wonder where names can evoke magical things. *The Hobbit* goes on:

> I suppose hobbits need some description nowadays, since they have become rare and shy of the Big People, as they call us. They are (or were) small people, smaller than dwarves (and they have no beards) but very much larger than lilliputians. There is little or no magic about them, except the ordinary everyday sort which helps them to disappear quietly and quickly when large stupid folk like you and me come blundering along, making a noise like elephants which they can hear a mile off. [P. 12]

Tolkien is instructing his son from a position similar to that he takes to instruct his audience in the *Beowulf* lecture. In each case he allies himself with his audience against some outsiders: "critics" they are called in the lecture, and "Big People" in the book, but they are obviously the same sort in each case. It is only the resolutely Anglophilic who like the voice of *The Hob-*

bit; others tend to find it too cozy and seemingly smug. The hobbits are recognizable English types, fond of beer and tobacco and good conversation, easily able to live without the restraints of police or women. C. S. Lewis's descriptions of the Inklings, the Oxford group that included Tolkien, Charles Williams, himself, and a few others, seem descriptive of hobbit life. Though the book is subtitled "There and Back Again," though there are adventures and dwarves and a magic ring, it is a static book; things happen but change is not possible.

The Hobbit is often taken to be a good introduction to Tolkien's major work, because it too is about hobbits, but if *The Lord of the Rings* needs any introduction at all, the Andrew Lang Lecture, "On Fairy-Stories," which Tolkien gave in 1938, provides the best. It is here he says that his love of fairy tales was quickened to full life by war, though he does not really explain the sentence. I am going to look at some parts of the lecture more closely later on; for now it is enough to say that here Tolkien describes what men in later days lost when they left behind the world created in fairy stories, and which we can begin to recover primarily through such stories. Fairy stories let us see or discover the world as we originally were meant to see it. We are left to imagine that the stupidity, barbarity, squalor, and horror of the war drove a sensitive young imagination toward the conviction that he was seeing the very opposite of life as it was meant to be seen. The horrors of World War I were trite, those of fairy tale brilliant and profound. Again we see that while withdrawal may have been a psychic necessity for Tolkien he made of it not just a journey away but a journey toward. Ironically, and wonderfully, as we will see, it was by means of his withdrawal and his imagining of a fairy tale that Tolkien could create one of the most powerful visions we have of the very world from which he was fleeing.

At about the same time, Tolkien was beginning this work to which the years of withdrawal and the slow flowering of scholarship and tale-telling had led him, though it was years before it was finished and published. For what he wanted to do, it seems, the scholarship on *Beowulf* and *Gawain* was too limited or too impersonal, the atmosphere of *The Hobbit* too confining, the point of "On Fairy-Stories" too doctrinal. His is a more capacious and inquiring imagination than perhaps anyone, including Tolkien himself, could have guessed in the late thirties. In any event, long after the modern age had passed and not only the first but the second war was over and Tolkien himself was near retirement, there appeared at yearly intervals the three volumes of *The Lord of the Rings*: *The Fellowship of the Ring* (1954), *The Two Towers* (1955), *The Return of the King* (1956).

As I have said, some people like to use some of Tolkien's early work as an introduction to the trilogy, just as some people begin reading Spenser with *The Shepheardes Calender* and Milton with the Nativity Ode, but the game is not really worth the candle. As we read the trilogy we can be reminded of this or that aspect of his other work, we are aware that he is an English don, a philologist, a writer in love with lore and naming, but all this is the soil of Tolkien's imagination, not the fruit. Tolkien needed his years of withdrawal, but not so he could glorify some way of life so long forgotten that it can be recalled only by the most nostalgic. When Tolkien says he wished he could have written the trilogy in Elvish, he is declaring his temperamental allegiance to the distant past, but the imagination plays strange tricks, seldom more strikingly than in *The Lord of the Rings*. Tolkien tries in many different ways to bring ancient values to life, but by and large he fails to do so. Neither his learning nor his fear of modern life could alter the fact that he is of the modern world, better able to render his own century imaginatively than any other. Technically the central action of *The Lord of the Rings* is a quest, and we know quite well that there are no modern quests, but

in fact the central action more closely resembles a descent into
hell. Tolkien could not have done this without displacing his
story into the fairyland of Middle Earth, without using many
ritual details of quest literature, but that does not change in
any significant way the fact that at its best the trilogy is modern
literature.

To say this, and to insist upon it as I will be doing, is bound
to seem at least a little impertinent to Tolkien himself who
might not understand this point and who, if he did, would not
like it. But *The Lord of the Rings* is what it is, a superb instance of the rightness of Lawrence's statement that we must
trust the tale and not the artist. I have called this chapter
"Tolkien and Frodo Baggins," and in a number of places I
speak of Frodo almost as though he were a free agent, separate
and equal to Tolkien. I do this, in the first place, because
it is Frodo's heroism that is clearly visible to us and is our guide
to see and understand Tolkien's heroism, which is not on view
in the way Lawrence's or Empson's is. But second and more
important, I do this as a way of stressing that Frodo is, unlike
a great deal else in the trilogy, modern, and that as a result
it is to Frodo that Tolkien's imagination responds most fully,
with or without his conscious knowledge. Because this may be
true without Tolkien's having been aware of it, it is difficult
to talk of his heroism, but the work makes clear that he is
heroic. It is as though Tolkien's imagination rescues him from
his convictions, and our best sign of this is the way the buttons
tell the truth: Frodo Lives. The buttons probably mean that
Frodo is alive and well in Argentina, and I mean that Frodo,
and the figures nearest him, Sam Gamgee and Gollum, live as
the major justification of the whole work, and that the work
itself never makes this clear.

Justice cannot be done to Frodo's heroism or to the ways it
is the key to Tolkien's heroism by treating Frodo alone. He has
a context, and it is his gradual emergence from that context

that makes him seem different and so impressive. We must begin by returning to the hobbits and to the way they fit into the fabric of Tolkien's imagination. In *The Hobbit* Tolkien is generally content to remain complacent about the hobbits' own complacency and lore, while in *The Lord of the Rings* he generally understands (for what it is) their desire to withdraw from any world more complex than a daydream—and so is able to place them critically. Occasionally Tolkien relaxes with the hobbits and pretends that buffoonery and schoolboy pluck are important responses to danger, but these lapses are infrequent and easily identified. The real issue at stake here is much larger than the hobbits' coziness, and that is Tolkien's love of lore, his endless naming, his ritual details, those qualities that are Tolkien's way of withdrawing and of making a world that is an adaptation of many older worlds. Tolkien will include anything as long as it bears no touch of the modern. The hobbits' names—Baggins, Sackville, Proudfoot, Gamgee, Took, Cotton— all are versions of names Tolkien might have found in a parish register in Buckinghamshire; their home is called The Shire. But we need a passage, and one about war rather than hobbits, to see how Tolkien uses his names to include many old things that are clearly not of our century:

> But everywhere he looked he saw the signs of war. The Misty Mountains were crawling like anthills: orcs were issuing out of a thousand holes. Under the boughs of Mirkwood there was deadly strife of Elves and Men and fell beasts. The land of the Beornings was aflame; a cloud was over Moria; smoke rose on the borders of Lórien.
> Horsemen were galloping on the grass of Rohan; wolves poured from Isengard. From the havens of Harad ships of war put out to sea; and out of the East Men were moving endlessly: swordsmen, spearmen, bowmen upon horses, chariots of chieftains and laden wains. All the power of the Dark Lord was in motion. [*The Lord of the Rings* (Boston, 1954, 1955, 1956), I, 416–417]

Anyone who finds this too stiff and pretentious probably will not be able to read *The Lord of the Rings* with much pleasure.

This is not Tolkien at his best, but it is characteristic. The reference to chariots, chieftains, and wains in the next-to-last sentence self-consciously places us in a preindustrial scene, and all the military details show that this is ancient, or at least old-fashioned, warfare, anything but the trenches of France. The names are also self-consciously chosen to convey a sense of scope and variety: Misty Mountains and Mirkwood are children's book names; elves and orcs come from fairy stories; Moria, like the country of the Dark Lord, Mordor, derives from Mordred, the faithless among Arthur's knights; Lórien, the forest of the elves, is one of a series of "L" words Tolkien uses to connote good, elvish things—its king and queen are Celeborn and Galadriel; Isengard combines the Old English *isen* and *geard* to form the kenning "iron-castle"; Harad is close to Arabic and so names a place far away from the main action. A full Tolkien entymology has not yet been done, so far as I know, but even a casual student of older English and northern literature will recognize over and over again sounds and combinations of sounds that show Tolkien adapting his names from earlier ones. The purpose is not to provide a riddle or a code, or to encourage a reader to feel he must be more learned in order to understand, but to evoke a world we know has long since passed away where naming is taken to be a matter of grave importance and where, therefore, all names are appropriate. An interest in names and the past they evoke is one major sign of the goodness of the "good" characters, just as evil is the effort to alter or destroy the right relation of namer to named, present to past.

This is the essential withdrawn Tolkien, and, as I have said, this is the soil of his imagination. We must now turn to his central story and myth, that of the Ring, to see how it transformed an important part of that imagination. In *The Hobbit* the Ring is just a ring, and part of just one more episode. Bilbo Baggins finds it in an underground tunnel near a dark lake, and he also meets there a slimy creature called Gollum who, it becomes clear, owned the ring and used it to make himself invisible so he could catch goblins. Gollum discovers his loss, suspects Bilbo has found the ring, and Bilbo discovers the ring's power to make him invisible just in time to escape. There is nothing in the episode to lead anyone to suspect what was going to happen. Shortly after he finished *The Hobbit* Tolkien began the trilogy, which could not have been written without Bilbo's acquisition having assumed major proportions in Tolkien's imagination. At the opening of *The Fellowship of the Ring,* Bilbo is planning to leave his home in The Shire, and he reluctantly leaves the ring for his nephew and heir, Frodo Baggins, who knows about it only through Bilbo's story of how he found it. Later Frodo is visited by an old friend of Bilbo's, a wizard named Gandalf, who tells him that his ring is The Ring, forged by Sauron, the Dark Lord, as a master ring, one that could bind and control all the rings of power that had been fashioned in an earlier age by the elves for themselves, dwarves, and men. Sauron lost the Ring in an earlier war, and by a series of accidents it came into the hands of Sméagol, or Gollum, one of some hobbit-like creatures that lived near the River Anduin, into which the Ring had fallen. Gandalf then shows Frodo the inscription on the Ring, which is the sixth and seventh lines of this poem, long known to the elves:

> Three Rings for the Elven-kings under the sky,
>   Seven for the Dwarf-lords in their halls of stone,
> Nine for Mortal Men doomed to die,
>   One for the Dark Lord on his dark throne
> In the Land of Mordor where the Shadows lie.
>   One Ring to rule them all, One Ring to find them,
>   One Ring to bring them all and in the darkness bind them
> In the Land of Mordor where the Shadows lie.

In a work filled with riddles, songs, and lays, this is the only poem about the Ring, and it is much the best and most important of the lot. Here, at the beginning, it mystifies both Frodo and the reader at least as much as it explains. Gandalf can tell Frodo about the three elven rings and the seven dwarf rings, but Frodo's response to such lore is not unlike ours: I have heard of such, but not in my world. Gandalf then tells Frodo that the Dark Lord, Sauron, has risen again in Mordor, and that he has gradually pieced together the history of the Ring and is at that moment known to be searching for a hobbit by the name of Baggins. Frodo asks Gandalf why they do not just destroy the Ring, and Gandalf tells him to try:

> It was an admirable thing and altogether precious. When he took it out he had intended to fling it from him into the very hottest part of the fire. But he found now that he could not do so, not without a great struggle. He weighed the Ring in his hand, hesitating, and forcing himself to remember all that Gandalf had told him; and then with an effort of will he made a movement, as if to cast it away—but he found that he had put it back in his pocket. [I, 70]

Frodo begins to understand, and also to see he is being asked to undertake something he feels is beyond him:

> "You are wise and powerful. Will you not take the Ring?"
> "No!" cried Gandalf, springing to his feet. "With that power I should have power too great and terrible. And over me the Ring would gain a power still greater and more deadly." [I, 70–71]

The Ring's only use is to bind and subdue others, just as here it has bound Frodo to the extent that he cannot choose to throw it in the fire. As it turns out, it would have made no difference had he done so, because the Ring would remain untouched. It can be destroyed only in the fire in which it was forged, on Mount Orodruin or Mount Doom, in the land of Mordor, home of Sauron, where the Shadows lie.

The idea of the Ring is really quite simple, and though it is not until much later that its ramifications become clearer and its power can be fully felt, even this early it is clear that the idea of the Ring can do much for Tolkien. The stronger the Ring-bearer the stronger his temptation to use the Ring himself and so be bound by it. This means that Tolkien can employ many of the traditional figures of fairy tales like wizards, dwarves, and elves, and can work to make them as impressive and powerful as he likes, but that they must always be a little irrelevant because Frodo, neither impressive nor powerful, is Ring-bearer at the moment, and is at least as able to accomplish its destruction as anyone else, even though he has no credentials as a hero whatsoever. No one is suited for this perilous quest. Frodo knows about dwarves and elves and the rest exactly what we know—what we have been told or read about—and suddenly he is asked to leave home and find out about all this for himself. He has no recourse but to see it as "adventure" even though he can read in Gandalf's tone a sense that much more is involved than he understands. The myth of the Ring gives Tolkien a double perspective, in this scene that of Gandalf and Frodo, lore-knower and bemused troubled innocent, and at the same time lets him show that the latter is at least as important as the former. In a poem that is at first glance as far removed from Tolkien as seems possible, Dr. Johnson asks: "What murdered Wentworth, and what exiled Hyde?" The answer is: "Power too great to keep, or to resign," which is precisely Gandalf's answer to Frodo's questions about destroying the Ring or giving it to someone more powerful than himself. It will take heroism of some kind, though of what kind no one can glimpse this early in the trilogy, to hold onto the Ring, to take it to Mordor, to give it up there, and thereby to avoid the fate of Wentworth, Hyde, and the fate Gandalf foresees for himself were he ever to have the Ring.

So Frodo sells his house and sends out word he is retiring to the home of his childhood, farther east in The Shire. Even before he leaves he learns he must hurry, because mysterious Black Riders who look like men come into The Shire and ask after a hobbit named Baggins. Frodo leaves stealthily, keeping away from the high road when he can, accompanied by his servant, Sam Gamgee, and the young hobbits, Pippin Took, and, later, Merry Brandybuck. All the other hobbits know is that Frodo is in danger and must go on a long journey, and Frodo himself knows little more. Gandalf has advised them to head eastward to Rivendell, the home of Elrond Halfelven. A group of friendly elves appears, then an eccentric named Tom Bombadil in an ancient forest, then barrow-wights, more Black Riders, then a Ranger named Strider who rescues them in a pub in the town of Bree after Frodo has given himself away by letting the Ring slip on his finger during a tavern show so that he becomes invisible. Through all these early chapters Tolkien moves deliberately, slowly expanding the world of the hobbits. Some readers who start by thinking they will not like Tolkien move through these episodes feeling that this is just a dressing-up of some old and musty story. But as anyone can see when he looks back at these chapters from some later point in the trilogy, Tolkien knows what he is doing. The hobbits are like us in their attitude toward the lore and mysteries of life outside their own province. They move provincially, clumsily, relating everything they see to what they know from life at home, as though their way of understanding the world, no matter how inadequate, was the only one they could possibly have. Thus Tolkien must move slowly, altering landscape and mode little by little, in order to trap the hobbits in their provinciality.

When Frodo becomes invisible in Bree, he reveals the location of the Ring to all the Black Riders, and so the hobbits flee, guided by Strider, moving circuitously now because the highway is constantly watched. Even so the Riders catch up to them one night and Frodo feels compelled to put on the Ring, which makes him invisible to his companions but which reveals his exact location to the Riders, one of whom wounds Frodo badly. Finally, after a dash along the highway, the hobbits, Strider, and an elf carry Frodo to Rivendell. Here Frodo can begin to heal, and here Elrond has called a council—Gandalf, Bilbo, elves, dwarves, and men are there—and the hobbits can begin to see how vast the world is and how much is at stake in their journey with the Ring. The part of the book that feels and reads like "adventures" is over, for them and us.

At the council Glóin, a dwarf, begins by telling of Sauron's efforts to use the dwarf-lord to find Bilbo and so regain the Ring; Elrond describes how the Ring was first taken from Sauron by Isildur; Boromir, a man from Gondor, announces that Sauron has moved out of Mordor to reoccupy land in Gondor taken from him in his last defeat. He also repeats a prophecy he heard in a dream that he could not understand:

> Seek for the Sword that was broken:
>   In Imladris it dwells;
> There shall be counsels taken
>   Stronger than Morgul-spells.
> There shall be shown a token
>   That Doom is near at hand,
> For Isildur's Bane shall waken,
>   And the Halfling forth shall stand.
>
> [I, 259]

Strider then stands forth with the "Sword that was broken," and Elrond tells the others that Strider is in fact Aragorn, heir to the kingdom of Gondor. He then introduces Frodo with the Ring, and the halfling stands forth.

Here lore and action meet, but not in a way that either hobbits or readers can readily understand. It does not really tell Frodo anything to learn that the Ring is "Isildur's Bane," and it cannot really matter to him that Strider is Aragorn. Lore is still only names and songs and stories about the past, and all that happens at the council can be significant only to those like Gandalf and Aragorn who already know what the lore signifies. Frodo does not even know what questions to ask that might give him answers to put together the fragments he has learned about. Boromir's prophecy and the rest are for him like the quotations in Eliot's poems for us: they recall something we have heard about but have never really grasped no matter how well we know the words themselves. And when Frodo does learn of something he can understand, as when Gandalf describes how he traced the passing of the Ring from Isildur to Gollum to Bilbo, and Bilbo tells how he later gave it to Frodo, he really only sees more clearly how irrelevant a good deal of it is to what he must do. The war seems to be between Sauron and the members of the council, but a great many there cannot really help Frodo. The elf-lords seem glorious to the hobbits but they are faded now, rulers of small lands, unable and uninterested in stirring abroad. Aragorn and Gandalf can do much more because they have knowledge and power to help show Frodo the way, and as long as he is with them they can forge links between the wisdom of the past and the urgency of the present. Still, Frodo is the Ring-bearer: "I will take the Ring, though I do not know the way." A fellowship is formed to go with him, south with the Ring: the four hobbits, Gandalf, Aragorn, Boromir the man, Legolas the elf, and Gimli the dwarf. But the fact that there is no need for a powerful army because that would only attract attention and an even more powerful army from Sauron, also emphasizes the limitedness of the help anyone can give Frodo. He is best armed, though he does not quite realize it when Gandalf tells him so, by the fact that Sauron will not conceive that anyone could want to destroy the Ring and so will not be looking for them to move toward Mordor.

The fellowship moves through Moria, the ancient underground mountain kingdom of the dwarves, and in a fierce fight there with a Balrog, Gandalf is lost and Aragorn assumes command. The company then moves out of the mountains and into Lothlórien, forest home of the elven-queen Galadriel, where "All that he [Frodo] saw was shapely, but the shapes seemed at once clear cut, as if they had been first conceived and drawn at the uncovering of his eyes, and ancient as if they had endured for ever" (I, 365). In Moria and Lothlórien the hobbits can begin to see for themselves the ancientness of life that had been, before this, only the lore of others. Once again, in *The Fellowship of the Ring,* as in *The Rainbow* and *Some Versions of Pastoral,* the would-be hero must become a historian first, able to explore the past in order to see its implications for the present.

In Moria the hobbits meet creatures, some merely ferocious and others really malicious, who know and care nothing about the Ring or the perilous journey: wargs, orcs, the Balrog. At one point Boromir casually throws a stone into a pool, and Frodo says: "I am afraid of the pool. Don't disturb it!" One can "disturb" the water of a pool by throwing a stone, but that is nothing to be afraid cf. Frodo is beginning to sense, however, that the world is alive in many and dangerous ways, and he is right: "Out from the vater a long sinuous tentacle had crawled; it was pale-green and luminous and wet" (I, 321, 322). In Lothlórien there is respite from struggle and danger, and also discovery:

In Rivendell there was memory of ancient things; in Lórien the ancient things still lived on in the waking world. Evil had been seen and heard there, sorrow had been known; the Elves feared and distrusted the world outside: wolves were howling on the wood's borders: but on the land of Lórien no shadow lay. [I, 364]

The rampant and threatening vitality of Moria, the preserved stillness of Lothlórien—"In winter here no heart could mourn for summer or for spring"—in one sense we are only passing through places on the way south, but these are anything but mere episodes because we begin to see what the journey is all about. The hobbits have no way to understand Gandalf at the beginning when he says The Shire is in danger, and in Rivendell they are so overwhelmed by the "memory of ancient things," they can only glimpse any relation between what had happened and what is happening. But in Moria an ancient kingdom had fallen—there are enchanted doors and winding stairs and great halls still left to remind—and what remains is unordered, fierce, not quite a chaos but almost. In Lothlórien another such kingdom is fading, and gradually Frodo and we see that these words, these civilizations, simply are following their natural course, rising and falling in the flux of history. The more clearly this is felt and understood, the more important the present becomes because if Sauron regains the Ring the whole process of history will be his to control. The Ring seeks and binds, and in binding it aborts process. Quite unlike Sauron, the Balrog in Moria fights and terrorizes the fellowship when he feels his territory is invaded; there is nothing friendly or good about him, but he is not evil. To be alive, Balrog or dwarf or elf, is to follow one's own nature, whatever that be. To be bound is to have the part of oneself that is unique destroyed. Just as lore is the means whereby sentient and articuate creatures assert and nourish their uniqueness by keeping their ties with the past, so war is the struggle to be alive fought against any who seek to destroy lore and the relations it implies.

Such a formulation is not made by Tolkien or any hobbit, but it can help to show how the trilogy reveals its subject. The word "natural," for instance, is unknown in *The Lord of the Rings,* but passages like the following make the word seem appropriate:

> "There lies the fastness of Southern Mirkwood," said Haldir. "It is clad in a forest of dark fir, where the trees strive one against another and their branches rot and wither. In the midst upon a stony height stands Dol Goldur, where long the hidden Enemy had his dwelling. We fear that now it is inhabited again, and with power sevenfold. A black cloud lies often over it of late. In this high place you may see the two powers that are opposed one to another; and ever they strive now in thought, but whereas the light perceives the very heart of the darkness, its own secret has not been discovered. Not yet." [I, 366]

This is stiff and ancient, but the magic is at work in it, too. Tolkien here repeats a verb, "strive," so that the subjects and objects moved by the verb make a kind of metaphor: the trees in the forest of Mirkwood "strive," and then the two powers "strive." Just as tree against tree leads to rotting and withering, so too light against dark leads to war. We know, or sense, that the trees are "real" trees, whereas the light and the dark powers are symbolic, but the effect of the comparison is to make us think of the ways the symbolic powers are behaving naturally, like the trees, and indeed, we recognize, rays of light do "perceive" darkness.

But "light," though "real" and "natural," does symbolize the moral power of goodness, or, rather, can describe and even explain what that power is:

> At the hill's foot Frodo found Aragorn, standing still and *silent as a tree*; but in his hand was a small golden bloom of *elanor,* and *a light was in his eyes.* He was *wrapped in some fair memory*: and as Frodo looked at him he knew that he beheld things as they once had been in this same place. For the *grim years were removed* from the face of Aragorn, and he seemed clothed in white, a young lord tall and fair; and he spoke words in the Elvish tongue to one whom Frodo could not see. [I, 366–367; italics (except "elanor") mine]

This is a stunning passage, but it demands the context of the whole work to this point to make it so. The italicized phrases all might be spotted as clichés if we were not forced to take them literally as well as metaphorically. In Lothlórien, for that is the point about it, the trees are now silent but once were not, so that the phrase "silent as a tree" does not mean, simply, "quiet," but something much closer to "deliberately silent." The light from Lothlórien shines from a vanished world, and the light that Aragorn once saw when the forest was alive now shines only as a memory. Yet because Aragorn can remember he can be wrapped in that memory and the light in his eyes thus does what lore is usually employed to do—it illuminates the present by remembering the past. All this is clinched with a simple and lovely ambiguity: in "as Frodo looked at him he knew that he beheld things as they once had been," the second "he" refers to Aragorn or to Frodo, and so to both. The light that wraps Aragorn in memory is seen by Frodo in Aragorn's eyes, and Frodo understands a historical relation as he never has before.

Thus "light" becomes not just natural force or a cliché for moral power, but also is descriptive of the historical "natural" motion of living things. Because Frodo is there to see and to discover the past, Aragorn's transformation into a "young lord tall and fair" is not the literary or fey magic of a teller of fairy tales, but the "real" or "natural" magic of seeing the present clearly and rightly because the past is, for the first time, clearly and rightly seen. The war, thus, is not just a struggle between the moral forces of good and evil, light and dark, but a fight to be "natural" and unbound when life is threatened. The "One Ring to bring them all and in the darkness bind them" now seems less an idea with which to animate a tale and more a threat to living things.

After leaving Lothlórien the fellowship moves south down the River Anduin, the boundary, much farther south, between Mordor and Gondor. Boromir tries to persuade Frodo to go with him to Gondor, but Frodo knows he must go straight to Mordor because there is nothing in Gondor or any place else that he can help or that can help him. Boromir has no way of knowing, because to him the Ring is just magic, Isildur's Bane, what Frodo increasingly is discovering, the awful and heavy burden of bearing the Ring, and so he thinks the Ring can and should be used like a weapon in the coming war. When Frodo insistently refuses, Boromir tries to force the Ring from him, and Frodo can escape only by putting on the Ring and disappearing across the river. Only his servant, Sam Gamgee, figures out what has happened and so follows him, while the others remain on the west bank and find themselves attacked by a band of orcs. The fellowship thus is broken, and the first volume ends.

It is a very good book, *The Fellowship of the Ring,* the one that most improves with each rereading. There are slow places near the beginning—Bilbo's birthday party, the first meeting with the elves, especially the long interlude with Tom Bombadil—and, furthermore, nothing in it matches the best things in the next two volumes. But Tolken has great limitations as a writer about battles and the heroism they demand, and much of the last two volumes is about battles. As a writer about danger, however, Tolkien hardly has an equal, and in *The Fellowship of the Ring* he often wonderfully shows how a world that is expanding and becoming more resonant and understandable is at the same time becoming more dangerous. At the beginning, for instance, we have the Black Riders, who are like villains in children's books; we accept them literarily and so do not in the least feel endangered by them. By the end of *The Fellowship of the Ring,* however, though the Black Riders have not changed, our view and Frodo's view of them have, because we know so much more about the power of the Ring. Thus Tolkien's naming of them must change too, and they are no longer the Black Riders but the Nazgûl, the Ringwraiths, the nine mortal men doomed to die, wraiths and doomed because bound, because cut off from other men, without lore or any vital relation between present and past, the very definition of shadow: "a dark shape, like a cloud and yet not a cloud, for it moved far more swiftly, came out of the blackness in the South, and sped towards the Company, blotting out all light as it approached." Frodo has not only learned about the Riders and been wounded by one of them but also has learned a great deal about light in Lothlórien, and so: "Frodo felt a sudden chill running through him and clutching at his heart; there was a deadly cold, like the memory of an old wound, in his shoulder. He crouched down, as if to hide" (I, 403). There is no sense of heroism or of any possible adventure here. What it means to bear the Ring, to become more bound to it, is becoming clearer in the very process of its being felt as a chill and a terror from which one wishes to hide.

In the next two volumes Tokien splits his narrative. The first part of each describes the coming of the war to the lands west of the Anduin—to the forest of Fangorn, the plains of Rohan and Helm's Deep, Saruman's castle Isengard, and finally Gondor—as it happens to the members of the fellowship left on the west bank of the river: Aragorn, Merry, Pippin, Legolas, Gimli, and Gandalf who returns from his fight with the Balrog. The second half of each volume covers the trip of Frodo and Sam to Mordor. This journey, where the trilogy reaches its greatest heights, is vastly superior in quality to the story of the war in the west, and for reasons that allow us to see why of all the kinds of heroism the war entails, only the modern heroism of Frodo really strikes resonant chords in Tolkien's imagination. As Frodo becomes heroic, so too does Tolkien; both, as it were, cast off all trace of the mustiness of the lore and the snugness of the living in The Shire, and move into the present and face it heroically.

I have tried to indicate how much of Tolkien's success depends on the hobbits, and on the perspective he gives them, and us. The story of the Ring shows what everything in Tolkien's Middle Earth is all about, but that story only gains its full force when "shows" means "shows a hobbit." As a simple matter of arranging words, Tolkien can make the world "live" by taking all the dead metaphors he knows and using them as though they were not dead—"the sun climbed the sky," "the wind fell still," "now a star had descended into the very earth" —it is an easy enough device. But, as we have seen in the passages where Frodo sees Aragorn wrapped in memory and the Ringwraith blots out the sun, when a hobbit is there to see and to respond, then the dead metaphor really can come alive. Tolkien himself seems to have understood this only imperfectly. There are times when he magnificently makes the whole tissue of aliveness the whole issue of the war by making one of the hobbits see something freshly, and by making us see a formerly dead metaphor gain great resonance, and Tolkien must have known that our seeing depended on the hobbits' seeing. But there are many times, especially in the last two volumes, when the wind murmurs or the shadow blocks and all we have is ornamental language being manipulated, and Tolkien seems unaware of how tired his writing can seem, how simply literary and old-fashioned, when the language is not his instrument for making someone see how literary and old-fashioned things can reveal the present danger.

There is a doctrinal point that needs to be brought in here. In his Andrew Lang Lecture of 1939, "On Fairy-Stories," Tolkien writes about the importance of having us see the aliveness of the world:

> Recovery (which includes return and renewal of health) is a re-gaining—regaining of a clear view. I do not say "seeing things as they are" and involve myself with the philosophers, though I might venture to say "seeing things as we are (or were) meant to see them" —as things apart from ourselves. We need, in any case, to clean our windows; so that the things seen clearly may be freed from the drab blur of triteness or familiarity—from possessiveness. Of all faces those of our *familiares* are the ones both most difficult to play fantastic tricks with, and most difficult really to see with fresh attention, perceiving their likeness and unlikeness: that they are faces, and yet unique faces. This triteness is really the penalty of "appropriation": the things that are trite, or (in a bad sense) familiar, are the things that we have appropriated, legally or mentally. We say we know them. They have become like the things which once attracted us by their glitter, or their colour, or their shape, and we laid hands on them, and then locked them in our hoard, acquired them, and acquiring ceased to look at them. [*Tree and Leaf* (Boston, 1965), pp. 57–58]

Tolkien says the essay was written "when *The Lord of the Rings* was beginning to unroll itself and to unfold prospects of labour and exploration in yet unknown country as daunting to me as to the hobbits," and the essay and the trilogy cast revealing lights on each other. I have called this passage doctrinal, and thereby have implied a pejorative point about it, but it would do almost as well simply to say that what is stated here about Recovery is what is enacted in the trilogy by the hobbits, by us if we are willing, and, in ways I do not think Tolkien was aware of, by Tolkien himself.

We "recover" something when we no longer possess it familiarly, when we see with the freshness of our childish seeing. Fairy stories make us see with the freshness our culture had before it too possessed the world around it. The psychological point about ourselves as individuals is true, and in ways we all easily recognize. The point about fairy stories being an important way to recover is something we all perhaps can vaguely assent to, but for Tolkien it is of much graver importance than it is for most of us, because fairy stories, like philology, are his means of locating himself in the past such that he can say about the present that we all live behind dirty windows:

The incarnate mind, the tongue, and the tale are in our world coeval. The human mind, endowed with the powers of generalization and abstraction, sees not only *green-grass,* discriminating it from other things (and finding it fair to look upon), but sees that it is *green* as well as being *grass.* But how powerful, how stimulating to the very faculty that produced it, was the invention of the adjective: no spell or incantation in Faërie is more potent. And that is not surprising: such incantations might indeed be said to be only another view of adjectives, a part of speech in a mythical grammar. The mind that thought of *light, heavy, grey, yellow, still, swift,* also conceived of magic that would make heavy things light and able to fly, turn grey lead into yellow gold, and the still rock into a swift water. If it could do the one, it could do the other; it inevitably did both. When we can take green from grass, blue from heaven, and red from blood, we have already an enchanter's power . . . in such "fantasy," as it is called, new form is made; Faërie begins; Man becomes a sub-creator. [*Tree and Leaf,* p. 21–22]

To write fairy stories, then, is to go back as best one can to the moment when Faërie began, and *green* was taken from *grass* and put on a man's face to make a horror. It is to Recover, to see green and grass as though for the first time, to write about them as though just discovering the power of words, to know how things were meant to be seen.

It is not difficult to imagine that the acquisition of this idea of Recovery was a very important step in Tolkien's development. Anyone who has worked at all with old languages or older forms of our own language knows that at certain moments a word can convey the sense that that word was made so we could know how something was meant to be seen: the Mediterranean really is wine-dark, the North Sea hrim-cald. At those points in our civilization men took an especial care in seeing and naming what was important: sea, sky, tree, sword, king. To become a student of those words and the historical periods in which they were made is amost always to become convinced that we in our own time have lost that care. For Tolkien the doctrine of Recovery was justification for his withdrawal, because it meant that he was not just leaving but going, and finding. To be able to see in the study of words and, eventually, in the writing of fairy stories, a way away from the ravages and complications of a world that seems mostly proud of its capacity to make gadgets and complicated social organizations is to give an almost religious basis to the Myth of Lost Unity. When he gained his sense of Recovery, of seeing things as they were meant to be seen, Tolkien found what George Eliot's Mr. Casaubon could not find, a key to all mythologies, and Tolkien was no longer withdrawn because defeated but withdrawn because finding.

Tolkien could at this point have been content merely to relax, to use his idea of Recovery as a fortress behind which he could then have proceeded to invent, to spin out words and worlds, to be elvish. He could also have done what C. S. Lewis did, to stand up behind one of the turrets on the fortress and inform the world outside of all it was missing. When Tolkien says that hobbits are still around but we Big People cannot see them because we make too much noise, he is being both relaxed and preachy, as he is in some stretches of the last two volumes we will look at later. But for Tolkien the idea is not just an idea, or a dogma; it is enacted. In *The Hobbit* this is not yet the case. When Bilbo Baggins leaves The Shire he has "adventures," he learns the lore of dwarves and elves and dragons as lore, and Recovers nothing. But in *The Fellowship of the Ring* this acceptance of the familiar as natural and the unfamiliar as adventurous is precisely what Frodo must stop doing. So too Tolkien forces his reader to give up his sense that he knows all about Middle Earth because he has read Kenneth Grahame and Beatrix Potter and has heard of dwarves and elves and thinks he knows what kind of book has such creatures in them. The hobbits are possessive of their world—they bind it to themselves—at the beginnng, just as we are possessive about books with hobbits, and both we and the hobbits are made free by the story of the Ring "from the drab blur of triteness or familiarity." Among the hobbits, Frodo is much more strongly forced into this new seeing because he carries and is increasingly burdened by the Ring that embodies the final possessiveness, the ultimate power to bind things apart from ourselves to ourselves. Sauron's weakness is precisely that he is bound by the Ring and so he cannot imagine others seeing the world differently than he does—"That we should try to destroy the Ring itself has not yet entered into his darkest dream," says Gandalf.

What is most striking here is recognizing what this imagining did for Tolkien himself. Tolkien is not the first to have an idea of Recovery, but almost all the others who formulated such or similar ideas continued to see the present, the world of their own life, tritely, possessively. So much in the idea tempts one to be backward-looking—that is not its point, one presumes, but it must have seemed so to many—and seems to offer a way to withdraw from the present and go back into the vision of one's childhood and the life of the early years of the civilization. And Tolkien, when speaking in his own voice, can indeed be very trite and unseeing about the twentieth century:

> Not long ago—incredible though it may seem—I heard a clerk of Oxenford declare that he "welcomed" the proximity of mass-production robot factories, and the roar of self-obstructive mechanical traffic, because it brought his university into "contact with real life." He may have meant that the way men were living and working in the twentieth century was increasing in barbarity at an alarming rate, and that the loud demonstration of this in the streets of Oxford might serve as a warning that it is not possible to preserve for long an oasis of sanity in a desert of unreason by mere fences, without actual offensive action (practical and intellectual). I fear he did not. In any case the expression "real life" in this context seems to fall short of academic standards. The notion that motor-cars are more "alive" than, say, centaurs or dragons is curious; that they are more "real" than, say, horses, is pathetically absurd. How real, how startlingly alive is a factory chimney compared with an elm-tree: poor obsolete thing, insubstantial dream of an escapist! [*Tree and Leaf,* p. 62]

And he ends another paragraph of comparing various things mechanical with various things "natural" with "Fairy-stories might be, I guess, better Masters of Arts than the academic person I have referred to."

But there is no need to trust the artist when we can trust the tale. Tolkien's vision of modern life in the second and third volumes of the trilogy will not be precisely that of a Lawrence or a Joyce, but it need not be, and it very definitely is modern life that Tolkien is envisioning here, and Recovering as well. Supported by his immense learning of Old things, emboldened by the idea that we can clean our windows and see freshly, Tolkien was thereby enabled to do what no one else, so far as I know, who shared or shares his beliefs was able to do: come back to the present, face the very things that had made him withdraw in the first place. To make a hobbit see the vitality and irrelevance of the past and the immensity of the world and of the Dark Lord's desire to possess it, is to see oneself in the present anew, and to be a modern writer.

At the very end of *The Fellowship of the Ring,* as Frodo is fleeing from Boromir, he climbs to a tower and is offered a vision of the power of the Dark Lord that is made spectacular by the fact that Frodo is wearing the Ring. Looking north and west he sees all the signs of war: fires, orcs, hordes of warriors and horsemen. Then, looking south, down the river:

> But against Minas Tirith was set another fortress, greater and more strong. Thither, eastward, unwilling his eye was drawn. It passed the ruined bridges of Osgiliath, the grinning gates of Minas Morgul, and the haunted Mountains, and it looked upon Gorgoroth, the valley of terror in the Land of Mordor. Darkness lay there under the Sun. Fire glowed amid the smoke. Mount Doom was burning, and a great reek rising. Then at last his gaze was held: wall upon wall, battlement upon battlement, black, immeasurably strong, mountain of iron, gate of steel, tower of adamant, he saw it: Barad-dûr, Fortress of Sauron. All hope left him. [I, 417]

Wearing the Ring gives Frodo superhuman eyesight, able to see the valley on the other side of a mountain range, and to identify the materials used in the making of a fortress in that valley, two hundred miles away. But this power is really Sauron's, not Frodo's, and Tolkien must try to build his rhetoric so that each name, each detail, evokes the horror of that power such that to reach the place where Frodo's gaze is held, Barad-dûr, is to realize that all hope must leave him. Every step Frodo takes after this vision will be solemn, foolish, heroic. To see freshly now is to see reasons for despair—that is the truth of the Myth of Lost Unity operating here—and to go on is to try to move in despite of that despair or those reasons.

Before following Frodo on his journey, we must look at the parts of the last two volumes devoted to the war west of the Anduin, and to see what Tolkien does with the hobbits there. In one place Tolkien succeeds beautifully even though he is not dealing with the Ring, which he usually needs to make his literary language work. In the grand fourth chapter of *The Two Towers,* Merry and Pippin discover the ents in Fangorn. This is much the best detachable episode in the trilogy, the best passage, furthermore, to read aloud to those skeptical of Tolkien to show how he works. One quotation may be enough; Pippin is describing the eyes of the ent Treebeard:

> "One felt as if there was an enormous well behind them, filled up with ages of memory and long, slow, steady thinking; but their surface was sparkling with the present: like sun shimmering on the outer leaves of a vast tree, or on the ripples of a very deep lake. I don't know, but it felt as if something that grew in the ground—asleep, you might say, or just feeling itself as something between root-tip and leaf-tip, between deep earth and sky had suddenly waked up, and was considering you with the same slow care that it had given to its own inside affairs for endless years." [II, 66–67]

Here is Recovery and escape from ordinary vision because Pippin is seeing the likeness of animal and plant; Treebeard *is* like a tree, but like a lake, too, and a well, and a man. The world is not suddenly alive, but suddenly Pippin sees that it is, and has been for longer than he can guess, and "was considering you with the same slow care that it had given to its own inside affairs for endless years." To be able to write a phrase like that is to be abe to show that the aliveness of the world is not just belief for Tolkien. He has taken ancientness from forest, mind from man, color and life from sun and tree, and made an ent; "in such 'fantasy'," as Tolkien has said, "new form is made; Faërie begins; Man becomes a sub-creator."

Unfortunately, much more often in these sections we have something like this, Merry's meeting with Théoden, King of the Mark of Rohan, outside Saruman's castle:

> "My people came out of the North long ago," said Théoden. "But I will not deceive you: we know no tales about hobbits. All that is said among us is that far away, over many hills and rivers, live the halfling folk that dwell in holes in sand-dunes. But there are no legends of their deeds, for it is said that they do little, and avoid the sight of men, being able to vanish in a twinkling; and they can change their voices to resemble the piping of birds. But it seems that more could be said."
>
> "It could indeed, lord," said Merry.

"For one thing," said Théoden, "I had not heard that they spouted smoke from their mouths."

"That is not surprising," answered Merry; "for it is an art which we have not practised for more than a few generations. It was Tobold Hornblower, of Longbottom in the Southfarthing, who first grew the true pipe-weed in his gardens, about the year 1070 according to our reckoning. How old Toby came by the plant . . ."

"You do not know your danger, Théoden," interrupted Gandalf. "These hobbits will sit on the edge of ruin and discuss the pleasures of the table, or the small doings of their fathers, grandfathers, and great-grandfathers, and remoter cousins to the ninth degree, if you encourage them with undue patience." [II, 163]

It is not Théoden who is unduly patient, but Tolkien, who loves to indulge himself, with the trite vision of hobbits discussing the pleasures of tobacco while sitting on the edge of ruin. Merry is not a perceiver here, but a performer, so there is nothing interesting for Théoden to Recover either. While this is only irritating, a betrayal of some pact an attentive reader thought he had made with Tolkien to use his hobbits as Recoverers, it goes along with something worse, useful only for showing the heroism Tolkien cannot write well about, the better to show the heroism he can.

The men in Tolkien's world are all cast in rather ancient molds—the Riders of Rohan are like Dark Age Germanic tribes; the citizens of Gondor live in a decaying Alexandria or Constantinople. So their heroism is also ancient: stern, solemn, filled with belief in portents and in absolute loyalty to tribe and city:

"It is not strong," said Faramir. "I have sent the company of Ithilien to strengthen it, as I have said."

"Not enough, I deem," said Denethor. "It is there that the first blow will fall. They will have need of some stout captain there."

"There and elsewhere in many places," said Faramir, and sighed. "Alas for my brother, whom I too loved!" He rose. "May I have your leave, father?" And then he swayed and leaned upon his father's chair.

"You are weary, I see," said Denethor. "You have ridden fast and far, and under shadows of evil in the air, I am told."

"Let us not speak of that!" said Faramir.

"Then we will not," said Denethor. "Go now and rest as you may. Tomorrow's need will be sterner." [III, 88]

This is so bad that it already seems like an S. J. Perelman parody, and Tolkien is capable of going on for pages like this, without pause for breath or blinking. This Old World of Men is very important to Tolkien in one sense, and he works very hard to have it seem important and impressive. But he simply knows nothing about men, or knows them only through books, and so all he can do is copy down their manners as he has read of them. The fact that he does better with elves and dwarves, and that he does best of all with his own inventions, the hobbits and ents, shows how far he had withdrawn—it is not difficult to see that he intended no irony when he said that a centaur is more "real" than an automobile. The price he had to pay, we can see, is that he is ignorant of men and unaware of his igno-rance. So we have, for a while in the second volume and for long stretches at the beginning of the third, false language and false manner that hurts everything; faced with Denethor and Faramir and the others, Pippin and Merry can either clown before them or else talk as they do, which is no choice at all.

To be sure, even the worst sections "fit" into Tolkien's whole conception, though that is nowhere near enough to save them. What keeps them moving is the fullness of Tolkien's intuition about evil, which told him that when Sauron resumed his ancient seat it was not only in Mordor that the shadows lengthened: those lesser than Sauron are smaller, even pettier, in their aims, but no less malicious. Saruman the White Wiz-ard studied Sauron and was corrupted, and so he tried to set himself up as rival conqueror and hunter after the Ring. He enlisted orcs and wolves; he subverted King Théoden of Rohan with a despairing counselor; he had trees cut down wantonly in the forest of Fangorn and thereby aroused the anger of Treebeard the ent; he corrupted some small town toughs far north, in Bree and in The Shire, and had them destroy willfully and meanly. Denethor, steward to the vacant throne of Gondor, also wrestled with Sauron and was deceived, though in his case the deception led not to dreams of conquest but to despair and suicide. The conception does hold up remarkably well. Tolkien needs all Middle Earth to show how evil invades, corrupts, makes small and possessive, because for him evil is not merely Satanic. Unfortunately, to fulfill this conception Tolkien has to write about people and ways he only knows about rather than knows, and when that happens the writing stiffens and the humorlessness becomes enervating.

But no one has ever rejected *The Lord of the Rings* because of this. In the first place the worst parts come in the third volume and by then the grand expansiveness of the design is so fully felt that the dullness of the writing matters much less than it would had these pages come earlier. In the second place, there are some fine moments here: the end of the battle in Helm's Deep when the ents appear to surround Saruman's forces; the appearance of the Lord of the Nazgûl before the gates of Gondor; the last council, which is Gandalf's finest hour. In the third place, we know while reading these sections that they will eventually give way to the story of Frodo and Sam on the other side of the Anduin in which a much different kind of heroism and a vastly more impressive role for the hobbits can be found. Here all that is promised in the first volume is delivered, and with a rare and wonderful and modern majesty.

The moment we move back across the Anduin to Frodo and Sam, we have landscapes, and for these Tolkien has no background of received tradition on which to draw, and the books he read could not tell him how to proceed. At the end of *The Fellowship of the Ring*, as we have seen, Frodo has his frightening vision of Sauron's power while he is wearing the Ring, and that is enough to show him and us his task. Frodo is of course not big enough to stand up to Sauron; he cannot go on wearing the Ring without sooner or later giving away his presence, so we come down. No one sees the doors of Barad-dûr in a wasteland of crags and gullies called the Emyn Muil:

> The hobbits stood now on the brink of a tall cliff, bare and bleak, its feet wrapped in mist; and behind them rose the broken highlands crowned with drifting cloud. A chill wind blew from the East. Night was gathering over the shapeless lands before them; the sickly green of them was fading to a sullen brown. Far away to the right the Anduin, that had gleamed fitfully in sun-breaks during the day, was now hidden in shadow. But their eyes did not look beyond the River, back to Gondor, to their friends, to the lands of Men. South and east they stared to where, at the edge of the oncoming night, a dark line hung, like distant mountains of motionless smoke. [II, 209]

The route through this world must be made rather than followed, and here Sam Gamgee begins to become more Frodo's equal and less his servant. In the first volume Sam is very much the servant or the slave of the nineteenth century, thinking only of Master Frodo, speaking in a crude slang designed to keep him in his place, tending strictly to domestic and logistical details. But given the trackless wild country through which Frodo and Sam are now moving, all that must give way to an increasing sense of mutual dependency.

Even before this Frodo and Sam are aware that they are being followed, by Sméagol, Gollum, the owner of the Ring before Bilbo. Back at the Council of Elrond, Legolas had said that Sméagol had escaped from the wood-elves who had been his guardians after his capture by Aragorn. Earlier still, after losing the Ring, Sméagol had gone to Mordor, had been broken by Sauron, and had been let go to try to find the Ring again. Now he has tracked the fellowship south, and on the lonely Emyn Muil he meets Sam and Frodo unexpectedly, and they capture him. Sam is all for getting rid of Sméagol, but Frodo remembers something Gandalf had said long ago, back in The Shire:

"I have not much hope that Gollum can be cured before he dies, but there is a chance of it. And he is bound up with the fate of the Ring. My heart tells me that he has some part to play yet, for good or ill, before the end; and when that comes, the pity of Bilbo [in not killing Gollum] may rule the fate of many—yours not least." [I, 69]

What we have here is more than a prophetic device to frame the story, because Frodo knows more than what Gandalf said. Sam sees Sméagol only as a dangerous nuisance, slithery, cunning, and obviously given to lying. But Frodo himself is feeling the weight of the Ring and can see, as Sam cannot and as Gandalf only could guess, why Gollum is more an object of pity than of scorn or anger. The natural kinship of similar creatures and the common bondage of those who bear the Ring become one:

"And what would you swear?" asked Frodo.
"To be very very good," said Gollum. Then crawling to Frodo's feet he grovelled before him, whispering hoarsely: a shudder ran over him, as if the words shook his very bones with fear. "Sméagol will swear never, never, to let Him have it. Never! Sméagol will save it. But he must swear on the Precious."
"No! not on it," said Frodo, looking down at him with stern pity. "All you wish is to see it and touch it, if you can, though you know it would drive you mad. Not on it. Swear by it, if you will. For you know where it is. Yes, you know, Sméagol. It is before you."
For a moment it appeared to Sam that his master had grown and Gollum had shrunk: a tall stern shadow, a mighty lord who hid his brightness in grey cloud, and at his feet a little whining dog. Yet the two were in some way akin and not alien: they could reach one another's minds." [II, 225]

Because outcast, Frodo can create the possibility of society.

One can only hope that Tolkien himself realized that this relationship between Frodo and Sméagol, as seen by Sam, is his masterstroke. In his instinctive wish to save and tame Sméagol rather than destroy him, Frodo creates his heroism. Just as he could see the light of ancient Lothlórien in Aragorn's eyes and so discover and Recover a young but ancient lord, so here he Recovers himself by looking at Gollum at his feet and seeing "himself" there, seeing his own struggle to stay alive against the force of insuperably great power and temptation. He does not know what Sméagol has in mind, and knows he does not know, knows that in Sméagol he sees what he might become very easily if he does not struggle.

Gollum tells Frodo and Sam of his first trip to Mordor:

"Once, by accident it was, wasn't it, precious? Yes, by accident. But we won't go back, no, no!" Then suddenly his voice and language changed, and he sobbed in his throat, and spoke but not to them. "Leave me alone, *gollum!* You hurt me. O my poor hands, *gollum!* I, we, I don't want to come back. I can't find it. I am tired. I, we can't find it, *gollum, gollum,* no, nowhere. They're always awake. Dwarves, Men, and Elves, terrible Elves with bright eyes. I can't find it. Ach!" [II, 222]

Sméagol is the expert on the journey because he also is the historian, the one who knows where they are going because he has been there. In this scene Frodo can see the past just as he could in the one with Aragorn in Lothlórien. Needing all that Sméagol can tell them, even though he can only guess when he is being told the truth, Frodo knows he must let Gollum guide them.

They travel by night and sleep by day. They move out of the gullies of the Emyn Muil and into the Dead Marshes, where lights like candles flicker in stagnant pools. Earlier Strider and Gandalf and Galadriel had told Frodo where he was by saying what had happened there; here Sméagol brings the Dead Marshes to "life":

"Yes, yes," said Gollum. "All dead, all rotten. Elves and Men and Orcs. The Dead Marshes. There was a great battle long ago, yes, so they told him when Sméagol was young, when I was young before the Precious came. It was a great battle. Tall Men with long swords, and terrible Elves, and Orcses shrieking. They fought on the plain for days and months at the Black Gates. But the Marshes have grown since then, swallowed up the graves; always creeping, creeping." [II, 235]

We understand the landscape by understanding history, and it is as though we are living through a microcosmic history of the Western world, so that long after the great battles, the hobbits come wandering in the Dead Marshes with an untrustworthy guide.

Then a Nazgûl looms up, "a black shadow loosed from Mordor; a vast shape winged and ominous . . . sweeping the fen-reek with its ghastly wings." When it leaves "Frodo and Sam got up, rubbing their eyes, like children wakened from an evil dream to find the familiar night still over the world." Not knowing which is worse, the "unreal" Ringwraith or the "real" Dead Marshes, they cower and hope uncertainly during the day, groping their way at night. Then, one dawn, "Frodo looked round in horror":

Dreadful as the Dead Marshes had been, and the arid moors of Nomen's Land, more loathsome far was the country that the crawling day now slowly unveiled to his shrinking eyes. Even to the Mere of Dead Faces some haggard phantom of green spring would come; but here neither spring nor summer would ever come again. Here nothing lived, not even the leprous growths that feed on rottenness. The gasping pools were choked with ash and crawling muds, sickly white and grey, as if the mountains had vomited the filth of their entrails upon the lands about. High mounds of crushed and powdered rock, great cones of earth fire-blasted and poison-stained, stood like an obscene graveyard in endless rows, slowly revealed in the reluctant light. [II, 239]

Children, lost on the way to the mountains of their doom, led by a wretched sniveling wight—in this bleakest of landscapes, now recognizably modern, every act is heroic. The old terms for the struggle of good against evil—courage, loyalty, honor, magnificence, fortitude—are mostly irrelevant now. We notice another of those brilliant repetitions of a verb that makes a metaphor out of two nouns: the day and the mud both "crawl," so the light is indeed "reluctant." This is the industrial slag of midlands England, and No Man's Land in France in 1916, and so we come closer and closer to the modern evil that is Sauron:

> One Ring to rule them all, One Ring to find them,
> One Ring to bring them all and in the darkness bind them

The ordering of such a deathly landscape is Sauron's triumph, and we may well remember that the trilogy is called *The Lord of the Rings*. It is his book, and Frodo can only become more bound to the Ring the closer he comes to Sauron. In the Marshes, on these foul plains before the Black Gate, then down the dark road to Minas Morgul, up the stairs into the mountains to Cirith Ungol—all that way we have no fight against evil but the effort to stay alive and the consequences of giving in to death.

So, though Tolkien may have been enabled to return to this vision of modern life by withdrawing, Frodo cannot hold back at all. Inevitably he becomes less able to do more than merely walk, and Sam must assume command. Frodo's last great effort comes after the stairs have been climbed and the hobbits discover that Sméagol has reached his destination, and kept his promise not to deliver the Ring into Sauron's hands. Instead, he has taken them to Shelob, a giant spiderlike creature who lives in the caves near the top of the mountains:

> There agelong she had dwelt, an evil thing in spider-form, even such as once of old had lived in the Land of the Elves in the West that is now under the Sea, such as Beren fought in the Mountains of Terror in Doriath, and so came to Lúthien upon the green sward amid the hemlocks in the moonlight long ago. How Shelob came there, flying from ruin, no tale tells, for out of the Dark Years few tales have come. [II, 332]

The lore pours out wantonly, and we sense in the story of Beren a nostalgic glance on Tolkien's part back to a world he would much rather have lived in than the one he in fact did, but his sense of the present is so strong that the glance is recognizably and almost consciously placed as being nostalgic, and the lore that describes Shelob herself is anything but that:

> Already, years before, Gollum had beheld her, Sméagol who pried
> into all dark holes, and in past days he had bowed and worshipped
> her, and the darkness of her evil will walked through all the ways of
> his weariness beside him, cutting him off from light and from regret.
> And he had promised to bring her food. But her lust was not his lust.
> Little she knew of or cared for towers, or rings, or anything devised by
> mind or hand, who only desired death for all others, mind and body,
> and for herself a glut of life, alone, swollen till the mountains could
> no longer hold her up and the darkness could not contain her. [II,
> 332–333]

For a moment Sauron himself becomes kin to the hobbits,
caring for towers and rings, things devised by mind and hand
as he does, and, by comparison with Shelob, he is lofty in his
aims and lusts.

We then learn why Gollum has brought the hobbits here: "It
may well be, O yes, it may well be that when She throws away
the bones and the empty garments, we shall find it, we shall
get it, the Precious." Also, and inevitably, Frodo is becoming
like Gollum because of the burden of the Ring, himself almost
cut off from the light and from regret in all the ways of *his*
weariness. But it is still "almost": he has light, in a vial given
him by Galadriel, and he has a sword given him by Bilbo, so
he fights and wounds Shelob. But he falls too, and Sam is left
in a quandary. First he decides to go on alone with the Ring,
then he follows a group of orcs who have dragged Frodo's body
away, and finally, after resisting the temptation to put on the
Ring and become a hero, he climbs into a large chamber where
an orc stands with a whip over something lying on the floor.
Sam rushes at the orc and wins the fight only because the orc
accidentally falls through an open trapdoor. He then turns and
finds that it is Frodo on the floor, alive, but wounded and weak,
unable to move any farther with his burden without help. So
Sam must guide them now as Sméagol had done earlier, and
Frodo's greatness lies in part in his ability to know this, and

to seek and gain the help and community of others because he cannot move alone. But the price he is paying is awful, as we see when he discovers that Sam now has the Ring, and he almost falls to pieces, Gollum-like:

"Give it to me!" he cried, standing up, holding out a trembling hand. "Give it me at once! You can't have it!"

"All right, Mr. Frodo," said Sam, rather startled. "Here it is!" Slowly he drew the Ring out and passed the chain over his head. "But you're in the land of Mordor now, sir; and when you get out, you'll see the Fiery Mountain and all. You'll find the Ring very dangerous now, and very hard to bear. If it's too hard a job, I could share it with you, maybe?" [III, 188]

Sam senses how terrible the burden is going to be for Frodo and also, he wants the Ring, if only in some small way, for himself. But Frodo can only see in Sam's want a reflection of his own much greater want, cut off as he is from light and from regret, bound and binding:

"No, no!" cried Frodo, snatching the Ring and chain from Sam's hands. "No you won't, you thief!" He panted, staring at Sam with eyes wide with fear and enmity. [III, 188]

For that moment Frodo is himself Sméagol, but then:

A mist seemed to clear from his eyes, and he passed a hand over his aching brow. The hideous vision had seemed so real to him, half be-mused as he was still with wound and fear. Sam had changed before his very eyes into an orc again, leering and pawing at his treasure, a foul little creature with greedy eyes and slobbering mouth. But now the vision had passed. There was Sam kneeling before him, his face wrung with pain, as if he had been stabbed in the heart. [III, 188]

Tolkien cannot say that Frodo is heroic because for him the passing of the awful vision is simply and implicitly part of Frodo's goodness, his aliveness; no act of will is involved. But we know that modern heroism need not and probably even cannot carry with it any strong conscious sense of willed achievement or triumph; for Frodo *not* to "triumph" over Sam is his heroism. He is Frodo still.

The hideous moment passed, Sam helps Frodo on with an orc uniform and they escape the tower to the valley of the Morgai. Gandalf has lured Sauron's army out beyond the mountains by pretending that the combined forces of Rohan and Gondor and elsewhere can actually challenge the armies of the Dark Lord, and he has done this knowing that the only possible help he could provide Frodo, assuming that Frodo is still alive, is in that lure. Frodo and Sam watch Sauron's armies march past them and out to the Black Gate, so that the road to Barad-dûr is almost deserted, but Frodo is nonetheless almost helpless. Sam has to carry him part way up Mount Doom, the end of the journey, but when they reach the brink of the chasm where the Ring was forged, Sam hears Frodo, and in a voice "clearer and more powerful than Sam had ever heard him use":

> "I have come," he said. "But I do not choose now to do what I came to do. I will not do this deed. The Ring is mine!" And suddenly, as he set it on his finger, he vanished from Sam's sight. [III, 223]

If the story were Frodo's to shape to his will, all would be lost, his heroism at last unavailing, his binding to the Dark Lord complete. But it is not his. Suddenly Sméagol is there, knocking Sam down and pursuing the vanished Frodo. Sauron too leaps in response:

> From all his policies and webs of fear and treachery, from all his stratagems and wars his mind shook free; and throughout his realm a tremor ran, his slaves quailed, and his armies halted, and his captains suddenly steerless, bereft of will, wavered and despaired. . . . At his summons, wheeling with a rending cry, in a last desparate race there flew, faster than the winds, the Nazgûl, the Ringwraiths, and with a storm of wings they hurtled southwards to Mount Doom. [III, 223]

But too late, Gollum is there first, struggling with the invisible Frodo. Sauron once had lost the Ring when Isildur cut it from his hand, and so now Frodo, Lord of the Rings for a moment, is attacked:

Suddenly Sam saw Gollum's long hands draw upwards to his mouth; his white fangs gleamed, and then snapped as they bit. Frodo gave a cry, and there he was, fallen upon his knees at the chasm's edge. [III, 224]

Gollum shouts that the prize is his, "And with that, even as his eyes were lifted up to gloat on his prize, he stepped too far, toppled, wavered for a moment on the brink, and then with a shriek he fell." As the Ring falls to its doom the mountain shakes; outside

Towers fell and mountains slid; walls crumbled and melted, crashing down; vast spires of smoke and spouting steams went billowing up, up, until they toppled like an overwhelming wave, and its wild crest curled and came foaming down upon the land. [III, 224]

This is fairy tale, and the Ring must destroy Sauron's world apocalyptically. But it is Frodo and Sméagol—neither of whom is grand, neither of whom at that last moment sought the Ring's destruction—who are responsible. Wars have always been secondary in this struggle, and at the end even Frodo's modern heroism, which is of primary importance, is unavailing:

"Well, this is the end, Sam Gamgee," said a voice by his side. And there was Frodo, pale and worn, and yet himself again; and in his eyes there was peace now, neither strain of will, nor madness, nor any fear. His burden was taken away. [III, 224]

The phrasing of that last sentence is precise, as Frodo makes clear right away. His burden was taken from him by the only one whose need to make the Ring his own was at that moment greater than Frodo's own. Peaceful though he is now, Frodo is bound still, and he must seek solace and compassion for his bound companion Sméagol.

In the end they are rescued and returned, first to Gondor

where Aragorn is crowned, then to The Shire, where the hobbits discover to their surprise and outrage that Saruman's cronies have been wanton, tearing down trees, setting up petty governments. The trouble here can be righted, however. Saruman is discovered, conquered, exiled, and killed, and afterward trees can be planted again, Sam can marry Rosie Cotton, and even eventually become Mayor. But for Frodo all is unreal; he could not fight much against Saruman, his wounds cannot heal, his bondage cannot be broken, he cannot really settle down in The Shire, though he tries. Merry and Pippin are now lore-masters in The Shire, with their tales of Rohan and Gondor and battles. Frodo, however, "dropped quietly out of all the doings of the Shire, and Sam was pained to notice how little honour he had in his own country." In an earlier age, we may remember, heroic deeds were rewarded with instant glory and renown. The Faerie Queene could know of and honor the deeds of any of her knights almost the moment they happened. In Shakespearean tragedy the hero is never properly understood by those around him, but Hamlet is given a soldier's burial and Lear's death is greeted, as Empson says, "with a sort of hushed envy." But for Frodo none of that is possible: "It is gone for ever," he says, half in a dream, "and now all is dark and empty." So he leaves The Shire and goes westward to the Grey Havens where, with Gandalf and the faded elves, he sets out to sea. He knows that this "defeat" is natural, that he was part of an age that is passing, that he was one of the instruments of its passing indeed, and a securer of the world's living. There is bang, then, in the destruction of Mordor, but whimper too in Frodo's discovery that his wounds cannot heal on Middle Earth.

So Frodo is finally of his time, just as Tolkien is of his, and both realize (Frodo perhaps better than Tolkien about this) that one can only live in the time in which he was born. Tolkien could write of Gandalf and elves and of ancient men, but because they were not of his time he could write of them only what he had read in books, and the resultant literariness never leaves them. Likewise he writes so wonderfully about Frodo because, by comparison with the others, Frodo is a modern, his landscape, his challenge, and his heroism all distinctively belonging to no earlier century.

"That virtue and intelligence are alike lonely," writes Empson at the end of *Pastoral*, "and that good manners are therefore important though an absurd confession of human limitations, do not depend on a local class system; they would be recognised in a degree by any tolerable society." Temperamentally there is little resemblance between Empson and Tolkien, for Empson is subtle and cheerful and pagan and Tolkien none of these. But Empson's sentence does as well in describing Tolkien's and Frodo's greatness as anything Tolkien himself might have tried to say in summary. When we look at *The Lord of the Rings* in retrospect, we see that Sauron cannot openly affect Frodo at all; valor and physical strength and the very idea of battles are not germane here. Sauron can bind Frodo only as Frodo binds himself and seeks to bind others, his virtue and his intelligence alike lonely, cut off from lore and aid. The landscape through which Frodo must move is Sauron's most powerful weapon, a valley of the shadow of death, and we know there are ways to see the book as being Christian and Frodo as a pilgrim. But the landscape is really much closer, as we have said, to the wasteland, the valley of ashes, and the nightmare cities of Rupert Birkin and Henry Adams than it is to the arbitrary and unclear landscapes of Spenser or Bunyan. Where Tolkien differs most from other modern writers is not in what he sees but in what he understands must be done.

If Frodo's virtue and intelligence must be lonely, then one way of describing his heroism is to reaffirm his "good manners," though that is not the most obvious way of saying it. In different ways both Sam Gamgee and Sméagol are better equipped than is Frodo to carry the Ring to Mordor. But they are also less virtuous, less intelligent, less courteous; they cannot sympathize or trust each other and they cannot understand Frodo's sympathy and trust for them both. Sam serves Frodo, Sméagol serves the Ring, and only Frodo can serve the heroic idea of the Ring's destruction. Yet though neither Sam nor Sméagol is of Frodo's stature, he is lost without them, and he knows it. His good manners toward both is an absurd confession of limitations of any so lonely, yet in his love for Sam and compassion for Sméagol he finds himself. As long as Frodo is thus openly dependent, the urge to possessiveness can be quelled by his good manners and his recognition of the blessed and cursed otherness of his servant and his wretched guide.

In a moment of respite on the stairs of Cirith Ungol, just before Sméagol takes them to Shelob, Frodo and Sam talk about the songs that will be sung of them after all this is over. Sam does most of the talking, but Frodo makes the key points: (1) "You may know, or guess, what kind of a tale it is, happy-ending or sad-ending, but the people in it don't know. And you don't want them to." (2) "[The great tales] never end as tales. . . . But the people in them come, and go when their part's ended." (3) "Why, Sam . . . to hear you somehow makes me as merry as if the story was already written. But you've left out one of the chief characters: Samwise the stouthearted. . . . 'And Frodo wouldn't have got far without Sam, would he. . . .'" (4) "It's no good worrying about him [Sméagol] now. . . . We couldn't have got so far, not even within sight of the pass, without him, and so we'll have to put up with his ways. If he's false, he's false." [II, 321–322]

We are in a story, but we have as yet no storyteller, only ourselves—such is Frodo's meaning and it is rather too much for Sam. But Sam does recognize the grim and yet almost sublime equipoise of Frodo's weary generosity—I cannot come upon this pending passage without feeling simply grateful to Frodo for being what he is here—and so, too, for a moment, does Sméagol.

Right after this conversation Frodo and Sam fall asleep and
Sméagol discovers them thus, peaceful in each other's arms:

A strange expression passed over his lean hungry face. The gleam
faded from his eyes, and they went dim and grey, old and tired. A
spasm of pain seemed to twist him, and he turned away, peering
back up towards the pass, shaking his head, as if engaged in some in-
terior debate. Then he came back, and slowly putting out a trembling
hand, very cautiously he touched Frodo's knee—but almost the touch
was a caress. For a fleeting moment, could one of the sleepers have
seen him, they would have thought that they beheld an old weary
hobbit, shrunken by the years that had carried him far beyond his
time, beyond friends and kin, and the fields and streams of youth, an
old starved pitiable thing. [II, 324]

This is Sméagol's finest moment, and so it must be Frodo's and
Tolkien's finest moment too. Beyond friends and kin, old, tired,
Sméagol loves the specialness that is Frodo's care of him. This
love is almost without its like in our modern literature, because it is not filial or sexual but the tentative, unbelieving
response to a caring so unlikely it seems heroic even to Gollum.
It suggests the story might go differently, but not just Frodo
and Sméagol are bound here, possessive, but Sam as well. He
wakes before Frodo and automatically accuses Sméagol of
being a sneak. By the time Frodo wakes Gollum is back to his
old whining and sniveling self, ready once again to lead the
hobbits to Shelob.

Frodo's uniqueness and greatness lie in his way of being returned to himself as he sees a light shine in others; no one else
in the trilogy, really, can do this more than fitfully. He faces
the strongest of temptations to give in and to make the world
only what he says it is, but of all the characters he shows fewest
signs of having yielded to that temptation. He turns out into
the world and so finds a means of self-knowledge, and in his
scarred and beautiful relation with Sméagol he finds himself
and lives by the light of the self he finds. He is saved from the
worst ravages of the Ring because of his lovely courtesy that

lets others be themselves and unbound, and therein finds a way to be heroic. This heroism may not be what *The Lord of the Rings* is all about, and almost certainly it is not all that it is good for, in Tolkien's scheme or anyone else's, but it is the cornerstone of its greatness. Over and over we are told of the prices that must be paid when one is called upon to pay them, and over and over Gandalf, Aragorn, Merry, Pippin, Faramir, and others pay such prices when they are demanded. But these are ancient heroisms, ancient prices and payments, and Frodo's heroism is not, and as all the "great deeds" are chronicled, we respond to what is most like ourselves because Tolkien does too. We see, without in the least needing to make that seeing into a formulation, what this version of modern heroism is and can be: lonely, lost, frightened, loving, willing, and compassionate—to recognize the otherness of others while reaching out to assert our common livingness.

*   *   *

Tolkien published *The Lord of the Rings* in the mid-fifties, when he was nearing retirement. Shortly thereafter word began to filter down from people who may or may not have actually talked to Tolkien, that he was at work on something called *The Silmarillion,* which was also about Middle Earth. That Tolkien has occupied this place of his with far more than ever got into the tale of the Rings is clear enough from the hundred pages of appendixes that recount tales and give genealogies of hobbits, dwarves, elves, and men that were published at the end of the third volume of the trilogy. Presumably *The Silmarillion,* which may be prose or poetry or written in Elvish, concerns itself with some of this material. In the meantime, perhaps in response to public cry for "more Tolkien," he allowed to be published *The Adventures of Tom Bombadil,* an exceedingly bad collection of hobbit poems; it barely makes a good Christmas gift for members of the Tolkien cult. Nor should one find hope in the promised *Silmarillion*. At this writing Tolkien is still alive and said to be at work, but he is also in his late seventies and there is no earthly reason why he should not be working in ways that amuse him privately and that maintain his withdrawal from all he finds abhorrent in contemporary life. Empson may speak of once again facing unresolved conflicts when one is "seriously old," but Tolkien's passage always was far different from Empson's. The conflicts of Empson's youth he faced, heroically, with his pastoral triumph over them. Then, as he has said, the conflicts were reduced or transformed into practical questions, and, as we have seen, into doctrinal answers. Tolkien, however, had to run from his conflicts, to find in his imagined Middle Earth Recovery not just things "as they were meant to be seen" but recovery from the oppressive wounds of the war, and it was only in fairy tale, in myth, that he could face and resolve the conflicts at all. It took years to accomplish this, Tolkien was writing about the pains and terrors of his twenties when he was in his fifties, and that in itself is miracle enough that one should not hope or ask that he should ever try again. Tolkien has never said anything to lead one to believe that he recognizes that what is greatest and most poignant in his imagination is its modernity, and anyone who tried to convince him of this would be both foolish and rude. Anyone who has read the denigrators of *The Lord of the Rings* knows how silly they can be when they try to make Tolkien out to be dangerously old-fashioned. The latest to come to my attention is by Catherine Stimpson in the Columbia Essays on Modern Writers series, and it makes great point of the fact that the women in Tolkien are not much, that Shelob herself is a terrifying Giant Mother, that symbolism of white and black, light and dark, is pernicious in our day and age. That all this is true enough in its way is only another way of saying that it is irrelevant, that except for his two lectures everything Tolkien wrote outside the trilogy is not very good, that *The Silmarillion* is not a work one can hope much for if one is not a cultist—that, in other words, *The Lord of the Rings* is something of a miracle.

One can only guess, but it does seem that Tolkien's having had to take over thirty years before he could write his heroic book about war hurt its chances of being read properly. Had he been able to write *The Lord of the Rings* at the same age that Lawrence and Empson were when they wrote their greatest books, the year would have been about 1922, and the way it rises to its greatest heights in its response to the circumstances of the modern world and the Great War should have been clear to many. By the fifties the modern age had passed and the war that did most to define it had been forgotten or else never known by those who read and adored Tolkien, and so *The Lord of the Rings* became a book fearfully abused. It afforded a withdrawal that was far less understandable or necessary than Tolkien's own in the years after 1918; it afforded ways of being chic and adolescently melancholy, too, and what it afforded beyond that was misunderstood or ignored.

For such a failure, however, we should not blame only the members of the Tolkien cult. This much is true about the heroism of our century, and it is probably truer of our century than of some earlier ones: it is rare, and it is not easy to recognize. A great deal of this book has concerned itself in one way or another with the reasons why this should be so, and if readers of Tolkien in the fifties and sixties could not see how he and Frodo are modern heroes, let us add right away that no one seems to know, as yet, what postmodern or contemporary heroism is. I can only hope here that something like recognition for Tolkien's heroism, and for Lawrence's and Empson's as well, can at least show that we had heroes as recently as a generation ago and that there is no necessary reason why we will never have any again.

Tolkien and Frodo Baggins

History is always creating the conditions of chaos, and for most people, undoubtedly, some grim or comic adaptation to those conditions is all that is possible or necessary. But it is in our nature to seek to reply to history as well as to acknowledge it, and if it is still true that the hero resembles the fool because he does what most of us would never do, we can and should understand that fact. Lawrence and Empson and Tolkien are not likely heroes, but then few ever are. In any age there is much to admire that is not heroic at all, but we deny much that has been achieved and much that may still be possible if we once imagine there can be no more heroes. Most intelligent and sensitive people at any time despair of the present and the future, and with good reason, too. But it is not the only way.

V. *Afterword*

The proper conclusion to any story is its own ending, and the stories told in this book have, I hope, ended. They have, nonetheless, been put into an intellectual frame, loosely constructed though it be, and it should be possible to suggest some useful limits for an inquiry into modern heroism. The best way to do this is to look at some other figures who seem on the face of it to be as likely candidates for the name of modern hero as Lawrence, Empson, and Tolkien—namely, Henry Adams, Yeats, and Conrad's Lord Jim. The aim is not to exhaust the possibilities, but only to indicate that there are limits to this kind of inquiry which common sense and our awareness of what is important can help to dictate. The difficulty with dealing briefly with figures as interesting as Adams, Yeats, and Jim is that the brevity of the treatment must tend to obviate the case. It has been necessary to move slowly in describing Lawrence, Empson, and Tolkien in order to render them as heroes, and had I tried simply to summarize my point about any of them I cannot imagine anyone would find them heroic. Still, the effort can be useful, if only to show that if the term "hero" is honorific it is not the only one we have. If, as it seems to me, Adams, Yeats, and Jim are not best described as modern heroes, they are not one bit less important for that reason.

Afterword

The last chapters of *The Education of Henry Adams* give us the earliest full version I know of the Myth of Lost Unity. Adams in these chapters is trying to account for the failure of his education to prepare him for the multiplicity and chaos of the twentieth century, and he has from the beginning made clear that for him both "education" and "failure" are sufficiently lofty terms to guarantee that we are not just inquiring into the details of one man's life. He also offers ample reasons why he might have given in to the mad powers of an industrial society and to despair of any possibilities for education remaining to anyone; the description of New York at the beginning of the last chapter of *The Education* is one of the first and most powerful evocations of the modern wasteland. Finally, Adams locates in the figure of the Virgin at Chartres a symbol of a world whose unity was lost in the years between 1200 and 1900 which he speaks of with reverence and nostalgia. The basic ingredients of a modern sensibility, thus, are all here. And along with them we see the impulse not to give in or despair or withdraw:

The movement from unity into multiplicity, between 1200 and 1900, was unbroken in sequence, and rapid in acceleration. Prolonged one generation longer, it would require a new social mind. As though thought were common salt in indefinite solution, it must enter a new phase subject to new laws. Thus far, since five or ten thousand years, the mind had successfully reacted, and nothing yet proved that it would fail to react—but it would need to jump. [*The Education of Henry Adams* (New York, 1931) p. 498]

Adams believed civilization would explode and he even spent a good deal of time trying to calculate the exact date of its doom. But he also believed it was possible to reply to the terrifying and accelerating motions of history, though the jump the mind would have to take just to adapt to the surrounding chaos would be a heroic leap indeed. Throughout the years of what he called his posthumous existence, Adams restlessly peered and searched for ways to bear up and then to defy the terms of the Myth he had created.

If all one were interested in was proving the existence of something like heroism in this century, the later chapters of *The Education* and many of Adams's letters would offer fruitful territory. But the game is not worth the candle; we could make a modern hero out of Adams, but finally it would be distorting to our sense of him to do so. If we survey Adams's work and locate what is most important in it, then that part we might call heroic does not loom very large. The superbly confident historian of the great *History,* the charming autobiographer of the opening six or eight chapters of *The Education,* the master unraveler of character of "The New York Gold Conspiracy," and the London chapters of *The Education*—there are many great Henry Adamses and most of these are not particularly amenable to analysis along heroic lines. The glimpses we get in the later work of a man defeated yet undefeatable, in despair yet curious and peering, are glimpses of a hero, but only glimpses nonetheless. We simply cannot say enough of the necessary things about Henry Adams by trying to make him into a modern hero.

The case of Yeats is different. If we want a heroic Yeats we will look at all the major poems, and I have often been tempted to try to say something new about these poems by writing about Yeats as a modern hero. Here we have someone who began his career, and not wholly in vain, by seeking for an old theme of ancient heroism embodied in Fergus, Cuchulain, Oisin, and the Countess Cathleen, and who also wrote a number of versions of the Myth of Lost Unity, of which "The Second Coming" is the most famous and *The Trembling of the Veil* is perhaps the most complete. But something happened. As he found more and more reasons to retreat from the modern world and to become the singing bird of an ancient emperor in Byzantium, he also found, apparently to his own surprise, access to great new energies that did not want to retreat into ancient heroism, nostalgia, or a palace of art. Alongside the despair and sense of loss we find toughness and defiance. The energy and force with which Yeats locates the foul rag and bone shop of his heart is itself a kind of countermotion to the absurdity of his decrepit age. Never, he says, had he more expected the impossible.

But to call this heroism is only a kind of rhetorical jugglery. The term "heroic" is only another name for qualities in the major poems we have long since recognized by other terms, and Yeats's energy and defiance do not so much imply a triumph over despair as they are his way of expressing it. In the triumph we have located in our three heroes, we have seen communities created, and in Yeats all the communities are in the past. The "we" that were the last romantics are dead, gone, and all is changed, the high horse is now riderless; if nothing drastic is done the town will lie beaten flat, but nothing drastic *is* done or can be done; the glittering eyes of the Chinamen who stare on the tragic scene are gay. We come closest to the bottom of the depths of this great man, I think, when we see him as a writer of epitaphs. He knew about communities, and he would have agreed that it would take a hero to create communities now, but his were lost and any attempt by a critic to claim that Yeats had somehow regained them is bound to seem irrelevant, willful, discourteous.

The case of Conrad's Lord Jim is different still from either Adams's or Yeats's. Though we can hardly call either Jim or Marlow historians, in the first half of the novel both are facing or trying to face the implications of their discovery that the unity they had presumed to govern their world was shattered when Jim jumped from the *Patna*. For Jim the unity had been provided by a boy's book image of himself as a romantic hero; for Marlow it was derived from the strength and strictness of the code of honor among men of adventure and the sea. When

Jim jumps, both men are in effect thrust out of their old world and into another that we can quite easily, given our perspective, call modern. Jim is wonderful, Jim is one of us, yet he jumped, and as Marlow tries to fathom that fact he speaks in sentences as confused, as intelligently unable, as those of the speaker of *The Waste Land*. But Marlow never faces the implications of his confusion, Jim tries to deny he was ever confused at all, and Conrad himself seems not to know where to take his story after the first long dialogues between Jim and Marlow are over. Had Conrad pushed on, had he, in other words, fully grasped the implications of the unity's having been lost, he might have created a modern hero, and he almost certainly would have written a better second half to his novel. Instead, by giving Jim a haven on Patusan where he can redeem himself at least in the terms of the boy's books that shaped his imagination in the first place, by letting Jim become a romantic hero, by giving Marlow a story he can tell mistily and comfortably, Conrad reverts to a distinctively nineteenth-century kind of romance and heroism, one we associate with Robert Louis Stevenson or perhaps Alexandre Dumas. What Conrad shows us in *Lord Jim* is that his imagination can move either in the direction of romantic heroism or in the direction of a modern agony, but it cannot do both at once. The really modern landscape of the London of *The Secret Agent* is one totally without any possibility of heroic action; the romantic heroism of Axel Heyst in *Victory* is, like Jim's on Patusan, not in the least modern.

In the case of Henry Adams, then, the modern hero is identifiable but plays a small part in the total career; in that of Yeats the term "hero" is not the one we most need to identify his central achievement; in that of Conrad and Jim the part that is heroic and the part that is modern never come together. I doubt if this exhausts the possible ways in which likely looking modern heroes fail to seem worth entering into these lists, but perhaps it does indirectly suggest two points I have been trying to make all along; there *is* something special about Lawrence, Empson, and Tolkien, for all they seem such an unlikely grouping, and it is probably beside the point to try to make a precise definition of modern heroism and then consider all the writers who fit the definition in one way or another. Fortunately criticism can be blessed with having a term like "heroism" to describe qualities it values without diminishing the importance of other terms and other values. The problem is finding out which ones to use when.

What there is that is special about Lawrence, Empson, and Tolkien, then, cannot be reduced to a definition, but it is possible, nonetheless, to make some generalizations about them in the light of what has just been said about Adams, Yeats, and Jim. In the first place, none of the three was eager to be a hero, though that is a quality they share with most of the human race and with some earlier heroes who felt that only a wretched spright could thrust their heroic tasks upon them. Nor, in the second place, did any of the three ever want to be modern, unless that can be said of the very young Empson. With Lawrence and Tolkien this aversion to their own time amounted to an almost hysterical hatred—you can sense great depths of contempt in Tolkien, and something like physical revulsion in Lawrence, when they think of cities, cars, coal mines. If this is not quite the case with Empson, we do not find in him any desire to accommodate his fastidious waywardness to the modern temper or to any ruling fashion. Lawrence, Empson, and Tolkien never really belonged, or wanted to belong, and their loneliness is not that of an alienated modern but that of a unique, isolated, temperament. There is, indeed, a central quality in this loneliness that perhaps can help us reach out toward some more inclusive statement about the three.

The quality I speak of begins with a certain imaginative rootedness in each writer. I call this rootedness imaginative rather than literal or geographic not because geography does not play a major part in creating the roots but because the pull of the roots could be felt regardless where the literal self might geographically be. This is most striking, perhaps, in the case of Lawrence, the world traveler, the wonderful travel writer, who spent as many of his mature years as he could manage outside of England, yet who never really left home. The visitor to the Lawrence country in and around Eastwood in western Nottinghamshire cannot but be struck by the narrowness of Lawrence's imaginative geography. The journey from Lawrence's house to Jessie Chambers's farm, the Haggs, which Paul Morel takes so often on foot and bicycle, is about three miles. Along the way, as one is reconstructing the landscape of *Sons and Lovers* in his head, one stumbles, as it were, on Lamb Close, the Shortlands of *Women in Love,* on Moor Green Reservoir, into which Birkin throws stones at the image of the moon, and, by one route, on Felley Mill, the Strelley Mill of *The White Peacock.* Four miles from Lawrence's home in another direction is Cossall, the Cossethay of *The Rainbow.* From there the marsh is only a few hundred yards away in one direction and the factories of Ilkeston are easily visible a few miles away in the other, so one can locate all the essential places of the novel just by turning around in the main street of the village. Seven miles away is Nottingham, where Paul Morel works and Alvina Houghton of *The Lost Girl* lives. This landscape, which would be moving even had Lawrence never written about it, with its farms giving way to small forests, with the landed gentry living almost next to the slums of the miners, with the mines themselves pitting the landscape here and there, dominates the three major novels, all the early stories, many of the later stories, *The White Peacock,* much of *Aaron's Rod,* all of *Lady Chatterley's Lover.* We can, if we like, and occasionally we should, associate Lawrence with some other places: Mexico and New Mexico, the Italian Alps, Cornwall. But these places

are all imaginatively alien to Lawrence, and much of the splendor of his writing about them depends on this alienness. Cen-
trally, crucially, his imagination never left home, and he was
saying more than perhaps he realized when he wrote Jessie
Chambers's younger brother in a very late letter that "whatever
else I am, I am somewhere still the same Bert who rushed with
such joy to the Haggs." There is no reason to believe that
Adams or Conrad or Eliot or Ford or Stevens could have written
a sentence anything like that.

Empson's relation to his roots is different except for its imaginative tenacity. We think of such a man as living inside his
own head and in his reading, and, when we compare him with
Lawrence especially, we note how little geography there is in
Empson's writing and how all the landscapes are literary or
symbolic. Nonetheless it is important to note that he said, when
leaving China for the last time and forced to return perma-
nently to England, that if he had to teach in "that country" he
would do so only in his native Yorkshire. It is doubtful if Sheffield, where he has lived for the last twenty years, is home for
him the way Eastwood is home for Lawrence or Oxfordshire is
home for Tolkien, but Sheffield is very obviously for him not
Oxbridge or London or part of any kind of establishment.
There are stories of how young admirers have found it difficult
to visit Empson, and of how it used to be that one saw him best
by accompanying him on his marches to the Early Warning
Station to protest English complicity in atomic weapons and
the Cold War. The image such stories create of him, striding
on the moors, lonely and resolute, seems exactly right. Empson
is in everything he writes charming and witty, but not cosmopolitan or urbane. He consistently has resented and resisted
fashions, and he is so obviously apart and alone that when he
does report on a current mode he speaks as an outsider, as one
who gathers his news by hearsay, as one who is at home some
place far away from where the news is happening. Speaking as

one who has enjoyed the graciousness of his hospitality, I can report that a pilgrimage to see Empson is just that.

In Tolkien, we know, the whole question of rootedness is recurrent and central. It is true that the hobbits grow imaginatively rusty in The Shire, and that Tolkien had to be uprooted from *his* Shire in order to make his heroic tale both great and modern, but these facts in themselves testify to the strength of the entness in Tolkien, the firmness of his roots in the Oxfordshire landscape. In an interview with Henry Resnick, Tolkien said:

Well, my parents both came from Birmingham in England. I happened to be born there [Bloemfontein, South Africa] by accident. But it had this effect; my earliest memories are of Africa, but it was alien to me, and when I came home, therefore, I had for the countryside of England both the native feeling and the personal wonder of somebody who comes to it. I came to the English countryside when I was about 3½ or 4—it seemed to me wonderful. If you really want to know what Middle-earth is based on, it's my wonder and delight in the earth as it is, particularly the natural earth. [Cited in Lin Carter, *Tolkien: A Look Behind "The Lord of the Rings"* (New York, 1969), p. 8]

Tolkien is so closely tied to his own landscape, furthermore, that he can extend his admiration only toward those who long for home, and he can convey much of his sense of evil by having Sauron and the Black Riders and the orcs and Saruman want to make living things homeless, in effect, by reducing every place to the same place. And when Tolkien relaxes, he becomes not only an inferior writer, but very much an Oxfordshire writer, as in the coziest parts of *The Hobbit, Smith of Wooten Major, Father Giles of Ham,* and *The Adventures of Tom Bombadil.*

All three writers, then, begin or sustain themselves in a fixed, imaginative landscape, and in the case of two of the three that landscape is also fixed geographically. The particular circumstances whereby each came to accept the terms of the Myth of Lost Unity vary in each case, but the results are similar in all three. For them, being uprooted, alien, lost, is not simply a matter of the whole culture or of the impersonal forces of history, but it is also a personal wrenching from a past known and felt to be fixed and whole. It might well be that the strange and indirect ways in which each becomes a historian is the result of their not originally feeling the unity that was lost as a cultural matter at all, but as a more private tearing loose from the early landscape. Unquestionably the original rootedness gave to each some measure of security and strength, but with none of the three is this strength simple or pastoral. Mixed with the rootedness are anger, fear, and frustration, nakedly expressed in Lawrence, clearly visible in Empson, easy enough to postulate in Tolkien, and these feelings too are personal rather than cultural. Thus, as the individual is uprooted, as the terms of the modern world and the Myth become known to him, the answering cry, the anguish, the protest are simultaneously those of a person and of a culture. At that moment heroism becomes possible, when the cry is not allowed to die down and accept anguish, and the private energy insists that protest or defiance is a necessity. That we know many others had experiences similar to Lawrence's, Empson's, and Tolkien's can only show us that there is mystery involved in heroic replies that no critical definition can possibly explain.

I realize that these statements about uprootedness are not as clear as one would hope for. Partly the difficulty is a shortage or absence of the kind of biographical details that might illustrate the case more clearly, and partly the difficulty is that the matter *is* a mystery, that the experience being described is a cavern that is at best difficult to illumine. Perhaps a comparison or two will help. If we think of the central modern voices as belonging to Eliot, Pound, and Joyce, we can say also that they are central because they were right for their time, in and of the modern experience. The terms of the Myth of Lost Unity we are most accustomed to are their terms, and it gave them their voices. They could sustain their own sense of loss with their modernist acceptance of loss; they could fit into their culture and thereby could do a great deal to create it. We might then think of those who feel the rightness of their roots and the wrongness of the modern world so deeply and easily that they suffered no pain or shock as they withdrew. They could turn their back on their own century, and mock it, or not accept it, or even agree that they were living in it. Most of our examples of this kind of person lie outside literature or even outside articulated experience because they were silent, but the other Inklings beside Tolkien—C. S. Lewis, Charles Williams, and Dorothy Sayers especially—offer examples, and we can find an almost ideal expression of the type in Winston Churchill. Even after World War II was over, Churchill could not bring himself to think that the Kitchener battalion had been disbanded at the beginning of World War I, and that there would be no more parades. And he could write a history of England which makes Trevelyan and Maitland seem terribly modern and still act as though doing so were not remarkable.

The experience of Lawrence, Empson, and Tolkien shares a good deal with both the more accepting and the totally refusing imaginations I have just mentioned. If we could sort out an individual's experience and put one attribute in one group and another in the other, then perhaps my three heroes would seem to be placeable about halfway between Joyce and Churchill. But experience itself does not allow for such sorting out and placing, and the real truth implied by the comparison is that Lawrence, Empson, and Tolkien were in some way trapped, too much in and of the modern world genuinely to ignore it, too much rooted in their own more unified pasts to accept its terms with any kind of fluency. They were driven from within and pressed from without, their intelligence insisting that the modernist view of history was correct, their personal rootedness urging them to withdraw into their old worlds, their anguish forcing them to defy but not to deny the existence of the trap. Each then is compelled to create a new sense of possibility which acknowledges that all that was precious in the old world has been lost but which insists a modern community can be made in defiance of history. Ursula showing Birkin the bell-heather, both forlorn and wanting; Empson, outcast himself, showing us Herbert and Jesus, because themselves outcast, creating the possibility for society; Frodo, trudging toward Mordor, insisting on his kinship with Sméagol to a distrusting Sam, creating thereby the community that could destroy the Ring—these *are* modern, not like the ancient Brangwens or the historical Herbert and Jesus or the old life in The Shire, but they are communities too, where experience is loving and shared as well as anguished and anxious. The communities are not created by writers who are spokesmen for the modern world, and in many ways they do not speak the language of that world. Each writer really is doing no more than trying to work out his own destiny. As a result they are bound to seem a little clumsy, a little provincial, if that is the right word, not cosmopolitan and so not masterful, certainly not really aware of the great importance of what they are creating. Even at their best all three convey a sense of struggling to gain expression of what they need to say, rather than a sense of successfully expressing it. Lawrence is constantly liable to being overcome by his sexual turbulence; Empson never quite frees himself of trying to turn his subtlety into a vice; Tolkien always carries with him the heavy freight that is his adoration of the past. The taproot of their power being local and personal, they collide with the modern world rather than meet it.

It is no wonder, then, that their ability to achieve their heroic and defiant communities is short lived. Their heroism is their fate rather than their goal, and, having achieved it, they had to go on, neither secure nor able to sustain their heroic energies. That is why, I suspect, when each, exhausted, began to subside, they did not fall into the accommodation of modernist irony and despair but into the solace that can be provided by dogma. Lawrence and Empson, achieving their heroic triumphs early, losing their greatest imaginative energies but not their great animal energies, could move into their later years only by insisting they were still fighting their essential fights. Both become more strident. Lawrence could even bring himself to think that his worst novel *The Plumed Serpent* is his best, and it would not be surprising if Empson said that his most important work is *Milton's God*. Tolkien's lot is different because his withdrawal into dogma took place before and became a condition of his eventual heroic success, but, having achieved it, he too could relax, the burden of his being a modern man having been lifted by his unwilling confession that that is what he is.

Of their time, but athwart it as well, propelled for reasons never entirely clear to create a heroic destiny out of their sense of loss rather than retreating into nostalgia—that will hardly do as a definition for all heroes, but it does not do badly for those heroes of the latter days since Shakespeare and Hamlet. Hamlet himself, being of his time, could dream of making mad the guilty, appalling the free, and amazing the very faculties of eyes and ears. Later heroes could imagine no such grand possibilities. Wordsworth, being of his time, could conclude the most famous of his explorations into his childhood terror, that episode with the stolen boat, by extolling the wisdom and spirit of the universe. Later heroes could not imagine that possibility either. If we insist on putting the case that way, if we must make the largeness of the arena crucial to our sense of heroism, then Hamlet is more heroic than Wordsworth, Wordsworth more heroic than any modern hero. If, however, we look at the heroes themselves, then we can see that Hamlet and Wordsworth, like Lawrence, Empson, and Tolkien, were also imaginatively rooted, however solitary. They too were uprooted by events and conditions beyond their control, and they too responded by recoiling into themselves in ways that express both their personal pain and the crisis of the culture outside. Hamlet cannot live in Claudius's Denmark, Wordsworth cannot live in Cambridge and London, any more than Lawrence, Empson, and Tolkien adapt themselves to the prevailing attitudes toward the Myth of Lost Unity. They defy, they set themselves apart by pursuing a something beyond acceptance or accommodation, and in the clumsiness of their pursuit they locate their heroism. They are too self-absorbed to sense they are being heroic, so their moments of self-justification or self-congratulation come later, when the heroic achievement is past and the capacity for self-delusion is strong. Hamlet, after all, can say to Horatio in Act V that his revenge can be performed in perfect conscience because Claudius has popped between the election and Hamlet's hopes—no late, mad assertion of Lawrence's is any more self-deceived than that. Wordsworth can heroically explore his childhood fear and hauntedness, and he can then proclaim not only that he is writing about the growth of his mind but that this story is only a prelude to some great philosophical poem— no claim by Tolkien that he would have rather written in Elvish is more withdrawn from the facts of the case than that.

Though I have chosen Hamlet and Wordsworth to use here alongside Lawrence, Empson, and Tolkien, a great many of the terms I have just used apply as well to Webster's Bosola, or to Milton's Adam, or to Tom Jones, or Dickens's Pip. This is certainly not the place to inquire how or in what ways Shakespeare was decisive in the history of heroic action, but it certainly is true that all later heroes share qualities with Hamlet or Lear or Macbeth that set them apart from any earlier heroism and which make the experience of the last four centuries seem roughly all of a piece. The heroism of my three heroes is different from the others in obvious ways—it is modern, and therefore more historically aware, more a matter of decision than of action, more a matter of action than of triumph, more a matter of triumph than of ultimate victory. But we are more than used to those facts. What does seem the case when we look backward in history from the heroism of this century is that, before Hamlet, it gets harder and harder to find heroes who seem akin to Lawrence, or Empson, or Tolkien, or anyone else who seems heroic in our century. One obvious reason for this is that earlier heroes are more confident and at one with their time. A less obvious one is that we ourselves have so completely accepted the Myth of Lost Unity that we cannot imagine a time much before Hamlet's that was not unified and where heroes were not defiant and self-conscious.

We are back to the old truth that Western history has been a history of change, and thus the nature of the hero has changed, and the quality of heroic experience has been its ability to respond to change. The uprootedness of which I have been speaking is built into Western experience, and the resultant kinds of heroism have of necessity expressed our general bewilderment with the fact that uprootedness is frequent and violent. Earlier centuries seem less like this than those more recent, and, by comparison, other cultures and other heroic responses seem nigh static and serene. But the one thing we have learned from modern experience is that we do not know. Empson very wisely refuses to go back before the generation of Shakespeare in his historical study, and Tolkien's efforts to take us back to a period before Shakespeare's fail markedly. The heroism with which this book has been concerned, thus, is only the outgrowth of the history that we can trace back at least three centuries before beginning to get lost in the mists of the past, lost precisely in those periods of "unity" imagined by the mythographers.

The heroism of our own age is of necessity more fugitive and less easily identified than that of earlier ages, but these facts could surprise us only if they were not true. If we could, like Hrothgar, recognize heroic action immediately and know as if it were our birthright the best terms for its praise, then we would know we were not natural beings of the twentieth century. Even praise itself has not survived as a fully accepted practice. So our lot is more like Horatio's than Hrothgar's, and we cannot begin to tell our heroic tales rightly until we acknowledge that we probably will not recognize what is heroic in the life and art around us until it is past. That does not, however, mean we should stop looking. We do not gather at the table to hear the bard chant and we do not meet in theaters to learn of the fall of princes, but heroes we have nonetheless.

> In the deserts of the heart
> Let the healing fountain start,
> In the prison of his days
> Teach the free man how to praise.

Index

Index

Index